Mission Theological Advisory Group

presence
and prophecy

a heart for mission in theological education

CHURCHES TOGETHER
IN BRITAIN AND IRELAND

CHURCH HOUSE
PUBLISHING

Church House Publishing
Church House
Great Smith Street
London SW1P 3NZ

Churches Together in Britain and Ireland
Inter-Church House
35–41 Lower Marsh
London SE1 7SA

Published 2002 for the Board of Mission of the
Archbishops' Council by Church House Publishing
and Churches Together in Britain and Ireland.

Copyright © The Archbishops' Council and
Churches Together in Britain and Ireland 2002

ISBN 0 7151 5548 2

GS 1442

Typeset in 10/12 Franklin Gothic

Printed by Creative Print and Design Group,
Ebbw Vale, Wales

The Scripture quotations contained herein are from
the New Revised Standard Version Bible, copyright ©
1989, by the Division of Education of the National
Council of the Churches of Christ in the USA, and
are used by permission. All rights reserved.

'Now I belong to Jesus', Norman J. Clayton,
copyright © Wordspring Music, Administered by
Copycare, P.O. Box 77, Hailsham, BN27 3EF,
music@copycare.com Used by permission. (p.141)

contents

the Mission Theological Advisory Group

The Mission Theological Advisory Group is set up jointly by the Archbishops' Council's Board of Mission within the Church of England and the Churches' Commission on Mission of Churches Together in Britain and Ireland. It includes members from the Church of England, Roman Catholic Church, Methodist, Church of Scotland, Church in Wales and Congregationalist traditions.

list of members (1997–2001)

The Rt Revd Dr Michael Nazir-Ali (Chairman)
The Revd Dr Brian Castle
The Rt Revd Richard Garrard
The Revd Canon Dr Graham Kings
Dr Alwyn Marriage (from 1999)
The Revd Joanna Penberthy
The Rt Revd Peter Price
The Revd Fr Frank Regan
The Revd Dr Chris Wigglesworth
The Revd Dr Janet Wootton
The Revd Alison White (to 1998)
The Revd Dr Martyn Atkins (to 1998) Methodist Apologetics Group
The Revd Dr Andrew Wood (from 1999) Methodist Apologetics Group

staff

Mr Simon Barrow (from 2000)
Mr John Clark (from 2000)
The Revd Donald Elliott (to 2000)
The Revd Canon Philip King (to 2000)
Dr Anne Richards (Secretary)

preface

why we did it

We offer this book to everyone involved in theological education. That means we offer it to the whole people of God, for all of us are caught up in a learning journey that is lifelong. On this journey, the call to follow Christ asks us to use our growing knowledge and love of God to witness to others, to nurture others in the faith and to serve them. We must therefore understand mission as being fed by our own continuing theological education. If we care about witness to Christ, we need to recognize and feed our skills and to know our prejudices and limitations.

Our work is offered to all Christians, lay or ordained, who are involved in any kind of training or learning. We hope this book may serve teachers and students in formal theological education, but it has something to say to all who love God and desire to live out a vocation of service. It is for people of all denominations whose Christian life contributes to the continuing *presence* of the Christian tradition in Britain and Ireland, for Christian ideas are deeply embedded in our culture even if they are no longer recognized and acknowledged. We see the missionary task as finding ways to recognize that presence and helping it to become an active agent of transformation.

We believe that Christian witness is also *prophetic*, since the missionary task also requires that we reflect on our own situation and try to discern the signs of the kingdom. By this means we create a picture of a Church for the future. We have therefore not defined theological education as just studying for an accredited qualification in theology, because we see it as being part of a range of different activities. Theological education can take place anywhere, in church, at home or sharing ideas and insights together in a local group. Our work is offered to encourage everyone to have *a heart for mission* in our changing world. We hope it can be used by everyone who cares about the Christian Church and its role in society today.

While we offer our work to everyone in theological education, we want to engage with *you*, the reader, in a particular way. The way in which we have carried out our work means that we have not produced an academic tome, a 'how to' book or a manual for mission with a definitive statement of how mission perspective is to be achieved in theological education. We know there are very many ways in which missiological perspective can be introduced and that it is often dependent on the ethos and orientation of the places where theological learning happens. To be prescriptive would be to go up against a fundamental condition of the mission thinking we offer: *that it is creative, it surprises us, it opens doors and discovers new possibilities*. That means that you, the reader, have an important part in the process. We are not trying to do the teaching ourselves, nor do we seek to place extra burdens on hard-pressed teachers or students, by suggesting that teaching and learning *must* be done like this. We hope to stimulate through mission perspective, so that what is already done well can be both enriched and sustained. Above all, we hope to provide you with a source of encouragement, and to provoke you to enquire: *what is God doing? what is God saying? what difference does it make?*

To do this, we have tried to provide pictures, snapshots, of what mission permeation of theological education could look like and what questions emerge in the process. Of course there are other such pictures, but the ones we offer are the ones we have enjoyed researching and examining as the journey of our work has unfolded. Your reactions to our pictures are valuable and indeed necessary in making the possibility of mission perspective real. We hope the material will challenge and inspire as we have been challenged and inspired. This will also involve struggling with different issues and looking at where our ideas cut across your experience and convictions. Challenge and debate in mission perspective is important in seeing more clearly how the overflowing love from the heart of God makes a real and discernible difference in the world.

For us, the task of doing theology has been much more than completing an agenda in a committee. We have sustained a long conversation, which, although we have finished the book, is still continuing. We have spent considerable time in reflection and prayer on issues related to mission in contemporary society, into which our personal experiences and ideas have been offered. By doing this, we have become a family, talking, praying, eating and worshipping together, having friendly arguments and reflecting on the way our understanding has evolved. Because our group has grown and evolved in this way we have had to acknowledge that mission thinking can be a risky business, challenging things we have taken for granted and pushing at the edges of our own faith and witness. We would like you to risk such thinking and wondering with us.

We have completed this work by means of extending our conversation to include dialogue with many others, and this has both challenged and changed us. We now hope you will use this book to become part of the conversation. We have seen our views of mission theology evolve and change and, to reflect this, we have included a section on mission as a specific subject in the curriculum. In this, we have set out some of the challenges to our own mission thinking we received from those we met during our work. We are grateful to all our consultants who gave generously of their time and expertise to help us think through the issues. We did not agree with everyone who came to us, but without people to prod and disturb us, we would not have had to think about some of the more difficult questions. We have come to feel more strongly that we are all part of a Church that is called to be present in witness within our culture and prophetic in its engagement and encounter with it. We hope you will too.

We could not have done this without the generosity of the Churches' Commission on Mission, which has been the gracious host for our meetings and has made it possible for our guests to come to us. Further, Westminster College, Cambridge, was the host for two consultations on the Hebrew Scriptures and on the New Testament. We are grateful both to the college and to all the participants for making this possible.

The Rt Revd Michael Nazir-Ali
Bishop of Rochester (Church of England)
Chair of the Mission Theological Advisory Group

acknowledgements

The group would like to thank all those people who came to MTAG meetings and gave of their time and expertise so generously:

The Revd Professor Dan Hardy, Dr Annie Hargrave, Dr Kirsteen Kim, the Revd Dr Sebastian Kim, the Ven. Gordon Kuhrt, Dr Ian Linden, the Revd Dr Michael Moynagh, Ms Ruth Musgrave, Mr Martin Palmer, Dr Suzanne Skevington, Dr Brian Stanley, the Revd Michael Stevens, the Revd Canon Vincent Strudwick, the Revd Ian Stubbs, the Revd Flora Winfield.

In addition, the group is grateful to all those who contributed further material to our work, including Dr Martin Davie, Ms Maxine Green, Professor David Hay, Dr Kate Hunt, Mr Frank Knaggs, the Rt Revd Roger Sainsbury, the Revd Jenny Savage, the Revd Dr Peter Stevenson.

We are grateful to all who attended our consultations on the Hebrew Scriptures and on the New Testament, and especially to the Revd Dr Chris Wright and the Revd John Proctor for helping us prepare the material. We also owe thanks to our correspondents who provided us with material for the section on Mission and Pastoral Care.

The CTBI Churches' Commission on Mission and its member churches and agencies would like to thank all involved in this report, and especially Dr Anne Richards, the secretary of the group and Mission Theology Adviser to the Archbishops' Council's Board of Mission. Her tireless, painstaking creative work has made this publication possible.

introduction

how it started

making Christ known

In April 1994, the Church of England's Board of Mission and Advisory Board of Ministry (as it then was) jointly organized a conference entitled *Making Christ Known, Mission and Evangelism in Ministerial Training*. This was a conference to explore how mission could both permeate and be focused in the academic curricula of theological education in the Church of England.

Professor David Ford of the University of Cambridge was invited to give an address. In it, he argued that three dynamics of the Church's ecclesial life may be identified: worship, community and mission. Without any of these elements, the whole life suffers. In general, he suggested, mission had been neglected.

mission is jazz

Professor Ford went on to offer some ways in which we can look at mission in theological curricula more creatively. Mission is not just another lump of information we can tack on to particular teaching disciplines. Mission is not a replacement for essential material or a set of rules to be followed. Mission is most definitely not a buzzword to be attached to educational material to make it more consumable, interesting or contemporary. Rather, mission can be improvisation on a set of themes we already use in theological education. Mission thinking and understanding can create new texture, explore new melody, or underlie and strengthen the harmonic depths of our theological understanding. Mission is *jazz*, the exploration of the new and the creative out of the strength of what is laid down by participants who know expertly how to play their instruments. This jazz is not just an experiment or whim, but emerges from a thoroughgoing knowledge of the tradition. By this means a creative dialogue is set up which permits something fresh, engaging and new. It is improvisation, but it also pushes us beyond comfortable boundaries. This is the understanding of mission that underlies our own engagement with theological education.

the heart of God

The text for Professor Ford's argument was the letter to the Ephesians. 'We need to improvise on Ephesians and generate an ethic of evangelism and mission from the heart of the Gospel.'[1] He suggested that the fundamental image of mission given to us is an overflow (*pleroma*) from the heart of God: 'The author of Ephesians seems to be weaving together God, Christ, Church, Christian living and the whole cosmos into a dynamic soteriology of abundance.' If this abundance is being poured out as a consequence or a sign of God's mission, then we *must* respond.

Such response requires that we pay close attention to Bonhoeffer's question 'Who is Jesus Christ for us today?' for 'it is essential that the interrogative mode be sustained in relation to Jesus Christ'. Asking questions and reflecting contributes to our ability to respond to the overflowing of abundance from the heart of God.

mission as Christ's hospitality

Finally, Professor Ford argued that Christian mission and evangelism 'is, precisely, an offering of "the hospitality of the face of Christ"'. Christian mission, then, is about response to the abundance of God poured into the creation; it is about reflection and questioning; it is also about being and doing in a way which provides essential witness to Christ: *making Christ known*.

METE

Following the conference, the Mission and Evangelism in Theological Education (METE) process was set up between the Church of England's Board of Mission and the Advisory Board of Ministry (now Ministry Division). This process is intended to provide access to consultancy and to resources for those in theological education wishing to explore improvisations in mission.

the search for faith and the witness of the Church

However, in 1996, following the publication of the ecumenical Mission Theological Advisory Group's *The Search for Faith and the Witness of the Church*,[2] it was decided that the place of mission in theological education was a matter affecting all the churches. Accordingly, MTAG decided to build on its work on contemporary culture in *Search for Faith* and go on to look at how those passing through theological education can be equipped to have a vocational sense of response to God's own missionary nature. This would require a questioning and reflective approach to the world around us and an ability to *make Christ known*.

what we decided

In this book, we decided, we would look at current issues in contemporary culture and ask what precisely are the contexts for ministry today. What kind of education and training is required for engagement with these contexts and what most helps Christians called to work within them? What styles of teaching and learning foster a heart for mission in this complex and changing world? These questions have been behind our conversations, our jazz. Beyond this, we looked at subjects offered in theological curricula and talked to those currently teaching in them. Our response has been to offer forms of mission-oriented improvisation that we hoped would keep a sense of God's purposes moving through the material. We have not treated ethics as a separate subject, but rather have sought to argue 'no mission without ethics' throughout. We have asked ourselves what generates people's moral decisions in today's society and have tried to understand this against our own Christian perspectives.

what we can offer

We hope that the book will make it possible for you to foster hearts for mission in the ministry of the Church in the twenty-first century. But it does not end there. Mission is a matter of partnership and we offer to you both resources and a journey of continuing dialogue. Words on a page need practical outcomes and facilitation. If we can help with the process of mission permeation in any kind of theological education, we will. We can offer practical resources for teaching and learning, from up-to-date bibliography and essay questions to consultancy and dialogue partners. Tell us your needs. Get in touch with us.[3]

part 1 settings

chapter 1

the world we live in

If our theological education is going to equip us for mission, then we have to ask questions about the sort of world we live in. What are the characteristics of contemporary western society and how do they affect the hearts and minds of people living in it? How are we affected?

Further, this has to be an ongoing process of enquiry and reflection, for the world we live in changes rapidly. When we began our work, we were concerned to be open to the global situation and to the voices of others outside the western world.[1] Since the destruction of the World Trade Centre twin towers on 11 September 2001, we have had to consider new and perplexing theological issues. What does it mean to have a modern day temple of Mammon destroyed by people with God's name on their lips? What does it mean to wage war in the backyards of the poor and powerless? Why are our churches full of people seeking ways to express their grief? What are the consequences for our relations with people of other faiths? If, for a government spin doctor, it was a 'good day to bury bad news',[2] should we perhaps look beyond exploitation of tragedy to determine what it really means to offer the good news to bewildered people? Yet we have to ask, are clergy and lay people trained to respond to the questions, the shock and emotions aroused by such events? How do we determine how to respond appropriately in such situations?

To see how we can develop hearts for mission in today's fast-changing world, we decided to look at three important processes that affect all of us, Christians included. These are: individualization, post-materialism and globalization. We also need to know how people live and how their thoughts are shaped. In this section, we refer to theological education, in its widest sense, as something the Church can offer to allow us to reflect on where our own ideas come from, and what difference our faith makes to our lives.

individualization

Individualization refers to the increasing emphasis on the importance of self over the importance of community. It means that individuals have rights that must be asserted over groups and partnerships. People take control over what happens to their bodies and to their relationships. It can be said that 'it is every woman's right to have a child' or indeed 'it is a woman's right not to have a child'. Television programmes and advertising present images of women and men as being young, beautiful and self-fulfilled. The slogan for one producer of cosmetic products is currently 'because you're worth it'. Consumerism encourages people to fulfil these prerogatives and it is society's responsibility to see that the demand for self-importance and happiness is not contravened or alienated.[3]

paying for services

The key to an individualized society is money. For those who can afford it, personal trainers and self-styled 'analysts' may be paid to bolster a person's sense of a fulfilled body or a healthy mind. Other professionals, such as lawyers and doctors, may be used as a means to preserving rights to health, money or possessions and may be very rarely thanked or even appreciated for the help they give.[4] Our culture is filled with the suggestion that we must get everything we are entitled to. There is a trend, if not fashion, for litigation in the USA and there is a similar rise in claims for compensation for a host of reasons in Europe. There is also an increasing number of cases coming before the European Human Rights Commission relating to issues of personal grievance and the 'right' to adequate financial compensation.[5]

satisfaction guaranteed

Clergy and lay people may therefore be faced with offering God's love to an increasingly thankless society. They may also be faced with being seen purely as service providers whose job is to contribute as fully as possible to a person's feel-good factor. For example, when a rural minister told a couple that the church was unable to provide a full home-grown choir for the occasion of their wedding, the couple were upset and angry because they assumed and expected that it was 'all part of the service'.

refusal offends

The other side of this is that persons in positions of authority (including clergy) may become a focus for people's anger and frustration when their needs are not fully met. People may feel their rights to self-fulfilment have not been respected or that they have been let down.

A man who came to fill in a banns form in an Oxfordshire parish, physically attacked the vicar's wife when she told him he could not automatically be married at the church of his choice. The man felt frustrated and thought that the Church was deliberately discriminating against him because he was not a regular churchgoer. He said strongly that he should be given 'benefits' such as those afforded him by the state and would not accept a Church that said 'no'.[6, 7]

post-materialism (not 'getting better' but 'having best')

Individualization works hand in hand with post-materialism. This somewhat clumsy term refers to an increasing emphasis on quality of life as represented by material possessions.[8] It goes beyond acquiring material things for making life easier, such as buying a car or a vacuum cleaner, and reflects people's desire to obtain the best set of material things to represent depth of quality. For example, the acquisition of a washing machine to replace hand washing and wringing by mangle represents a material improvement. Owning a washing machine with a range of functions A to Z even if only B and F are ever required, falls into the realm of post-materialism. 'Things' obtain status beyond their utility, so some people have ambitions to own 'a Dyson', for example. All sectors of society are seduced by post-materialism even if the items to be desired are beyond the pocket of those desiring them. 'Quality is a right not a privilege' was a recent advertising slogan for a make of car.

read all about it

Again, effective engagement in post-material values depends on money. Nonetheless, if you cannot afford luxury cars or top of the range household appliances, you may still vicariously participate in the post-material search for lifestyle options by reading magazines about them. There are many such 'lifestyle' magazines on the market, creating for the consumers a virtual world of marvellous possibilities, such as cars, video cameras, hi-fi or computers for life enhancement. Utility is inextricably entwined with leisure and pleasure. Women and men may be targeted with magazines about other people's luxury homes, or designer interiors. People are encouraged to want and demand what is best for them and expect the right to exclude from any package deal whatever does not suit them or fit their self-image. This extends as readily to religious matters as it does to all other parts of life and can create problems with seeing Christianity as a whole life experience, which is relevant to anyone and everyone. How can we focus on making the mystery of the Incarnation real for people when Christmas shopping starts in September?

rapid turnover

Both these sociological forces mean that life is very fast changing in these early years of the new millennium. Yesterday's model TV/video/camera/ tape is out of date, to be replaced by today's digital technology, plasma screens and Windows XP. Suddenly, everyone seems to own a mobile phone (12.2 billion text messages were sent in Britain during 2001 – 42 million messages a day).[9] These changes pose real challenges to a Christian viewpoint that is based upon the truth, relevance and meaningfulness of events that happened 2000 years ago.

dislocation

Conversely however, many people in our society are increasingly trying to address a feeling of rootlessness and dislocation. This shows up at the larger level as passionate espousal of nationhood in the face of threatened fragmentation, together with hostility towards different ethnic groups. This was seen clearly in the Balkans and has been seen in public reaction to the World Trade Centre destruction. Elsewhere, the feeling of isolation and rootlessness can show up as an interest in local history and conservation projects, which take on special, even 'sacred' significance. People will hang on to their sense of a meaningful past even when this compromises regeneration projects for social improvement. In the midst of a need to find roots and things that endure, and as people go on pilgrimages to their own real or invented past, the Church needs to manage change in faithfulness to God's enduring story of love to the world.

Church and world

How theological education can equip us to understand and deal with these aspects of society is a profound missiological question. All of us are affected by the pressures of individualization and post-materialism whether we like it or not. We do not live in a hermetically sealed environment, but sometimes our experience of theological education may make it seem as if we do. Residential courses, for example, can create safe and secure environments where the sense of communal support and mutual care is very strong. Students can be greatly sustained and nourished by such kinds of training, but then emerge to a highly uncertain world in which all the goalposts are constantly being moved.

retreat from engagement

Living out Christian witness means that we are asked to provide an interface between the Church and the world, to create a valid engagement and to bring a theological world view to others. But has the equipping for this interaction between gospel and culture taken place? If it has not, there is the danger that, for some new clergy, church life may in fact become a shelter and a protection from this risky endeavour. They may retreat into clergy groups using the solidarity of this fellowship as an attempt to recreate the 'safe' world of the believing community. For many lay people and non-stipendiary ministers this is not possible; the engagement with the world is a daily question asking them either to compartmentalize their lives or to struggle continually with the overlapping worlds in which they live. On paper, 'mission' appears clear-cut, an extension of living out God's call. In practice, it requires daily engagement and a commitment to a rapidly changing world and the challenges it poses to Christian faith. Even the best theological education can leave students ill-equipped to make that transition from learning to living.

For example, beyond theological education, which may have included powerful experiences of corporate worship, where is the understanding of a world where people may use Gregorian chant as a relaxation tape or as 'music to sleep by'? Out in 'the world' the form and content of the music have been separated, so that people are attracted by the music as 'wallpaper' rather than as a means to praise God. Conversely, the same people have rocketed religious communities, who have praised God in the same way for centuries, into the commodity-driven heart of the music industry.[10] This is where equipping for mission through theological education can make a real difference.

See Chapter 10, 'mission and worship'.

globalization

We noted that individualization and post-materialism depend on the flow of money in our affluent western society. It is no surprise, then, that another significant factor in the way we live our lives today is the interdependent situation in which our society functions. Globalization is a multidimensional phenomenon. It has profound political, cultural and ecological effects of which we must be aware if we are going to speak prophetically of our vision of God's will for us. All of these matters require theological investigation and reflection, but here we concentrate on financial effects as being related particularly to our individualized and consumerist society. Financial affairs are as globally networked as human living so that a number of processes come into play that affect all our lives. These include:

- The revolution in IT and communications;
- The rapid increase in capital flow since the mid-1980s;
- The significant increase in global trade, especially from 1984;
- The growth in foreign direct investment (fdi) as a component of capital flows;
- The rising power of multinational corporations;
- The growing globalization of production and distribution.

A mission perspective on such a world requires each of us to be aware of the knock-on effects of even the small economic decisions we make. If we desire to live according to God's will and to build the kingdom while remembering the poor and underprivileged, then we will need a more sophisticated understanding of economics in order to make right decisions. Do our various forms of theological education provide this? In each local situation there may be a reflection of the global picture in which employment, wages, crime and social apartheid all have a part to play. Understanding the global economy may therefore allow important insights about the best strategies for mission in a local area. An encounter with 'third'[11] world poverty by fostering links and cross-cultural encounter can also open up fresh understanding of domestic poverty. For example, Ruth Musgrave, one of our conversation partners, told us:

> The experience of women's groups from Bangladesh who have used role-play to address conflicts with landlords has empowered them to solve difficulties in real life. Some of these women have assisted other groups in this country to address the consequences of conflict and change on council estates in Newham, London. Creative Bible study can forge important links between different sets of experiences which have the capacity to energize and empower people for change in their lives.

Ministers and lay people need to be able to encourage groups to analyse and learn about deprivation and encourage sharing to build up hope. The missionary task of building up the kingdom of God therefore requires proper decision making and an understanding of the consequences of decisions. Where in theological education does this take place?

For example, advances in communications technology mean that the financial centre of a company can be geographically thousands of miles away from other sectors of its economy. Some major airlines do their ticketing in 'third' world countries where appropriate simple skills and cheap labour suffice to do the job. Those who fly regularly are not encouraged to think of the human rights issues, such as exploitation and unfair wages, which may underlie their ability to do so. Similarly, car buyers do not consider the integration and precise timetabling required to assemble car components from eighteen different countries. The ordinary shopper may not ever think that the registration of goods passing out of supermarkets instantly generates new supply. To think more widely about our part in the culture of individualized society requires a certain kind of discernment and reflection. Where Christians have presence there should also be prophecy.

communications

The transformation of communication also has other effects in politics and culture. For example the African market is flooded by Asian video films:

> A friend of mine studies village life in central Africa. A few years ago, she paid her first visit to a remote area where she was to carry out her fieldwork. The evening she got there, she was invited to a local home for an evening's entertainment. She expected to find out about the traditional pastimes of this isolated community. Instead, the evening turned out to be a viewing of Basic Instinct on video. The film at that point hadn't even reached the cinemas in London ... We live in a world of transformations, affecting almost every aspect of what we do. For better or worse, we are being propelled into a global order that no one fully understands, but which is making its effects felt upon all of us.
>
> We are the first generation to live in this society, whose contours we can as yet only dimly see. It is shaking up our existing ways of life, no matter where we happen to be. This is not – at least at the moment – a global order driven by collective human will. Instead it is emerging in an anarchic, haphazard fashion, carried along by a mixture of economic, technological and cultural imperative.[12]

We are bombarded by information, surrounded as we are by access to new media. One consequence of this can be that satellite TV reports beamed instantly to public TV sets create a tide of public opinion that motivates ad hoc policy generation, which is neither considered nor informed. The disaster movie pictures of 11 September 2001 generated aggressive and hostile words. *The Times* headline for 12 September was 'When war came to America'. The inside pages were subheaded 'Bush vows to defend freedom from cowards ... Bush plans to hit back ... biggest manhunt in history.[13] Yet most of the world did not see the images on TV, did not have access to Sky or CNN. Our theological understanding has to take account of our responsibilities in the face of these processes and this asks questions of our ongoing theological education. Are we equipped to know how our purses affect supply and demand, how shopping affects workers outside our western society, to understand our own reaction to instantaneous reporting of international affairs?

virtual money

There are also questions relating to the fact that 90 per cent of international currency flow is now currency speculation, and the amount of money in flow can be 100 times greater than some government reserves. We live in a world filled with virtual money and the way we ourselves speculate and invest contributes to the bigger picture. We often hear a call to move from 'maintenance' to 'mission' but we have to ask how we move in ways that do not buy into the speculation ideal. Although to have 'vision' sounds like mission as speculation or wagering on the future God has promised us (with the risk of losing everything), we should not assume that concepts of investment and risk have the same meanings in God's economy. A Church that is called to make its presence engage robustly in a world like this, must have a prophetic edge arising from our Christian understanding of economic reality. Do we have it, and does our theological education help us to obtain it?

God's 'investment' in ourselves

Where do we start? The Gospels are full of illustrations about comparative worth. Jesus himself asks us to think hard about how monetary systems must be balanced against God's absolute investment in humankind. In looking at the different levels of the parable of the talents (Matthew 25.14ff.; Luke 19.11ff.), one question that may be drawn out is about what each of us does with the one life we are given.[14] If we do nothing, risk or dare nothing in making decisions about what we really believe, then spiritually we end up with nothing. On the other hand, surrendering our lives to the gospel brings us 'treasure in heaven': a spiritual richness and depth that we cannot foresee. The parable of the labourers in the vineyard (Matthew 20.1-16) similarly asks us to revise our ideas of investment and reward, for God gives the same to all who are 'hired'. Yet how do we help others to think about this in a society where we are encouraged only to have short-term, self-serving financial goals.[15]

It is often harder to think about investment in global terms and about our part in it. Foreign direct investment sounds like a good thing with money being passed from the rich to the poor, but in fact there are relatively few such flows. We need to realize that money more readily passes from the rich to the rich, with new industrial powers such as SE Asia being favoured and Africa becoming a 'write-off' area. Further, money also continues to pass from the poor to the rich. We can also see what a volatile situation this produces; over the past few years there has been particular recession in Asian markets and a monetary crisis in Russia. Further, such foreign direct investment is more readily spent on mergers and acquisitions rather than on plant and machinery, leading to ownership by large multinationals and eroding indigenous industry. Where such indigenous industry is lost poor nations become poorer.

challenge from theology

All of us who care about the mission of the Church have to be aware not only of the economic global realities but also of what we can do to build up a kingdom ecclesiology. Theological education can help us to explore these things more deeply. We need to challenge economic orthodoxy and determinism, and this needs to be done at the theological level. We need to understand the nature of the self-interested power bloc, which might not be conducive to issues of compassion or of justice. We have to be aware the concept of structural sin and understand that some ills of the world have a life of their own. This is true of apartheid and of the tragic examples in recent years of attempts at ethnic cleansing. Ways of moral reasoning therefore become crucial to people acting in mission and this responsibility needs to be passed on to all those who hold positions of power. There are openings and opportunities to create responsible moral and political agency. This can be done at local level, such that a church or congregation works towards becoming a model of a moral community. Theological education can help us to do all this, but there is a further task which *only* theological education can provide. The Church must also do its own power analysis – we too are the rich and powerful in many parts of the western world. We must also see to it that a self-critique is at the heart of our mission. This is a thread that has run throughout our work.

Theological education must equip us not only for better understanding of the world we live in, but also for *transformation* of that world. In terms of engagement with a globalized society, this might mean that we should resist the view that markets cannot be bucked and that market forces are such that nothing can be done about them. This makes the fight against the kind of discourse that disempowers people a mission matter. We can enable people and give them tools to shape their own economic locality (credit unions, corner shops, family businesses, partnerships with superstores, etc.). Such action can become part of witness to Christ in any given place. Holistic mission means helping all kinds of investors to see that if they have rights, they also have responsibilities: for the environment, for social needs and for right action towards others. There is currently a great concern about global and domestic debt,[16] which is being challenged at the political level. At the G8 summit in Birmingham in 1998 the leaders of the G8 countries were presented with a petition asking for a billion people to be freed from their countries' debt at the beginning of the new millennium. This is not the whole of the matter, however, as Clare Short explained to the General Synod of the Church of England in November 1998:

> *I want to ask whether the international campaign for debt cancellation can be broadened into an alliance to eliminate poverty? I was extraordinarily heartened by the many thousands of people who came to lobby the G8 Summit in Birmingham. But debt relief alone will not produce the result they seek. Debt relief can be an essential step in ending poverty. But we must not stop there. The biblical concept of Jubilee itself goes far beyond debt – slaves were to be freed, land was to be restored, tools given to people. In short, nobody was to be left in extreme poverty. That is what we should strive for – and for the first time in human history, it is possible. The question is can we work together to make it happen.[17]*

jubilee

Debt cancellation is also being challenged at the theological level, as can be seen in Pope John Paul II's call for countries held in thrall by debt to be relieved of their burdens by wealthy countries. He did this to emphasize the millennium as a year of jubilee.[18] This concept is taken from the idea in Leviticus 25, which:

> *enunciates the practice of the Jubilee year, a celebration of the fiftieth year (after seven sevens), in which there will be a return to one's property and one's family – a homecoming – and in which family land which has been forfeited in the normal transactions of business is returned. This is a remarkable provision, for it relativizes all economic transactions for the sake of rootage in the community. It is also a wise and cunning provision, for it recognizes the limitations of practice (v v. 29-33) and the capacity for exploitation and opportunity to take advantage that are present in the provision itself (v v. 13-17).[19]*

This is also related to the sabbatical year provisions for debt cancellation in Deuteronomy 15. Although some have argued that the jubilee provisions were never implemented, there was, in fact, widespread provision for this within different cultures in the Middle East.[20] We should also not forget that Jesus himself took up the idea of the 'year of the Lord's favour' on reading Isaiah 61 in the synagogue (Luke 4.16-21). Here he applied the mandate to 'bring good news to the poor … release to the captives … recovery of sight to the blind … let the oppressed go free' to himself. This is not just a stated good intention either, for Jesus says: 'Today this scripture has been fulfilled in your hearing' – causing uproar. The new order, the reality of the kingdom of God, is manifested through these ways of bringing change to people's lives within the whole of God's world. Theological education that is engaged with social reality can turn jubilee from a biblical concept to a mission strategy that effects real transformation.

If we argue that this is part of Jesus' *missio Christi*, we can see that following Jesus demands that we encourage governments and other agencies to recognize the impossible situation of debt burden in impoverished countries. God's option for the poor asks us to work for relief of this burden by cancellation of debt, and also to urge our governments to provide adequate economic support for other struggling economies. Beyond the political, however, there is the missionary drive to transform unjust structures and allow people to reclaim their land and livelihood from the necessity of always giving into the pockets of others. This places new burdens on us, so that a heart for mission includes understanding how our financial decisions – how we shop and how we consume – affect those who provide us with our consumer goods and services:

> The Jubilee, therefore, opens up to us part of what discipleship is all about. Because it is only part of discipleship, we cannot afford to settle only for the sorts of demands offered by Jubilee – the Kingdom of God involves much deeper social transformation than that. But because it is an important part of discipleship, neither can we afford to ignore the call to Jubilee. If some of the requirements of discipleship have a more eschatological character, the relevance of Jubilee is that it has a more incarnational character. That is to say that it can, in large measure, be put into practice now. The political economy of Jubilee is such that key practices of release are clearly in the interests of rich and poor alike and enable a degree of justice to be realized which may give us the confidence to dare to believe that Jesus calls us to even more.[21]

This shows how the contexts for ministry we come across provide us with the ability to make change happen. The desire to enable change emerges from theological reflection on the tasks laid upon us by the creator God. In a climate where we must all think more carefully about where our resources come from, mission can mean focusing on the recovery of community together with responsibility for control of and use of capital. Jubilee concepts have much to do with mission and arise as a result of people using their own economic power and refusing deterministic ideas. This empowers people to make businesses implement codes of conduct and affect the conditions of workers in countries on the other side of the world. Solidarity with those suffering in the global marketplace therefore becomes a mission issue. Theological education can provide Christians with a framework of ethics that can have particular outcomes in and through ministry. For example, we might support (and know why we support) Christian Aid's Fair Trade Campaign.

ethics

A heart for mission within the contexts for today's ministry requires a foundational understanding of Christian ethics. Yet we want to argue throughout that it is not just a matter of understanding and working with ethical principles. There is an urgent need within a globalized world to give attention to the consequences of our actions as well as to the ethics of intrinsic value and duty. When we enter into ministry in our pluralist and postmodern world, we need to get back to first principles to see more clearly what needs to be done. What is right behaviour for building up a missionary community in a consumerist society? Theological education can equip people in training to ask this kind of question. Without being urged by others to think in this way, we run particular risks about acting in complicity with oppressive economic structures. For example:

> A rundown and impoverished community was offered a regeneration project which would bring in both money and jobs. However, this was at the expense of environmental concerns about traffic and pollution and included the displacement of some peripheral communities, such as travellers. The local churches were involved in discussions about how the money should be spent, but were effectively advised that if they voiced concerns about the environment and the travellers this could compromise improvements for their own people. What was it right to do? Should leaders accept the argument for the greater good, be prophets dissenting in the wilderness, or refuse to enter into dialogue altogether?

The world we live in can put us in awkward situations like this. How can we decide what is the right thing to do to bring about the sort of transformation *God* wants? Theological education can equip us to make such decisions, not least through the history of social teaching, Christian witness and by the example of the lifelong commitment of priests and ministers in the poorest and most deprived of areas.

Theological education, however, cannot equip us for mission in a vacuum. The contexts for ministry today ask us to go further than this. If we are to have a heart for mission, we need to have more than information about sociological changes in our culture. We have to have some understanding of both how people live and how people think. This might seem obvious, but there is a temptation to believe that the people with whom we live and with whom we interact should think and behave just as we do. When they do not live up to our expectations, we can fall into judging people, without considering whether this is in reality a challenge to our Christian witness. Where have we failed and what can we do to make transformation possible in people's lives?

how people live

networks

Community underlies Christian faith. Where 'two or three are gathered in my name' (Matthew 18.20), there is the beginning of fellowship. Christian faith comes with a history of both community and geographical territory – a circuit, a parish system or whatever it may be. Often our experience of theological education is very good because it provides us with ready-made community where our well-being is nurtured and our faith affirmed. If we are lucky, that sense of strong community is sustained in the congregations where we live out our ministry, but is this a misleading lens through which to look at the world?

In our contemporary western society many people live in communities of networks rather than in geographically based communities. That is, people relate to each other across wide geographical distances and according to interest groups. Networks are centred on places of common gathering or interest such as work, school, leisure centres or shops. People may use cars or stay in touch by telephone or email rather than engage in face-to-face meetings with others in their network. Networking enables relationships to be pursued where distance would otherwise be a problem and satellite links and global communication mean that people can be linked with each other all over the world day or night. Through websites, the Internet has become a meeting place for groups of people who ordinarily could have no possible contact. We will put this material on a website to make it as widely available as possible. Networking accelerates the rate of change, but it can also erode the sense of 'local' relationships and even mean that neighbours telephone each other rather than knock on each other's door and speak face to face.

This poses interesting questions for us as Christians trying to offer access to our community of faith. The prevalence of networking may pose a significant challenge to mission. People who are used to organizing their lives by phoning, may find an interview or meeting with a stranger about a baptism, marriage or funeral discomfiting. It may be difficult to care for a networked family, in which parents and children may all live far away from each other. Similarly, it may be difficult to build up a cohesive congregation as a community modelling the Body of Christ where people have indistinct notions of corporate sharing and community life. Belonging may tend to be loose and peripheral and church be reduced safely to an interest network or occasional leisure interest in people's minds. For example, a non-churchgoer at a church fête was heard to remark, quite without irony: 'God likes to see us all pulling together'!

Handling networks and getting alongside people where they are may be primary skills in ministry for mission. It requires sensitivity to networking in a particular area, and the vision to see beyond the parochial or other boundaries, to identify the mission potential in deaneries, circuits or other areas. Church planting recognizes 'underchurched areas', for example, as a mission strategy that may be wider than the smallest unit boundary.[22] Adroit networking may also discover particular interest groups, such as cancer help or women's issue groups who may be sympathetic to Christian witness within a wider church group. On the other side of all the networking, there can be other opportunities for an outward-looking church. Loneliness may leave many people who are pursuing the self-realization dream feeling cut off even if they have a large circle of casual friends and acquaintances. Christian presence that is proactive in seeking out such isolated people can make a great difference. Befriending schemes can introduce them to a non-threatening church network. Some examples of successful schemes include approaching people who advertise in newspaper columns for friends, providing Christian taxi services and forming Christian babysitting circles.

science and technology

Another result of the technological revolution is the increasing reliance on scientific understanding. In an individualized and post-material world, people become increasingly reliant on technology to run their lives and may have high expectations of machines that they are unable to understand. Most cars and many household appliances cannot be fixed with a screwdriver or a drill, but require specialized repair centres. Computers and software require online technical support. Individualization then paradoxically creates a particular kind of reliance on others and may place the minister as the 'fixer' for spiritual problems. For example:

> *A teenager arrested for shoplifting blamed her local minister for failing to resolve ongoing tensions within her family. The shoplifting was a 'punishment' to highlight the minister's failure as a 'fixer' and to involve him further in sorting out the ensuing difficulties with the police, school and her family. At no point did the teenager accept that she had a responsibility to herself and to her family; her actions were caused by the failure of others to keep her out of trouble.*

the image of perfection

Within the world of 'fixers', people may sometimes have to make complex decisions about their lives in relation to technology. Christians too have to take account of this and think through the implications. This may arise simply because *in vitro* fertilization or some forms of cosmetic surgery are seen as the latest thing to have in pursuit of the 'right' to what you want (or what other people want of you). However, the most difficult decisions may stem from cases where developments in (say) reproductive technologies and genetic counselling enter intrusively into people's family lives.

For example, if an unborn child is diagnosed as having a disease that will be fatal in later life, or if an infant is born with physical or mental disadvantage, parents may look for answers in emerging technologies that 'cure' such 'defects' or make decisions about abortion that cause lasting distress. The TV soap, *Eastenders*, ran a storyline about Bianca's decision to abort her daughter with spina bifida, which involved the local vicar encouraging her to name her baby and grieve for her as a person. These episodes brought to the surface many people's latent feelings about this most difficult of ethical debates. A Christian witness to how we are made in the image of God and valued equally as children of God may make a tremendous difference to people struggling with these issues, but are we equipped to do this?

Advances in technology demand that we understand new strains in people's lives. People may have to choose between a bewildering array of variously costed treatments for their problems and be expected to be responsible for their decisions in ways that are perplexing and distressing. Some people end up not knowing whom to trust. It is therefore a mission imperative to help people see through the maze of choices and to offer them Christian faith as something which can make sense of a whole life, in sickness and in health. Prophetic witness also cuts through the prevailing idea that useful people are young, beautiful and capable. Our faith tells us that under God everyone can contribute to the kingdom no matter what his or her physical or mental capability. This requires a sympathetic understanding of the effect of technology on people's lives. Theological education can begin to equip us for the difficulties we may all run into if we have to make choices about procedures and processes we cannot understand.

what people think

The unprecedented public reaction to the death of Diana, Princess of Wales in 1997 showed with extraordinary clarity the depth of implicit religion in the people of this country. Here, the work done on implicit religion in *The Search for Faith and the Witness of the Church* (Church House Publishing, 1996) was prophetic of what needed to be done to help people make sense of the events following her death. An upwelling of extraordinary emotion, expressed in myriad rituals and offerings, showed that people have deep feelings of religious impulse which become overt at moments of personal shock, crisis, or unusual corporate grief. We have seen it again in the disbelief and emotion following the events in New York and Washington on 11 September 2001. The focusing of these critical moments of self-questioning and the search for meaning is something to which our Christian witness can and should respond. Many people look to the Church at such times. Here, we need to take account of the non-rational elements in people's implicit faith which can be grounded and given expression through the Church's own life of worship and pastoral care.

A heart for mission then can require a sensitivity to the importance of life crises and significant moments in people's lives, especially at baptisms, weddings and funerals. Such events may provoke a much deeper response than the surface encounter may suggest. As Christians, our witness and pastoral care may have to break through the 'service provider' perception, to nurture some of the implicit religious expression that may surface at this time. For example:

> *A child at nursery school became depressed and withdrawn following the death of a pet. After consulting doctors to no avail, the parents finally turned to a local minister who talked to the child and helped him improvise a ritual to make sense of the pet's death. This helped to allow the child to say goodbye to the pet and remember it joyfully. This attracted criticism in the local paper, which saw it as a pet's funeral service, which it was not. The child was helped to sort out confused and unarticulated feelings about loss by means of drawings, photographs and prayer, which helped the child's pain to heal and which also helped to strengthen the faith of the whole family.*[23]

religious plurality

It is another challenge to the mission of the Churches that contemporary western society is also characterized by religious plurality. This refers first to the fact that significant proportions of different geographical areas may be made up of communities professing one of the major world religions. Christian mission must then find an appropriate way forward in communities with significant numbers of Jews, Muslims, Buddhists, Sikhs or Hindus. Witness, sharing, dialogue with and care for people of other faiths are particular mission matters and those in ministry need to be equipped with proper understanding of world religions from within their own Christian perspective and context. One of the particular questions we need to ask in this book is whether theological education has provided this.

the 'narrative of the lie' and the 'domination-free order'

Some theologians, such as Hans Küng in his *Global Ethic*,[24] have sought to identify common values to undergird the world of religious plurality and to make it a safer place for us to live in mutual understanding. Robert Schreiter, in his book *Reconciliation*,[25] presents a theology for true dialogue and exchange, wherein another person's faith story is allowed proper respect. Aggressive confrontation and overwhelming others in the name of evangelism otherwise turns the gospel into the 'narrative of the lie'. His argument also helps us to identify how the global interaction of religious belief can result in fundamentalism and ethnic chauvinism such that the 'narrative of the lie' can become the only story on offer. This is far from God's intention for a kingdom of mutual loving relationships established within the creation, in what Walter Wink has called God's 'domination-free order'.[26] It is another particular thread of our mission focus that we consider carefully what it means to live among, and be in dialogue with, people of other faiths and none.

spirituality

Beyond this our Christian witness is also surrounded by a wash of less well-defined religious ideas and feelings. 'Spirituality' is something that has been appropriated by our consumerist culture and people may express their deep-down religious feelings in things they can buy. The holistic nature of contemporary spirituality is not necessarily 'pick and mix' but can be very well integrated in people's lives. For example, many young people express their spirituality and religious understanding in terms of self-created journey.

They talk about:

- Being in control of their own spiritual path;
- The need to feel good about themselves and their spirituality;
- A need for a short-term good feeling about the future and a real hope;
- A concern for the natural world, especially animals, and often passionate espousal of green issues for a better world.

conceptual diversity

After individualization, post-materialism and globalization, we may also see the presence of conceptual diversity as a fourth important factor in contemporary society, which challenges the way we have traditionally engaged with others in mission. People may increasingly hold different sets of ideas in their heads at the same time, even if some of the ideas are contradictory. When people receive competing pieces of information, they may simply compartmentalize them in their minds. This leads to a both/and mentality. For example, some people may visit a doctor for conventional western medicine, but also consult an alternative therapist even if they receive different advice. Similarly, people may say they are committed Christians, but also say they believe in reincarnation, spiritualism or in other non-Christian religious practices. While these different sets of beliefs may not appear to be compatible, nonetheless many people seem to be able to hold on to different sets of ideas without difficulty. The problem for us is that they may only ever tell us one side of the story – the part we want to hear.

a 'Christic' theology

Conceptual diversity in contemporary spirituality is a challenge to Christian witness, because we can often be unprepared for the hold it has on people. Nor is it something that only affects people outside the major faith communities. Conceptual diversity can also exist among Christian believers who may privately hold personal beliefs about reincarnation or about the paranormal, which they hold in tension with their public statement of the creed in church on Sundays. For people inside and outside the Church, difficulty with orthodoxy may lead to a 'Christic'[27] theology, whereby they do not accept Christian teaching for themselves but wish Christ to bless their struggles. Sometimes this is adopted deliberately to exclude the rigours of discipleship or any suggestion of church culture.

Christ outside the Church

People may speak of encountering Christ outside the Church and claim him for their own. This is the faith they offer when they encounter the Church. There may be a strong feeling that they want to have a real relationship with Christ but not with Christianity. The singer Tori Amos, for example, claims that 'the Christian God is alive and well and I usually go out with him every six weeks. Just for a good binge'.[28] The meeting of the Church with people who offer their own Christ to us is an urgent mission matter. It can either have great potential for the Church, or create a terrible stalemate in the engagement between Church and world. It brings us straight back to Bonhoeffer's question, 'Who is Jesus Christ for us today?'

What role, then, does Christian mission have within plurality? What is the ultimate aim of mission: should conceptual diversity be reduced to one (Christian) understanding, or do other ways of thinking of God enrich the Christian picture? Here theological education has a vital part to play in the presence of the Church and its prophetic word in society. Yet this is a part that can be misjudged or misrepresented. For instance, if matters of plurality are addressed only by teaching inclusivist and exclusivist arguments, these may have little practical application in the engagement with the world where issues are much more blurred. The same kind of question occurs about notions of 'Church'. For example, lay and ordained people working within a mission agency like the Mission to Seafarers, must rely on the creation of moments of grace on board ship for people who are often of different faiths. The welfare of these seafarers and their spiritual well-being is bound up with the practice of mission, but cannot take place without respect for the others' integrity. The question of what we learn from the holiness and spirituality of people of other faiths and spiritualities also becomes acute. This is not, however, something which many people's theological education has either the time or the ability to address.

the spirituality of non-attenders

Theological education tends to be 'for' Christians, so there can be underlying presuppositions about what people can and do believe. Further, these are often attached to presuppositions about Church, which prevents us asking a crucial question: 'what sort of Church do we want for what sort of world?' One way in which a missiological focus can begin to answer this question is to consider what can be learned from people belonging to no established religion or who have fallen away from attendance. In *Understanding the Spirituality of People Who Don't Go to Church*,[29]

David Hay and Kate Hunt showed that there has been a dramatic rise in people reporting a sense of a transcendent providence, especially at times of joy or sadness. Many turned to prayer at such times. Another commonly reported experience was of a sacred presence in nature, but also an increased awareness of the presence of evil in the world. Hay and Hunt thought that the increase in people reporting this kind of spiritual sense might not be a true increase, but that social permissions to tell this kind of story were now more relaxed (Hay and Hunt, 2000, pp. 13–14). While this suggests that Christian mission has a role to play in encountering and helping people to make sense of these stories, Hay and Hunt also showed that people may have very negative feelings about the institution of Church, which should give us pause.

This is 'Matthew's story:

> ... it seems so very often that you, people that are believers, they've got it, they know, you know? The fact that you don't know means that you, yes, you don't know, you're stupid. You know, it's the arrogance, um it's a very well dressed up humble looking arrogance, but it's arrogance nonetheless however, you know. That's what annoys me. Um, You know, you're not with us, therefore you're against us. No, I'm with you, but I'm not sure, I'm not against you, and I just want to know, you know. If you know, how do you know? Do you really know all the time? (Hay and Hunt, 2000, p. 19)

It is a difficult question to face for all of us concerned with ministry and mission, but how guilty are we of 'a very well dressed up humble looking arrogance'? In the many different contexts for our ministry today, is this what people see in us? More to the point, is this what theological education makes of us? Others in the study reported fear of ridicule or humiliation in telling their stories to others or embarrassment in being shown up at church. Should part of Christian witness be gentleness and reassurance?

cynicism

Hay and Hunt also reported that cynicism about the religious institution was more or less the 'default mode' for people being asked about their opinions of the Church. 'Mary', whose devotional life was entirely Christian and founded on daily prayer, said that the Church has an obsession with control (the Church should be a servant); is living in the past (God is a God of the living not the dead); fails to be concerned with humanity as a whole and fails to show genuine commitment (occasional collections for the poor of the world are mere tokenism). 'Mary' argued that her experience of Church had caused her to stop going altogether, but that she had not lost her faith (Hay and Hunt, 2000, p. 30). Commitment to mission as an overflow from the heart of God reaching out into the lives of all people, means that we have to learn a sensitivity to the thoughts and feelings of those exploring their spirituality outside the institution. How can our theological education make this possible?

God's story, our story

One obvious tool of Christian mission is telling God's story as our story. But there may be a need to have the creative ability to tell the 'old, old' story in a new way. This means we must first make sense of the 'Christic' presence in people's lives and be aware that the language people use to describe their feelings about God may be very far from conventional ways of speaking about God in the Church. We have to be alive to all the forms of engagement through which people encounter and are moved by God.

Contact with the arts may open doors for God to work in people's lives, whether through an abstract painting, a best-selling novel or a pop video.[30] If we develop appropriate forms of discernment, popular culture can be an important aide to our Christian witness, providing sense-making experiences and encounters with the transcendental for those who find Church incomprehensible.

For example:

> An artist in Los Angeles, who describes himself as a lapsed Roman Catholic, has drawn considerable attention with his installation of a figure of the Virgin in an empty room containing within her body a large conduit. Stairs at the end of the gallery lead up to nowhere. Yet below grids in the floor are images of extraordinary beauty that can only be glimpsed but not reached. This installation powerfully reminds onlookers that what we see in this world is not all there is and that if we look carefully we may be allowed glimpses of the transcendental reality.

Conversely, we should be aware of what our cultural heritage says about ourselves and what our galleries and museums tell visitors about who we are. What kind of images do we bury in our 'time capsules' as being the most meaningful? Have we asked adequately what the Faith Zone of the Millennium Dome really meant for visitors?[31] How do our churches and cathedrals present the rich legacy of the faith of generations in a way that also makes it clear that the gospel must be proclaimed afresh in each generation? This in itself is also a mission question. Where, in our theological education, can this be addressed?

holy places

Conceptual diversity also means that the recovery of a feeling of sacredness in particular locations can be an important mode of encounter. Many people feel drawn to the numinous and holy sites of Britain and Ireland; some Christians have reported a feeling of greater relationship with Jesus when climbing Glastonbury Tor at sunset. For many people such sacred sites allow them to 'earth' their spiritual feelings and their apperception of God. Preservation and care of holy places also can resonate with concern for green issues and for conservation, as can sympathetic attitudes to green cemeteries and other nature-based memorials. Again it is a task of mission in ministry to be aware of tourists and travellers who may pass through a place of Christian heritage or worship. We need to be equipped to see the opportunity for Christian witness in such encounters.

Hay and Hunt showed: 'The church building was typically seen as sacred space open to all, and not the sole property of churchgoers. Individuals spoke of going into empty churches and appreciating the atmosphere. Somehow there was a different quality to the atmosphere in a church than in other, secular buildings' (Hay and Hunt, 2000, p. 32).

'Graham' remarked:

> *Now as I've said, I'm not particularly religious. I don't go to church. But the feeling of calmness inside there [Ripon Cathedral] and the feeling of humbleness if you like, you know, is, it was amazing ... It was a strange, strange feeling, strange feeling. To say that, um, I don't really feel particularly religious, it was, it was a calming, calming atmosphere.*

It may be possible for us to provide an encounter with a 'Christic' presence that will bear fruit in another place and time. We need to know how to allow a natural and unforced progression to the Jesus Christ of the Christian community who afflicts the comfortable and comforts the afflicted and who provides entry into life in all its fullness.

The mission of the Church, then, is served by radical engagement between Christian witness and the fast-changing world. The conceptual plurality of society coupled with a supremacy of technology and a globalized economy makes the world a difficult place to live in effectively according to the gospel. Unless engagement for appropriate transformation takes place, the Church is perceived as falling behind and having ever less to contribute.

Theological education must therefore contextualize its teaching in terms of the encounter between Church and world. But is this as easy as it seems?

chapter 2

the world as God sees it

If this is the kind of world in which we now live, what story shall we live by? What kind of theology can help us thread a path through the complexities of this technologically advanced and fast-changing world? In this section of our work on 'settings', we ask, through our understanding of mission theology, what the world looks like to God and what that perspective means to us. We also set out what the word 'mission' means for us. This also helps us to ask what theological education is *for*: is it to equip people for ministry *and* mission, or ministry *or* mission, or do these terms become polarized – or even contradictory?

mission as overflow from the heart of God

Mission theology speaks of the *missio Dei* – the mission of God's love to the world. It assumes that God, having created all that is, both allows the creation freely to unfold in its own way, and at the same time retains a purpose of love towards it. This purpose is made known to us through God's revelation and we are offered a share in the process of achieving it. John V. Taylor writes:

> The divine insistence upon sharing responsibility with a human partner underlies the central idea of the Covenant. God's commitment to his people is a commitment to a mutual relationship. God surrenders unilateral sovereignty in order to involve them in responsibility for the future. Divine actions are not predetermined, for God is continually responding to the reactions of his people. That interaction all the time through history is God's partnership with wayward humanity.[1]

As partners with God in the mission of love to the world, we can see that God's intention is a reconciling work which has ultimate ends: the full realization of the kingdom of God and ultimately a new creation, 'a plan for the fullness of time, to gather up all things in him, things in heaven and things on earth' (Ephesians 1.10) in which 'God may be all in all' (1 Corinthians 15.28, cf. Revelation 21.22). The sovereignty of God is not compromised by this, but we are included as active workers, invited to participate in God's intention. We are not asked just to submit to God's will, but freely to become involved.

Mission, then, is not just a theological category describing human endeavours, but is first a function of God's own being. We need to be very clear what we mean however, because, as John V. Taylor also points out, the term *missio Dei* can be used in a very vague way: 'It can be made to include anything under the sun that anyone considers a Good Thing' (Taylor, 1998, pp. 1,2). In order to avoid this, we need to see that God's purpose of love towards the creation stems from what we understand to be the dynamic inter-relationships of the Trinity. The *perichoresis*, or co-inherence of Father, Son and Holy Spirit in love, sends out that love. We can therefore see mission as the heart of God:

> A trinitarian approach to the missio Dei *is therefore important. On the one hand, this promotes a more inclusive understanding of God's presence and work in the whole world and among all people, implying that signs of God's presence can and should be identified, affirmed and worked with even in the most unexpected places. On the other hand, by clearly affirming that the Father and the Spirit are always and in all circumstances present and at work together with the Word, the temptation to separate the presence of God or the Spirit from the Son of God, Jesus Christ, will be avoided. The mission of God is the source and basis for the mission of the church, the body of Christ. Through Christ in the Holy Spirit, God indwells the church, empowering and energizing its members. Thus mission becomes for Christians an urgent inner compulsion, even a powerful test and criterion for authentic life in Christ, rooted in the profound demands of Christ's love, to invite others to share in the fullness of life Jesus came to bring (John 10.10). Participating in God's mission, therefore, should be natural for all Christians and all churches, not only for particular individuals or specialized groups.*[2]

the constancy of God

The mission of God to the world is constant. God's love never gives up nor is it ever withdrawn, even though to human beings, with our imperfect understanding, it may be difficult to see God at work or what the Spirit is doing in any one contemporary snapshot. Reflection on history may show us God's work more clearly, however, although this may depend on our attitude to and handling of Scripture and tradition. God is known to act, to reveal the divine presence, to work in people's lives, to occasion change, to make known the divine promises. Taylor explains this as *Idea* (the Father's mysterious purpose), *Expression* (the Father's Idea manifested in the life of Jesus) and *Recognition* (the Spirit's affirmation of the missionary purpose at the heart of God, the divine 'Yes!') (Taylor, 1998, pp. 3–4). In these various ways God ministers to the creation and in so doing reveals more of the *missio Dei*. We are called to respond and to participate.

the mission of Jesus

The mission of God to the world finds its definitive expression in the person and work of Jesus Christ. This *missio Christi* is shown to us both as the outworking of Jesus' own ministry in obedience to the will of the Father and as the focus of the *missio Dei* in the events of the cross and the resurrection (Taylor, 1998, p. 5). Through the *missio Christi* we are able to make sense of the work that is given the Church for the rest of human history, for in Jesus we have been shown a servant God who suffers with us even as he has become the means of our salvation. Particularly, this mission of love is revealed to us in the Incarnation of Jesus. In the Incarnation, God's own mission and ministry become one, for God does not simply cause or intervene in human affairs, but becomes fully human, interacting with the human condition at every level. Jesus is said to have his own 'ministry', which writers often use to refer to his works of teaching, healing and caring for those around him. Or we can identify a particular ministry, which springs from Jesus' consciousness of having been sent into the world for a purpose. This purpose is worked out and demonstrated through serving and teaching others. Jesus' teaching is profoundly exemplary and by this means the new order is offered to humanity. Jesus both inaugurates and makes possible the kingdom as a sustainable reality in the material world. This restricted use of the term 'ministry', however, is also set within the larger context of Jesus' revelation of God's purpose in his life, death and resurrection and in the further working out of his teaching in the coming into being of the Church. This is the fulcrum of the *missio Dei*, which requires us first to respond to God's mission with our own sense of being sent – 'As the Father has sent me, so I send you' (John 20.21) – and to call our sharing in God's loving purposes a 'ministry' because God makes the divine presence known through dynamic love, by giving up his own self, for us, in Jesus' death on the cross.

problems of using the words 'ministry' and 'mission'

In practice, however, 'ministry' and 'mission' can become extremely slippery words resisting closed definition. This is because what is covered by either term can be quite small: a 'ministry of healing', a 'mission statement', or conversely broad and loose: 'a ministry to the whole people of God',

'Mission 2000'. Further, the terms are used by different people to mean a whole host of different things at different times. Mission can mean activities designed only to add members to a church, or activities aimed at those far away from the Church. Some people confuse mission with evangelism and see a division between those parts of church life directed *ad intra*: to the Church's inner life, and *ad extra*: to the Church's influence on the world outside its doors.[3]

Some would go further and say that the Church's inner life is defined by ministry and everything else is mission – with the added effect that if all the available energy is directed into the Church's life, with nothing left over, then mission is seen as 'impossible', another burden added on to the problems of church life. From this arises the distinction between 'mission and maintenance' with the inbuilt assumption that maintenance is always static and unproductive and mission always dynamic and changing. A further problem in recent years has been the use of the word 'mission' as a feel-good word to be introduced into titles and scripts to obtain the general feeling that mission is 'a good thing'. Maintenance is 'a bad thing' and can make us look negatively at the ministry that goes on within a church struggling to maintain the status quo. We can then become distracted away from the perception that both ministry and mission can take place simultaneously and successively to people inside and outside the Church. Such a perception also takes no account of Robert Warren's exposition of the idea of a 'missionary congregation'[4] or Lesslie Newbigin's assertion that the congregation is a 'hermeneutic of the Gospel'.[5] In the work of these authors, the fellowship of the congregation proclaims the truth of the gospel in and through its engagement with the daily life of the world, such that Christian faith moves from the enclosed, private realm to colour all aspects of public life. Further, Daniel Hardy suggests that:

> The call to mission for individuals and churches arises not only from the discernment of God as 'sending', but also from the 'finding' of God where God has not been 'taken'. Hence, mission is not so much a 'propagation in foreign parts' as a theological discernment of God's Trinitarian action already operative in other people and contexts, in ways which cannot be predicted from 'outside'.[6]

Alongside this, we could look at the holistic way in which some Christian communities are working. For example, in some African countries churches are engaging with material poverty and political oppression, including in those places where the structure of life has been decimated by war, famine and atrocity. Christians have responded positively in order to build community through reacting to the political situation and its consequences and have come up with many resources, including creative worship, within which hymn-singing can play an important part in the process of responsive engagement.

We can see that within the Church 'ministry' and 'mission' are words which are inextricably bound together in describing the activity of Christians, but which are often used as if they belong in different categories. Ministry can be understood as the practical exercise of Christian vocation towards others, and as such is exercised by all members of the Christian community and is not restricted to members of the clergy. Indeed it can even be the case that to become an ordained person constrains that person's gifts or ability. The mission theologian David Bosch sees ministry by the whole people of God as a form of mission in a way that 'ministry' defined as a role for the clergy is not.[7]

ministry as mission

If we see ministry as the practical exercise of Christian vocation towards others, then we can see mission as the directional arrow for such ministry. For example, ministry will carry with it the intention to spread the gospel, build God's kingdom and prepare for the eschatological reality that God has promised us. Ministry does not take place in a vacuum, but ministry by and to the whole people of God works within the context of God's promises and according to God's purposes. This happens because God calls people and equips them through the Holy Spirit to work in partnership for this end. Similarly, we may say that the *missio Dei*, God's mission of love to the whole of the created order, is the *context* by which ministry is teleological. Ministry has purpose, value and meaning because it operates not for its own ends, or even for the ends of the Church, but for the reality of God's intentions for the whole of creation.

chapter 3

the 'marks' of mission

If we know something about our contemporary settings and apply our understanding of mission theology to them, then we can speculate on what we should expect to see happening in the world. Various authorities have pointed to characteristics of the transaction between ministry and its missionary effects and have tried to determine the 'marks of mission'.[1] These 'marks' are the responsibility and result of all Christians acting out their vocation in the world and are not brought about by activity restricted to just one part of the Church. They ask this challenging question which is at the heart of mission perspective: *Who do you think God wants us to be?* The answer to this question helps to define a missionary witness that is prophetic in both its action and its effect.

The Anglican Consultative Council defines five marks of mission, which are general pointers for the Church, as follows:

> To proclaim the Good News of the Kingdom;
>
> To teach, baptize and nurture new believers;
>
> To respond to human need by loving service;
>
> To seek to transform unjust structures of society;
>
> To strive to safeguard the integrity of creation and sustain and renew the earth.[2]

But, these are only 'marks' if there are visible results of these statements of intention to act. What does the intention in these statements actually *mean* and what relevance do they have to the contexts? We now look further beyond the surface statements to see what these marks of mission are about.

to proclaim the good news of the kingdom

This suggests to us that the self-understanding of the Church in mission is about *communication*. Such communication presupposes the existence of metanarrative, a foundational story, and with it the existence of a Christian epistemology in which meaning, value and purpose can be found. Proclamation means that we cannot be satisfied with just keeping this Good News to ourselves; we must share it with those around us.

However, a prophetic witness in today's society requires us to imagine new ways of saying things – finding a vocabulary and a language that build bridges to the jargonized, superficial world (including our own 'church' world). This 'mark' of mission only becomes effective when communication is lively and engaging. Yet something else, something rather more risky, is built into this process. We need to acknowledge that every encounter between any two people changes both of them in the process of speaking and listening. Proclamation can be shaped and altered by both sympathetic and critical attention to the response. Only this process avoids making the Christian gospel into a lovely story that we tell to ourselves for our own sense of satisfaction and superiority – 'the narrative of the lie'.[3]

to teach, baptize and nurture new believers

This 'mark' of mission suggests that the self-understanding of the Church in mission is rooted in *education*. Yet what sort of education is it if we can no longer assume a foundational knowledge of Scripture and tradition in the face of the erosion and loss of a common 'Christian' language? If knowledge of the Christian faith is assumed to be where value, purpose and meaning are found, how do people get to be 'new believers'?

We would suggest that a prophetic witness in today's society requires education certainly, but education offering insight and understanding by means of exploration and discovery of those things that are significant to ourselves and to others. What is it about books, films, TV, pop music, Internet sites, that feeds imagination and fantasy and provokes questioning and reflection? How do we discern what of the Christian narrative and its imagery resonates for us in parts of our culture? For example, in the film, *Gladiator*,[4] the great leader who will not succumb to the temptation to compromise his integrity, becomes a slave, carrying before him always the hope of heaven. Inspiring other oppressed people, he endures injury and pain and finally sacrifices his life to free his people from tyranny. He takes hold of the transcendent reality, which he sees ever more clearly before him, and enters into a final reconciliation with all he has lost, a homecoming in which his murdered wife and child run to welcome him.

to respond to human need by loving service

This 'mark' makes it clear that mission is inextricably related to a ministry of service towards other people. Mission shows its outworking in terms of discernment of need, in pastoral care, and makes sense of how we respond to God's loving mercy towards the poor. Our loving service enables us to discover Christ in others and so find God at work with us in all parts of our society.

If we ask what this means in terms of prophetic witness, though, we find that we can end up in a trap of our own making. For loving service is not just 'doing to' others, but much more 'doing among' and 'being done to'. For example, allowing a homeless person to assert his or her dignity by buying you a drink can feel uncomfortable because of the urge to be the one who helps, but acceptance of that drink without qualification is a mission act, a kingdom reality. Prophetic witness in service means showing others whenever we can what the kingdom is really like. It can cost us. It can be difficult to admit that others can touch our need with loving service too.

to seek to transform the unjust structures of society

This 'mark' suggests the self-understanding of the Church in mission is about change for the better in some way. This requires us to identify the need for change, find out what is necessary for change and to accompany the process of transformation. This is how our 'presence' can make a difference. But this transformation is not the end process. We have a further duty as a prophetic people to help others see the injustice so that it cannot happen again. The 'mark' places upon us the difficult task of helping others see, and want to change, unjust structures.

This kind of prophetic witness suggests strongly that there is no mission without ethics. We cannot take the splinters out of others' eyes until we've dealt with the planks in our own. This requires us to deal unflinchingly with the concepts of repentance and forgiveness – not just empty hand wringing. This is achieved by deeper and closer attention to the ethics of intrinsic value and duty assumed as consequences of of our actions. We need to help ourselves and others work through the consequences of decisions, not just satisfy ourselves with assessments of right and wrong, or even with retrospective rereading of what Christians have done in the name of God in the past. We need to know *why* it is that Christians have acted in various ways throughout our history and to understand the consequences of those actions in ourselves. For example, blaming others for the failures in a church in the past may ignore the need to address what is wrong in the present situation.[5] We need to see poor decisions as learning experiences and to help ourselves and others to turn around to make new journeys together. Dealing with mistakes can make us a more discerning missionary people.

to strive to safeguard the integrity of creation and to renew the earth

This last 'mark' of mission reminds us of the larger picture. The self-understanding of the Church in mission includes issues of stewardship and partnership with God in the process of *ongoing* creation. It is also about the Church's role in ecology and environmental matters, something which can often be forgotten when the life of the Church seems so much to be only about people.

A prophetic witness, then, requires that we make sense of our stewardship at both local and global levels. The way in which we engage with stewardship also determines the way we see ourselves belonging to a common journey of Christian witness from everywhere to everywhere. Questions of renewal are not just about saving and sharing resources, but about seeing the Holy Spirit at work in the whole creation, not just the bits of it we think we would like to be involved in.

what sort of things could we do?

How do people engaging in theological education gain a heart for mission in the workplace that expresses itself in these ways? We can identify various possibilities for all those called to serve God in Christian witness:

- We may seek to identify where God has been and what God is doing in the contexts which we encounter.
- We may seek to discern God's will for the context, seek to prepare the way of the Lord, and to allow the Holy Spirit to work in the situation.
- We may be possessed of a firm vision of what can be achieved to further the kingdom and possess a sure hope in its promise of fulfilment.
- We may witness to what God has done in Christ by word and deed and by setting an example of what Christ calls us to be.
- We may be able to evangelize and nurture believers and to build up the spiritual heart of a congregation.[6]
- We may be able to share and speak about the faith sincerely and to reach out in witness, dialogue, service and pastoral care to people of all other faiths and none.
- We may also have an understanding of holistic mission, such that mission does not relate solely to people, but includes care for God's creation and concern for issues affecting groups and nations and the way they relate to their environments.

We have created this list of suggested opportunities to show that response to the marks of mission requires an ability to engage radically with the world. Our job is to create realistic bridges between the world as we believe God wants it to be and the world we really encounter. We need special gifts, tools and skills to do this, as we have to make sense of rapidly changing contexts, and to learn fast in complex situations. Experience undoubtedly has a large part to play in being mission-oriented in contemporary western society, but this is not just years chalked up as a nurse or an accountant or as a minister, but real experience which has been reflected upon theologically and which has thereby become a tool for mission. For this reason, theological education that equips us with these skills and allows us the space to reflect theologically is now more critical than ever in making the Church a relevant, transforming force in our contemporary society.

chapter 4

people in ministry and mission

who will go for us?

Theological education is not restricted to institutions but is part of the life and function of the whole Church. It takes place on many levels and is part of the Christian witness that seeks to make Christ known. In what ways, then, does the Church's formal theological education in colleges, courses and schemes interact with the day-to-day ministry of the whole people of God and how is it equipped to deal with the contexts which Christians face daily? To see how theological education and training does this, we need to look at its range.

We believe that all people are called to serve God and to discern and develop their gifts in ways that represent their response to the *missio Dei*. The majority of those whose search for faith brings them to a Christian commitment serve God by worship, prayer and by seeking to live out their faith in all parts of their lives. This is not a casual statement since it implies that our faith should thereby affect every part of our life in society, including how we relate to others and how we make decisions.

faith and work

For example, our Christian faith may demand that we work to transform unjust structures and to support the poor and disadvantaged. John Battle, a Roman Catholic MP, argues that his Christian faith is more than church worship but includes walking around his local area praying for his constituents as well as using his office to help improve their lives.[1] We may feel called to work for the care of God's creation, or to strive to make a Christian voice heard in global politics. Many kinds of ministry and mission may be involved here, and the possibility for both is latent in every single human encounter, no matter where it takes place or what the circumstances. Our life of prayer and worship sustains our consciousness of these opportunities and helps us grow in confidence to make the most of situations. Therefore mission and ministry go on in small, but not insignificant, ways all the time. Teachers confessing their Christian faith in a school assembly may have a profound impact on many pupils to whom this may not make sense for years. A shopkeeper who remembers customers' names and asks after their families may make important human contacts that pave the way for pastoral care. God can use any relationship and any encounter to enter into people's lives. Many Christians, then, are involved in ministry and mission by virtue of their faith and never have recourse to any kind of formal training or accreditation for what they do. This should never be undervalued.

specialized training: opportunities for lay people

Since all Christians are called by God, and all have opportunities for encounter, it follows that every kind of person, of every age group and from all walks of life, may enter full- or part-time theological training through a college, course, or scheme or other study opportunity. Many reasons may lead them to do so. Lay people may be called to grow in their faith through learning and may also take on authorized ministry – as evangelists or as special pastoral assistants, for example. In other circumstances, they may take on other full-time church work, or work in specialist posts. Lay people may also combine work for the Church with another form of employment. Ministry, however, is not restricted to that part of a person's employment life that relates to Church. People whose lives cross daily between church responsibilities and a non-church job must also carry over their service of God into every area of their lives.

ordained ministry

Some Christians feel called by God to train for the ordained ministry. For those who are called and who are then selected to train for the ordained ministry, successful completion of a period of theological training will usually result in the taking up of a post with particular kinds of responsibility. For full-time stipendiary clergy, this may mean posts in parish or congregational ministry, mission work at home or overseas, chaplaincy or teaching work. Some may also enter specialist sector ministry. In these cases the contexts for ministry will often be defined by the boundaries of the job responsibility and have certain immediate characteristics. It is possible, for example, to speak of people entering urban, suburban or rural ministry, hospital chaplaincy or youth work. It is also possible to move from one of these characterized ministries to another, assuming the transfer of some skills and the acquisition of others in the new context. However, this does not presuppose that any given responsibilities in a job cut down the person's ability to be mission-oriented, only that some kinds of context are more likely to be encountered than others.

For non-stipendiary clergy responsibilities will be to sector ministry, or to a particular congregation, which may be combined with a secular job. Such clergy may be retired, be parish focused or work focused. There is considerable variation in how such ministries are deployed.

a holistic view of mission/ministry

Theological education that involves equipping people with a heart for mission is not about helping people only to serve God in a church context; rather it is about helping people acquire a holistic understanding of the relation between the Church and the world. Such a holistic view helps to nurture and refine our ability to interact with a whole set of contexts as the whole people of God goes about living in a complex and changing world.

What, then, distinguishes those who have been through a period of theological education in terms of mission? The Ministry Division of the Church of England, for example, highlights mission-orientation, asking selectors to consider whether candidates have thought through the message of the gospel and their contribution to sharing it, and further:

> *In proclaiming the Gospel and witnessing to their faith, ministers need the ability to communicate not only with those who are Church members but also with those who are not. They need to live the Gospel as well as speak about it. In many instances it is what ministers do and are rather than what they say which promotes faith in others. However, the ability to communicate and inspire by word remains of great importance. Ministers should be able to convey their faith and its meaning in the style of people around them. They need to be able to discern God in the present moment and in the lives of those with whom they come into contact in order to further God's revelation.*[2]

The whole Church in mission, however, comes about as a result of a partnership between those so selected for ministry and the people served by them. In what ways, then, can all Christian people facilitate mission through their ministry? What are the end results?

chapter 5

some stories

We have talked theoretically about the contexts for mission, but what kinds of situation are we talking about? Here are some illustrations of ministry and mission working together in ordinary people's lives, but which might be overlooked as such because we have stereotypical images of what we mean by these words. All of them convey a sense of journey. None of them is 'finished' but the reality of God's love coming into the situation through the ministry of others has made a difference and allowed God to change the direction in people's lives. The stories also show that God can and will use any situation and that we can find ministry in unexpected and unlooked for situations.

> *Margaret, in her eighties, and a lifelong member of her local Roman Catholic church, was tending her husband's grave in the municipal cemetery when she began talking to another woman sitting crying on one of the benches. This woman was recently widowed and very distressed. After sharing the grief of their loss together, the two became friends and shared their mutual love of gardening with trips together to the local garden centre. The lady who was recently widowed was also invited to accompany her friend to other things, including church, but persistently refused. One day, Margaret was doing the flowers for a wedding in church and asked her friend for help and on this occasion she agreed. They both remained for the service, sitting at the back out of public gaze. This helped the reluctant widow to overcome her fear of church as the place where she had to say goodbye to her husband. She now attends church occasionally and has been able to share her sense of bereavement with others in her new family.*

In this story, Margaret's ministry to the widow has taken the form of pastoral care, befriending and sharing her own faith and Christian life in a non-threatening way. The pastoral care has centred on the woman's bereavement and on ways to help her through that. But this is also a story about mission, for it involves honest faith-sharing even if this took place gradually through relationship and not in any immediate evangelistic way. The person outside the Church has been offered a home, not just as a problem to be solved or cured, but as a whole person valued for her gifts and knowledge and as a friend. There is an intertwining of mission and ministry here: the mission act cannot work without the ministry to the bereaved; the ministry cannot work without the holistic missionary impulse to share faith and witness to God's healing love. There is a Zacchaeus principle in mission where we need to recognize those whose view is blocked but who are still hoping for a glimpse of Jesus. Discerning their need allows us to offer to them a possibility in their own lives of providing hospitality for Christ. A willingness to let Christ in further opens up the hope of conversion and repentance.

> *When we look round our churches in Rwanda, two-thirds of the congregation are younger people. That's on Sundays. This has been a challenge to the Church – how to nurture these young people. At the end of the day, when you look at registrations for weddings in the church, you see maybe two or three people are celebrating their marriages in the church. You have this paradox: you see many young people coming to the church, but few of them are having Christian marriage.*

> *So as a response to this challenge to the Church, we see being developed a kind of 'uncle and auntie' approach, which we have borrowed from our culture. We have a list of uncles and aunties, and they meet young people every Tuesday of every week, and one Saturday a month. This has led to a kind of outreach to people in the town and the rural area. We have outreach which has embraced street children. The results are there: two of the street children are now members of our choir. The results are the offspring of the uncles–aunties approach which is proving so fruitful in our church.*[1]

In this story, ministry among young people is undergirded by the importance of relationship. These 'uncles' and 'aunties' are not artificial constructs for Christian outreach, but relationships that already have important functions within the culture. These are made possible by the Church in order to reach further out from the town to the rural areas and to the street children who have no family and no sense of belonging.

the importance of prayer

> *In a strong, dynamic Anglican church there was a very active group of people who thought of themselves as the core group. These were involved in a mission and evangelism team. These people were 'doers', delivering literature, knocking on doors, running courses and house groups. For a while, though, there seemed to be an imbalance in the church, with other people being viewed as redundant if they were unable to be part of the mission team. This changed, however, when an elderly disabled person in the congregation began to pray regularly for*

people known to her working in mission overseas and received from them letters telling her how important her prayers were. Eventually, she was able to recruit more people to do nothing more or less than pray for the work of the church's own mission team. This made the 'doers' feel strengthened and supported and allowed those involved in prayer to feel they were contributing in a real way to the work and achievement of the active core. Meetings in the local sheltered housing were set up to strengthen and consolidate the life of prayer, creating a spiritual heart to the work of the church.[2]

In this story, we can see that overemphasis on the buzzword 'mission' led to a loss of confidence in the 'ministry' of the whole people of God. Evangelism was taking place in the community but it lacked a link back to the will of the *whole* congregation that people in the community should hear the Good News. By building up the life of prayer as a ministry to undergird those involved in visible mission work, the ministries of all the participants were able to build up the health of the congregation and give worth to both the internal and external functions of the church.

good Samaritans

In the Balkans, a soldier was shot by a sniper while his patrol was attempting to reach a Muslim family in a wrecked house who were cut off from aid and under fire. The family risked their own lives to get him under cover and looked after him until they could be rescued. They tended his wound and shared their food and water, although he was fitter, stronger and much more likely to survive than they. Although a non-practising Christian, the soldier later said that while he was sheltering with them and waiting for the rest of his group, he could not stop thinking of the parable of the good Samaritan: 'I was supposed to be risking my life for them.' While in hospital, reflecting on what had been done for him by complete strangers, the soldier decided to re-evaluate all his important relationships. Once home, he made peace with his estranged family and expressed his commitment in a proposal of marriage to his long-term girlfriend.

In this story, we can see a contemporary example of one of Jesus' most challenging parables. The questions 'where do we expect ministry to come from?' and 'who is my neighbour?' receive surprising and difficult answers. The soldier expected to serve, not to be in need of service. He had superior training, equipment, back-up and technology, yet found himself in a situation where those who had nothing could and would give him everything, resulting in a 'conversion experience' in his own life and relationships. This experience did not result in a commitment to Christian faith, but what is interesting is that the picture that was present in the soldier's mind came from a powerful recognition of the reality of a parable, a seed planted perhaps in Sunday school or in an RE class or school assembly.

problems with power

On a council estate, a lay worker began to jeopardize the health of the church by demanding more and more work from the ordained ministers in her area. Her ministry was incredibly important to her, but it was primarily engaged in feeding her own need to feel powerful. Her work with baptism and marriage preparation became a matter of her feeling she had been given authority over people's lives and she would attempt to force people to make decisions for which they were unprepared. Over time, this resulted in factionalism within the church, families fighting among themselves and a number of relationships breaking up, including the working relationship between the lay worker and the ordained ministers. The church membership fell dramatically, which only served to make the lay worker work even harder and to perpetuate the cycle. It took the presence of a sister from a nearby religious community, brought in to work on the estate, to heal the multiple rifts and to challenge the lay worker's view of ministry. No other help was offered to the lay worker.

In this rather different story, it is possible to see how a skewed view of what ministry is about can damage the mission of the Church. Where there is an abuse of authority and listening to and respecting other people's stories does not happen, people cannot grow and may turn away to follow their search for faith outside the Church. Sensitivity to the context matters. If Margaret, in the first story, had been purely concerned to recruit the bereaved widow and had not addressed her feelings of loss and her need for friends, then the result would quite likely have been a strong rejection of the Church and all it represents. Another difficulty raised by the lay worker's situation is the lack of resources for her problems. What was being covered up by her need to exercise ministry?

changed by music

Frank, a man in his forties, with a long history of personal troubles, was used to coming to church to receive unfailing sympathy and support from the minister and the congregation. Worship, for him, was dominated by the anticipation of unburdening and receiving ministry. In general, he felt bored and isolated during the service.

One day, however, the first hymn was 'O Jesus, I have promised' and Frank realized that he was paying attention to words which formerly he allowed to wash over him. He realized that the congregation was fulfilling the promise in supporting and ministering to him, but that he was not one with them because he was not fulfilling his own promise to serve. He also felt that 'I shall not fear the battle' meant that he could find the strength to wean himself off his dependence on the kindness and sympathy of the congregation, which he had been seeking as an end in itself and not as a means to an end. He now felt that the worship could become the support he needed.

After the service, he volunteered to make the coffee and wash up, much to the astonishment of all his friends. In due course, he managed to make some improvements in his personal life and become more integrated in the serving ministry of the church. He found that the more he engaged in ministry towards others, particularly the sick, the less he was preoccupied by his difficulties and troubles, although these did not lessen or go away. The congregation suggested that he consider some more formal way of his ministry being recognized, though Frank himself resisted this.

In this story, the change from being served to giving service comes about as worship suddenly becomes alive and meaningful in a person's life. A passive role and a persistent drawing from others within the church community were gradually replaced by a more outward-looking, active approach to Christian life, even though Frank's personal difficulties did not change. The congregation's response was to seek to validate or express formal recognition of this ministry, but it is interesting that Frank himself did not want to change the basis on which he carried out his promise to Jesus. While it is important that vocation is acknowledged and supported from within congregations, different journeys must also be affirmed and sustained.

a Church centre

On another council estate, a 'Church Centre' was established with the church premises being used for access to all kinds of professional help. Although, initially, Christian people were the leaders in providing a ministry of pastoral care to those attending the centre, increasingly a non-Christian community worker and other professionals such as health care and social workers began to be those who were most active in addressing the various needs of a whole community. This meant that the perception of a 'Christian' or 'church' ministry to the community began to be redefined as ministry from the community into the church, freeing up the congregation for mission. This was a very unsettling experience as the church members had to relinquish their initial roles and release them to others with superior skills, trusting non-Christians with pastoral tasks. Similarly, work with dispossessed people, where homeless people or refugees begin to bring their own gifts into the congregation, can challenge notions of who should be serving whom and change perceptions of who the 'ministers' and the 'ministered to' are.

This story reminds us that ministry and mission depend on the goodwill of other partners outside the safe walls of the church. While undoubtedly, in some situations, ministers may be the only professionals available and may be called on for advice about all kinds of matters beyond their expertise,[3] in other contexts, ministers may fail to recognize the importance of partnership with others.

what we learn from the wider world

In the global arena, we can see further questions about who must practise and who must receive ministry. In Korea, some of those who have suffered most at the hands of oppressors have found a way to reflect theologically on their experiences and to break out of the vicious circle of suffering and revenge. These 'minjung' meditate on their situations and approach what they call 'critical transcendence' to leave behind the bitterness and hatred arising from personal vendettas and from scapegoating in community situations, to find a way to forgive those who have hurt them. They understand that by this means a radical change is effected in the world, which is wider than the individual, so that salvation and reconciliation are poured into the empty spaces where the loss of relationship, through anger and despair, has torn holes.[4]

The Church all too often preaches forgiveness towards the sinful world without considering how the world can offer the Church forgiveness and the chance to change. In the Church Centre described above, 'critical transcendence' was coming from the interaction between the jobless, deprived families on the estate and non-Christian facilitators of the recovery of their self-esteem. We talk about issues of justice and peace without considering how reconciliation needs to come from those whom we would serve. How far are we guilty of creating underclasses of people by whatever means, in order to have someone to serve?

chapter 6

styles of teaching and learning

a theological exploration

We have argued that mission is a response to the overflowing love from God's very heart. We have set out a picture of life in contemporary western society and suggested that the engagement between God's mission of love and the world we live in is complex. We have considered what the ministry of the whole people of God means in this situation, but also how the Church commissions ministers to fill jobs that are available for lay and ordained people. What else is necessary for people taking these jobs to engage in mission? We have also argued that theological education is critically important in equipping people for effective mission.

Now we need to ask: in what ways can people best be helped to develop a 'heart for mission' through theological education? What needs to happen to equip people to engage effectively with the contexts for mission? Answering this question depends not only on *what* people are taught, but also on *how* they learn and *how* they afterwards apply that learning. Later we will look at the content of aspects of theological education through a mission lens, but in this section we look at styles of teaching and learning and ask which may help people better to grapple with the mission issues of twenty-first-century life.

where we're coming from

We decided it would be useful if we looked at our own backgrounds and tried to assess what our training had given us and what relation it had had to our passion for mission. If we were biased in some way because of our own formation, we would be able to see that in the process of sharing with one another.

Not all of us came from Christian homes or backgrounds, and some of us had had difficult early experiences. A few of us were called by God as teenagers and planned our training accordingly. Most of us were very aware of positive experiences of God as young adults among fellow Christians, but also of the effect of our immediate training at that time. For some of us it was a positive and exciting experience, for others frustrating and difficult. Some of us 'travelled' from our starting point within a particular church background to end up elsewhere. Cross-cultural encounter was fundamental to a number of us and changed lives forever. For those of us who are ordained, training for the ministry was both formal and traditional. Further, most of us are academics and many of us come from backgrounds in which academic excellence is paramount, something, which we felt, might colour our assumptions if we did not take this into account. Some of us recounted our debt to inspiring teachers who left lasting impressions. Although all of us have passed through some form of studying theology, this was not necessarily where we began. Within the group we have people who studied English, languages, the social sciences, classics, geology. All of us have been involved in teaching others.

What was interesting was that we had all worked through the rather formal, academic and intellectual aspects of training to find that emotional engagement made a difference to our having 'hearts for mission'. For some of us that means being fully engaged with justice and peace issues, or with politics. For a number of us, engagement with the arts makes a difference, with a particular emphasis on words and music in worship. Subsequent experiences of church life have also shaped and changed us, but especially perhaps Christian life lived in other cultures and in ecumenical situations.

One of us said 'I owe a deep debt of gratitude for my theological training',[1] while others of us found we had to get beyond what we had been taught to see more clearly what God wants of us. We were surprised by the diversity among us, but grateful for the chance to see how different paths and backgrounds had converged into a group that is able to enter into fruitful theological conversation.

Having shared our backgrounds, we then decided we would offer a theological exploration of styles of teaching and learning.[2]

what are we supposed (allowed) to know?

> *They heard the sound of the Lord God walking in the garden at the time of the evening breeze, and the man and his wife hid themselves from the presence of the Lord God among the trees of the garden. But the Lord God called to the man, and said to him, 'Where are you?' He said, 'I heard the sound of you in the garden, and I was afraid, because I was naked; and I hid myself.' He said, 'Who told you that you were naked? Have you eaten from the tree of which I commanded you not to eat?'*
> (Genesis 3.8-11)

Christian theology traditionally attributes omniscience to God. Does this then mean that learning is merely a human activity and a consequence of our existence in time? We see from the creation narratives in Genesis that one of our prominent archetypes, also present in many other cultures, relates to the idea that human beings should not aspire to the level of knowledge and understanding found in God. All too often human beings, impossibly curious, disobedient, full of pride, or desirous of equality with God, make the attempt on divine knowledge and bring on themselves ruin and despair. Adam and Eve do it. Prometheus does it. The builders of the Tower of Babel come tumbling down with it. Does this mean that we are not meant to know the things that God only knows? Or does it indicate that with education comes responsibility, and more questions yet to be answered and a whole host of moral and ethical questions for which we may not be adequately prepared? Does it indicate further, that theological education *in particular* places burdens of purpose upon us? What is this knowledge *for*? What is this learning *for*? Asking these questions may mean that a person's theological education may in many cases be intimately linked to a sense of vocation, of a purpose in life, and while it may strengthen that person's calling and sense of purpose, it may equally challenge it in unexpected ways. Some forms of theological education set out to provide this challenge, others to strengthen conviction and purpose; yet again, for some people it may provide the first opportunity and safe place to explore doubt. From the mission perspective, however, whatever learning in theological education takes place, God still asks for our partnership in the divine mission to the world. Our imperfect understanding is called to be instrumental in the reconciliation of the creation to God's own self.

can God learn?

A mission perspective suggests that learning in theological education is not just about the acquisition of facts, theories and interpretations, but also about relationships, including the relationship between human beings and God. But this creates a complex missionary question. One strand of biblical material certainly suggests that God is omniscient: 'I am God, and there is no other; I am God, and there is no one like me, declaring the end from the beginning and from ancient times things not yet done' (Isaiah 46.9,10). However, another strand of biblical material seems to suggest that God learns about us through relationship with us as free beings. This is important, because it relates to how a missionary God is involved in the creation itself.

We can see from Scripture that where God forms partnerships with human beings as part of the unfolding of the *missio Dei*, the evolving understanding of humans through events and experiences is reflected in God's own response. For example, in the sign of the rainbow after the Flood, God is understood to reflect with human beings on the destruction and waste and to implement the Covenant with Noah on the basis of this: 'I establish my covenant with you, that never again shall all flesh be cut off by the waters of a flood, and never again shall there be a flood to destroy the earth' (Genesis 9.11).

what does this say about a missionary God?

In the history of Israel, God's relationship with the chosen people continues by virtue of this mutual learning of each other in the process of partnership as history unfolds. God expresses regret and anger at wilful disobedience and sin, but satisfaction and delight at the return of the faithless people. Although God gives instruction to the chosen people by means of the giving of the Law, it is the application of the Law to the life of the people that defines the relationship with God. Living in accordance to the Law and as a holy people allows the people of Israel to understand more of God.

The prophetic voice is also a means of learning, as are signs and allegories, prompting God's people to reflect on meanings and to gain spiritual insights. In Jonah, for example, a profound learning experience must be undergone in mind, body and spirit, before the prophet is equipped to help the people of Nineveh learn about God. In Job, experience and reflection through suffering open the doors to an understanding of God's majesty. This suggests that all our theological learning is not a matter of 'catching up with God' but a much deeper process by which we offer our experiences, and our intellectual and emotional life to the economy of the divine will.[3] If the *missio Dei* really does ask for true partnership with human beings, then God can and does respond to the use we make of our free will. This response requires that we add discernment to all forms of our learning and understanding. As Christians, the offering of our learning may be obedient, but discernment does not mean comfortable acceptance. We shall show that theological learning may require asking hard, critical questions about a missionary God. Who *is* this God who tests Jonah and Job in this way? God may be the God of surprises, but are we capable of surprising God by our capacity for love and sacrifice, or conversely, for evil and inflicting of suffering? These may be very pertinent questions in our own times, where people are struggling to understand the love and the evil of which we are capable.

Jesus as one who learns among us

Another biblical strand concerns Jesus' growing up and acquiring knowledge as we do: 'And Jesus increased in wisdom and in years, and in divine and human favour' (Luke 2.52). Jesus studied the Hebrew Scriptures as we do and his learning formed the foundation of his teaching ministry. This is helpful to us in making sense of a theological model of learning, since through Jesus we do not have to choose between an omniscient God and a God who has the capacity to learn. The most important event may be Gethsemane, where Jesus surrenders his will to leave the outcome of events in the Father's hands. Our learning, then, can show us more clearly what we do not know, so that we may accept the need for obedience to the will of the Father.

Our discussion of these ideas led us to an image that may help us to reconcile the ideas of the omniscient God and the learning Jesus: the Ascension.[4] In the Ascension, Jesus takes his human life, which he has lived and experienced as we do, back into the heart of God. For this reason, we can imagine that all our learning and growth, as far as we are capable of these things, is received by God as part of our ultimate destiny.

Jesus as teacher

In the New Testament, we see Jesus teaching in the rabbinic tradition in the synagogue and teaching his disciples and crowds of followers in the open air. Although we see some asking direct questions on points of law or religious practice, we also see people asking larger questions, which open up the possibilities for a new relationship with God: 'Good Teacher, what must I do to inherit eternal life?' (Mark 10.17). Jesus also teaches by means of experience, as in the healing miracles, and by means of parable. The parable is a self-enclosed story whose many layers of meaning can only be accessed by the listener's own participation in reflection and meditation. By means of stories with which his listeners can identify, Jesus breaks open each parable's narrative enclosure with a focus on the God whose kingdom stands among us. By this means learning also becomes a matter of seeing the world differently and reviewing our knowledge in this new light. It can sometimes involve the painful process of unlearning and letting go of previous understandings that are no longer adequate. By this means too the mysterious and secret becomes accessible, even if what is accessed is beyond our understanding. We have a forum to acknowledge what is baffling and puzzling about the world and about God without recourse to gnosticism or mysticism.[5]

In the Epistles, we are given other forms of discourse, by which we can learn more about how the mystery of God in Christ is revealed. But, if we are thinking with a heart for mission, what use is all this if those among whom we live have no faculty for sharing our interpretative tools. Are we just being trained to be 'insiders'?

how do we learn anyway?

teaching and learning in relation to spirituality

We might argue that learning is a fundamental feature of human existence, as, from the earliest stages of foetal awareness, we acquire learning both through information and experience. Learning, and use of memory, allow us to survive. On the basis of information and experience we acquire the ability to make decisions about how to live. The mere possession of information is not sufficient to help us make our way in the world – a child who knows the Green Cross Code must also be able to apply it to real situations on a busy road. As we grow according to our specific abilities, we aggregate knowledge both for ourselves and as a consequence of our social relations with others. We share knowledge with others in families, social networks and in communities. By this means, we learn complex social interactions, such as when to speak and when to keep silent. We also learn to make judgements about the value, meaning and purpose of the information and understanding we possess. Our parents, friends and teachers and all our everyday experiences contribute to these processes. This means we not only have a multitude of examples with which to compare our lives, but also the tools to control our own learning and to make decisions about what is important to us in the future.

are we allowed to ask questions?

Even so, learning is not just a matter of filling our minds with information or of acquiring social skills. It also relates to our ontological and existential perceptions, and to our faith development. This matters, especially if we have a heart for mission, because the culture in which we live does not necessarily take this seriously, as we shall show. In one view, we are all in a process of continuous creation, continually recreating ourselves on the basis of what we did yesterday and are doing today. We can constantly take on some meanings and reject others, constructing a reality from what is on offer. But, at the same time, people may have foundational experiences of God that remain unacknowledged or untapped, so that the experiences are not shared and never have the chance to contribute to faith development.[6]

the spirit of the child

For example, David Hay and Rebecca Nye have shown that children very often have profound religious experiences that become reinterpreted or even put down by adults. Consequently, the learning and growth potential of these experiences can often be repressed or left undeveloped for years, until in later life they may become significant in the faith development and understanding of the person. For example, Hay and Nye cite a conversation with Rachel, aged ten, about plants:

> *Well, there must be somewhere, somehow – or else, how would it keep reproducing? Like it [?] made a flower, a dandelion. Where did the wind come from to blow all the petals off to make them fall to the floor to make more? … [in a whisper] It's puzzling.*[7]

It is worth wondering what significance this will have when Rachel becomes an adult. How can Christian witness answer her question for her and will her sense of awe and wonder be nurtured and allowed to grow? Sadly, it appears that, for many people, this is not the case.

Scientific answers may satisfy questions of cause and effect, but not deal with the larger question of purpose or the relation of the human self to a world where plants behave in this mysterious and wonderful way. Hay and Nye believe that children display an innate 'relational consciousness' that makes them aware of God, and recommend specific actions to nurture the spirit of the child as follows (Hay and Nye, 1998, p. 162ff.):

● Helping to keep an open mind;

● Exploring ways of seeing;

● Encouraging personal awareness;

● Becoming aware of the social and political dimensions of spirituality.

Hay and Nye believe that these aspects of teaching and learning have been largely neglected in recent years and, therefore, we need to be aware of the deficit and to try to redress the balance. More to the point, from a mission point of view, how far are foundational experiences of God, no matter how bizarre or unformed, acknowledged within theological education and training? *Are we allowed to ask questions?* Is exploration of other ways of seeing encouraged within the educational programme and is it linked to spiritual development? Manifestly, unless theological education includes permission for this exploration, we may miss the opportunity of helping the many Rachels we may meet or, indeed, Johns:

> *Well once I went um … in the night and I saw this bishopy kind of alien. I said 'who are you?' and he said, 'I am the Holy Spirit'. I did think he was the Holy Spirit.*

> *When, in his shock, he called out to his mum and explained what had just happened, John was told that the Holy Spirit looks like a ball of fire, and his version of events was rejected. He seemed to accept his mother's authority concerning this sighting, though he added, 'But I often felt the Holy Spirit in me' (Hay and Nye, 1998, p. 102).*

Powerful experiences of God, fundamental to a sense of vocation, can often be ignored, belittled, or worse, reinterpreted with the stamp of authority, which shuts down the experience and refuses to value it as a means of learning and spiritual growth. Theological education is perhaps especially prone to doing this, because it is properly concerned with delivery of the knowledge of God and because there is often not sufficient time or resources for explorations of this kind. But the development of a heart for mission demands that resolution of such experiences take place so that we may look for it, acknowledge it in others and help them to use it. For example:

> *Peter had been in parish ministry for ten years and was feeling more and more as if he was just going through the motions. For years too he had had a terrible fear of heights and of falling, which became deeper and darker until he began to feel a sense of vertigo in the pulpit or even walking down the street. Finally, he reached a point of no return. It was the death of a baby, a cot death, and the parents were distraught. Despite all his training in bereavement counselling and years of experience, he discovered he had nothing to say or to offer. He stood over the grave and felt as if he was going to be sick, or he was going to fall in. The ground would swallow him or he would collapse. He thought then that if he couldn't deal with this, he couldn't go on in parish ministry.*

> *At the couple's home, the mother told him she had had a vivid dream of a baby falling from a high building. But just before the child hit the ground, a man stepped out from the gaping crowd and caught her. She ran after him but he and the baby were lost in the crowd. She felt an aching sense of loss but also gladness that the baby was completely safe. She said that she had the same feelings now about the death of her child – in spite of the aching loss, there was a sense of safety, a promise of salvation. It occurred to Peter then, like a blinding light, that*

that was his trouble. He had preoccupied himself with the idea of loss of faith and falling to destruction. He saw himself on the precipice always. But the mother's dream made him ask himself if there had ever been that same sense for him, of the one who steps forward out of the darkness at the very bottom and breaks the fall. He thought back to his ordination and before that, when he was sure that God wanted him for ministry. He remembered that he had had a similar experience of Jesus supporting him and holding him up when he had doubts in himself and in his capability to be a priest. But he had never discussed this with anyone. No one had ever asked him about anything pertinent to it. He had just forgotten all about it.

This story shows that even the theologically educated can have powerful experiences of God's love locked away inside them that need to be released in some way. Learning and reflection are not done in a specified period and then left, but need to be engaged at all times. Part of being equipped for mission, then, is asking of every situation: *what am I ready to learn from this?*

theological teaching: what should we expect people to know?

A group of Oxford students was discussing a nineteenth-century short story in a seminar group. One of the themes of the story was that of betrayal and the betrayals were arranged in threes. On seeking to elucidate the theological foundation for the story, the group was asked what background they could imagine for the text. One of the group said, 'Wasn't there some bloke in the Bible who betrayed another bloke three times?' The group was asked for further information about this foundational story, but nobody knew. Once the story of Jesus and Peter had been supplied to the group, they were amazed at the way this unlocked the text they were studying. Some of the students were indifferent and felt it was interesting but not fundamental to their enjoyment of the story. Others were struck for the first time by the power of the gospel narrative.

One of us in the group was the teacher on this occasion and it had a profound effect on her to realize that the stories that live deep inside us may never have been assimilated by even the most well-educated other people. This example shows that we can no longer assume that people have any sophisticated inherited knowledge or understanding of the Christian narratives. This may be as relevant to those seeking some form of theological training as for any other group and it may be that much more foundational work may be necessary than was true previously. This obviously puts a strain on the teaching burden, such that there can be a tension between where teachers would *like* to begin and where it is *necessary* to begin. For this reason, greater emphasis on pre-theological training is perhaps required today.

teaching and vocation

However, even if people do not come into theological training with a large amount of foundational knowledge about the Christian faith, this does not mean that they have not had extremely important experiences of God, or that they do not experience a strong and compelling sense of call. Indeed, this strong sense of vocation may be the most important factor in determining their ability to be mission-oriented and their desire to enter into theological training. The problem is that this may be neglected or even lost, if a great deal of time needs to be put into teaching students the basic information they need to know. From a mission point of view, however, it is not enough just to value and affirm experience.

Efforts should be made to value and affirm what people have done before entering training. It has been an unfortunate by-product of some forms of teaching that people's lives and experiences have not been given value in this way. Consequently, 'formation' has been seen as something imposed by training rather than something nurtured by God. A further issue arises: how far has this experience has been in dialogue with others in the tradition, past and present, and what difference this has made to the development of a person's faith. This may need to be analysed and understood as part of developing a heart for mission. Notwithstanding, as with the children whose experiences are reinterpreted or put aside by adults, so people who have passed through training have often found that who they were before they entered training has come to the surface. This can be precipitated by times of crisis or in situations for which training has not prepared them. For example:

Ray was selected for training, was ordained and went to work on a large inner-city council estate. Although he had come from the same kind of background as most of the people on the estate, he found it increasingly difficult to avoid being seen as 'other'. His theological training and education set him apart from those around him and often seemed to become a stumbling block. An old man in a pub accused him of having 'a mouth full of hard stones' when he tried to talk to the pubgoers about the Christian faith. A breakthrough came for him when he was talking to some local youths who were trying to fix up an old car. Ray had trained as a car mechanic in his younger days and was soon able to help the young men get the car on the road. Later, he was invited to ride in it. Soon, other youths on the estate began coming to the vicarage to get help and advice about fixing up old cars and Ray soon found that his skills as a mechanic were the avenue that God could use for his witness to the gospel. He said, 'when I said what I'd been taught I was always using other people's words and it showed. A spanner and an oily rag were still the only languages I had.'

Jasmine, a lay woman working for a Pentecostal church had been trained as a teacher and as a nurse. She thought that God was asking her to use her communication skills and her abilities with people to build up her local congregation and to provide pastoral care. Very soon, however, she discovered this task was becoming impossibly hard and she became depressed and anxious about her ministry. Eventually, when teaching some children in a church group she realized she was making no impression at all and finally dried up. Her husband, leader of the music group, suggested that she get out her flute and play her feelings about the teaching point. When she did this, the children began to clap and sing and finally to dance. From then on, communication was much easier. She reflected later that she knew God had given her the gifts to do this work, but she had simply assumed it would be the gifts her training had given her and not her natural, musical skill. Now she extemporizes on her flute to illustrate stories and to inspire both children and adults. For her, now, 'nothing could be more natural'.

discernment of gifts

Who people are, what they have done and where they have been may be exceptionally important for the ability to witness to the gospel and to be mission-oriented after theological training has ended. For this reason, these aspects of people's lives need to be accepted, nurtured, affirmed and reflected upon as part of the training process, even if these included negative or bad experiences. But this is no mean task if a great deal of time needs to be spent on 'catching up' to a required level of knowledge. Because of this, perhaps the best way of encouraging people to make their contribution is to ask them to use a learning resource among themselves. For example, the *Telling Our Faith Story*[8] material helps people to get to grips with talking about their most private and intimate stories of God in their lives. It also strives to overcome the embarrassment or awkwardness some people can feel about their sense that God has purpose for their lives. The process of charting one's life as a journey, with its different shares of highs and lows, also allows people to think of their life experiences as a continuous process, all of which is under the influence of the Holy Spirit. Encouraging people to reflect on the ways in which all their life experiences have equipped them to be missionary in the light of all other learning, helps people to value all that they are and to see others as whole persons loved and desired by God. For this reason, some basic reflective questions can focus the mission orientation of any person entering theological training, such as:

- Where is God in this?
- What does it mean to speak of God in this situation and what is the most appropriate language to use?
- What experiences and/or gifts do I have to draw on in this situation?
- How can I offer this to God's will?
- What or whom else do I need to do God's will?

These kinds of questions can be helpful to people throughout their theological education.

teaching methods

Yet we are aware that to fulfil academic expectations and requirements pressure is often put on teachers to deliver a required amount of knowledge and to have that knowledge tested by means of essays, group assessment, or examinations. There are also time constraints in part-time, non-residential courses. Delivery of knowledge is traditionally accomplished by the 'banking method', by means of lectures, seminars, group sessions, or tutorials. We ourselves are used to teaching in these various ways. The tutor is cast in the role of fount of all wisdom, while the pupils' role is usually one of reading and research as an accompaniment to the basic instruction laid down by the tutor. Here, the learning space is the classroom, there are homogeneous cultural norms implied and power is held by the teacher and not by the student. There may also be hidden agenda about performance and about the suitability of public and private life. These are held up in the training processes and then trained into the students, who then faithfully reproduce these attitudes within the Church.[9]

performance

Theological education can, therefore, be dominated by an orientation towards performance and this is a problem with our acceptance of an over-professionalized society. All of us, those involved in mission included, often conspire to uphold this notion of some normative 'performance'. Further, some congregations also hold their own ideas of 'performance' and apply their own sets of criteria to those in ministry. This means that gifts can be overlooked and people are ignored or shunted into positions for which they are not intrinsically suited. But if mission is about partnership with God for God's own purposes, then greater discernment, beyond 'performance', must surely be applied. Some of the resources we suggest help to break down these prevailing notions of what is expected of people and look towards greater understanding of people's potential.[10]

roles

Another difficulty for these traditional methods of imparting knowledge is that they set up rigid roles out of which there is often simply not the time to break. This can be very frustrating for both teaching staff and the students. Teachers are prevented from further learning themselves by the sheer amount they are required to get across to a wide variety of people. Yet teaching which enables people for mission can be a risky business, for it requires teachers and students to have a mutually recognized relationship. In some situations, the teacher can be more of a facilitator, whose skill is to draw out from the students ways of making progress for themselves and ways of helping them to educate others. This may take more time than is available and this becomes a problem to be addressed.

Rigid roles can also be dissolved when the teacher is willing to be changed by the business of teaching, not just through intellectual challenge, but as a person who is also on a spiritual journey. Yet this, for some, can feel like disempowerment and a confusion of purpose, with authority and responsibility for delivery of information being undermined or dispersed. But it is only by enabling relationships to prosper that people in training can be allowed to assume responsibility for growth and to understand their theological education as a means of God's much larger lifelong purpose for themselves. They need to be able to do this, because people who have a heart for mission have to continue asking missionary questions long after they have left initial training and must feed them into their lifelong learning.

For example, in training their lay missionaries, the Columbans hand over responsibility to the students after an initial period, so that the next exercise in learning becomes discernment of 'what do you need from us?' This is an important part of the training process because the new missionaries will need to be able to see clearly both what is required and what can be discarded in the missionary situations they will encounter in other parts of the world.

some ways of learning

On the other hand, many people entering training come with preconceived ideas about how to learn. Many *expect* to be spoon-fed information and to regurgitate this in a pattern bred into them from school. For those who have not been in school for some time, this may feel familiar, but profoundly retrogressive. It may also be unhelpful where those who have come from jobs requiring the exercise of responsibility and proper decision making are forced back into passive, unquestioning roles.

Learning for mission requires the ability to ask the appropriate questions, which itself requires the space to reflect and reconsider what those questions might be. Creative reflection cannot often be marked or given an examination grade, but may have a crucial role to play in allowing information and experience to become assimilated and to make sense. Also, creative space may make it possible for people to articulate fears, doubts and lack of faith, which can then be explored and given value. Where those sending or supporting people entering theological training expect them to be possessed of a strong faith, creative reflection may make it possible to examine the burden this imposes and to seek solutions to it. This may prove invaluable in later ministerial situations that are characterized by apparent impossibility and failure (see Peter's story, above pp. 51–2). If people are also empowered to take on responsibility for their learning and to determine what is needed, a feeling of liberation and trust may make it easier for them to focus on what God wants of their lives.

What is required is a pedagogy of the question rather than a pedagogy of the answer. This means that new knowledge and information are imparted but with a context of questioning and reflection about how it relates to the learner's experience as well as to the current context. Freire suggests:

> At root human existence involves surprise, questioning and risk and because of all this, it involves action and change. Bureaucratization however, means adaptation with a minimum of risk, with no surprises, without asking questions. And so we have a pedagogy of answers, which is a pedagogy of adaptation, not a pedagogy of creativity. It does not encourage people to take the risk of inventing, or reinventing. For me,

to refuse to take risks is the best way there is of denying human existence itself.[11]

adult education as jazz

If we have suggested, following Professor Ford, that mission is jazz, so we note that this view of Christian adult education is sometimes likened to jazz. Jazz has traditionally been played by trained and skilled musicians who are also interpreters and innovators of a given stock of musical ideas. This allows, musically, something new to emerge, with new influences and fusions. Players of jazz need to have perfected their technique before improvisation can be meaningful. If an original set melodic and harmonic framework is not laid down, then musicians cannot improvise. This has implications for the way we think about theological education as formation and as transformation. Further, as jazz arose as a reaction to a controlling and repressive tradition and has a subversive quality, so creative reflection can break out of the 'banking method' and open up new possibilities.

the importance of placement

The period students spend in unfamiliar environments is vital for mission orientation and understanding. Students may spend significant amounts of time in places where they have no cultural references and no real links and, therefore, have to deal with feelings of marginalization, unfamiliarity and alienation. Coping with feelings of being lost, cut off, even deserted, can focus the reality of God's presence and make questions about vocation and purpose very sharp. Dealing with these feelings and overcoming them are part of the integral learning experience of the placement, perhaps beyond the overt purpose of the placement itself. For example:

> I set off for Denmark with a fear of being alone, a fear of being lost, and a fear of the dark. I was to arrive in Denmark at 10 p.m., catch a bus and get off at a stop I couldn't pronounce, and someone I had seen once would pick me up. The plane was two hours late – would the bus still be running? I knew that God wanted me to go to Denmark but, waiting in the airport, I had the feeling well known to Jonah when God told him to go to Nineveh. It would have been much easier to go home. Why was I afraid of being alone, lost and in the dark? These were things I questioned on retreat (during the placement), where had they come from?... It was made real to me that God is with me at all times and there is nothing to fear. God revealed that to be alone is not to be lonely because wherever I am God is always there. Through the journey I

became more confident, and by the time I arrived in Denmark I was like a new person, especially as the pastor was waiting for me at the airport, an answer to prayer. On retreat, Psalm 139 received new meaning for me: 'You trace my journeying and my resting places, and are familiar with all the paths I take ... You keep close guard behind and before me and place your hand upon me ... The night is as light as the day, to you both dark and light are one.'[12]

More particularly, cross-cultural encounter beyond Europe and North America may prove a profound life-changing experience that brings an entirely new perspective to a person's life and ministry. Indeed, it may be precisely this experience that opens up an understanding of God's mission of love to the world and a realization of how much we all need continual evangelizing by the love and vibrancy of Christians from many different parts of the world. The application of what has been an intellectual experience, such as Bible study, may come alive where stories and events in the Bible can be compared with real events in the world. Making comparisons between a theologically constructed model of the world and the world as it is directly experienced can both shock and sustain. Further, experiences that have been examined creatively in other situations may assume a freshness and vitality of use when applied at home. In making this point, we do not suggest that this is important merely to students, teaching staff have found that inter-cultural encounter has changed their lives too.

For example:

Many churches in West Africa suffer from a 'brain drain'. Able ministers are lost to the mission of the Church in Africa because people travelling to Britain and the USA for theological study often do not return home. One small attempt to reverse that flow is represented by a developing partnership between Spurgeon's College in London and the Ghana Baptist Theological Seminary in Abuakwa-Kumasi.

This partnership has developed out of a relationship going back at least to 1997 when three Ghanaian pastors flew to London to begin work for the MTh in Applied Theology. After attending introductory study weeks they returned to continue their studies and their ministries in Ghana. Their participation in the study weeks enriched the experience for other students by highlighting a fresh range of issues and perspectives. The experience of working with these students has helped us think through some of the practical issues concerning how best to support students working in a very different context. More importantly, it has opened eyes to fresh perspectives on ministry and mission. Reading their assignments has not only offered glimpses into the challenges facing

Christians in the two-thirds world, but has also prompted fresh thinking about the issues facing Christians in Britain today.

As a theological educator, involvement in this initiative has deepened my conviction that, in an increasingly multicultural world, knowledge of what God is doing in other places is vital if we are to engage in effective mission in Britain. If the vibrant growth of the Church in places like Africa is a source of renewal for the tired Church in the affluent West, then we need to pay greater heed to what the Spirit is saying to us through our sisters and brothers from the two-thirds world.[13]

theological training institutions as placements

Perhaps, more simply, students should be encouraged to see their time spent with a training institution as 'placement'. This can be true whether the particular course they have joined is residential or not. If people come from a place which has nurtured them and if they have any sense of being 'sent' from that place or congregation, then it makes sense to think of the new environment to which they are being 'sent' as a placement, the experience of which they can take back to their communities and family, or on to their first appointment. Often, people coming forward for lay or ordination training do so as a consequence of being sponsored or encouraged by their home community. It follows that that home community should be the place where the person gives back the insights and ideas gained by contact with the training environment.

which is the 'real' world?

This needs to be realized as a responsibility, because people sometimes speak of getting away from their 'placement' and back to the 'real world', as though this were somehow more comfortable. This is sometimes fostered by the sense that placements within training courses are indeed sometimes especially constructed situations. The idea of the training period as a placement in itself might counter any sense in which the person is seen by the home community as being sent off to be trained into an 'officer' of the Church. All too often 'who' is replaced by 'what' in people's minds and to this perception is added that of 'formation' as moulding to a pre-specified shape rather than as growth. Yet, surely, people entering training with a heart for mission will want to share their experiences and bring feedback from their places of origin. When the 'placement' is over, the sense of continuity of a spiritual journey pursued in the company of others is continued in whatever old or new milieu the person's ministry is worked out. Exactly where that feedback takes place is also significant for, in some Christian denominations, some may (for example) take up a first appointment straightaway with responsibility for a team ministry, and without the apprenticeship of doing the job once round in the company of a more experienced minister. A new congregation waiting to be led may be less sympathetic to receiving the lessons of the training placement, and inadequate sharing and growth from the experience may be the result.

continuous teaching and learning

Learning on any placement is about the whole of life. Every daily activity makes a difference. Similarly, teaching and learning is not confined to the allotted teaching sessions within a college, course, scheme or other mode of theological training. Teaching and learning go on all the time, and the way in which daily life is lived by students also contributes a great deal to the way people are equipped for mission. Times of fellowship, eating together, worship and prayer all help to consolidate mutuality and support, while times of solitude and reflection offer time for considering personal growth. The dynamics of these times of corporate and individual reflection vary with residential and non-residential courses, but their value needs to be assessed and accounted for in the whole educational process of the institution. The ability to become a family and to create fellowship is drawn from both outside and inside relationships and helps to provide a basis for collaborative working and the building up of community. The idea of training as placement may also provide the context wherein people can make mistakes safely and learn from their experiences. Perhaps there should be more attention paid to this aspect of training. It may seem odd to suggest that theological education is about making mistakes, but this may be the only time that a people can use experimentation, exploration and risk in their spiritual journey without the danger of compromising others. Times of tension and difficulty need to be worked out and processes of reconciliation and forgiveness put into place. These can often be expressed powerfully in times of worship. If the training institution is recognized as a more particular kind of situation, a placement, then other aspects of the community's life such as group dynamics or personality types can be explored. By this means the consequences for ministry situations in the daily world can be acknowledged.

immersion

The notion of 'placement' should not, however, be seen to undervalue the immersion which takes place in residential training courses. Rather, the experience of immersion in a community of teaching and learning friendships can be significant in allowing mission perspective to develop within a 'placement'. What could be encouraged is the provision of space and time for reflection on placement and for assessment of what people do with their experiences in the context of support and mutual learning. This can become invaluable when, later, people may be subjected to disappointing or difficult experiences in their ministry and need to be able to work through them. The ability to find and enable support networks may then become paramount. For example, a clergy group support system suggests:

> *Knowing oneself can also become a catalyst for inner healing on a personal level and for others. As Christian leaders in the community this is an important aspect of spiritual growth and development, and offers a more balanced and sensitive approach to leadership and to life generally.* [14]

beyond theological training

Education for mission is part of lifelong learning and this too needs to be acknowledged in Post-Ordination Training, forms of Continuing Ministerial Education and in Ministry Development. People need a forum into which more of their experiences can be placed and reflected upon, particularly where loss of group support and the loss of immediate friends from the initial training period have resulted in feelings of disorientation or in retreat into networks of like-minded people. A clergy chapter or group meeting can become a place to hide, and can prevent the development of shared ministry with lay people. A heart for mission, responding to the overflow of love from the heart of God, needs a desire for self-education and development and a determination to build on what is already known, in pursuit of God's purposes. The need to find God in situations and to wait patiently on God's will is part of mission orientation and requires an ability to reflect and ask questions even in times of crisis.

the widest view of placement

The ability to look for help and to collaborate effectively with others is also part of seeing the mission potential in daily life, as is the confident use of whole-life experiences. The notion of 'placement' may be helpful again in this much broader context, if we consider that our ultimate home is in heaven and that our life on earth is given to us as a kind of placement and as a preparation for our ultimate destiny.

learned behaviour: ministry as dominance and exercise of power

Becoming equipped for mission within the contexts for ministry is not just a matter of acquiring information and experience. People with a heart for mission also need to learn and have self-understanding about how we relate to others, because mission is based on encounter and relationship. Yet it can be a consequence of the teaching process in some training institutions that people are treated as children, to be given information with limits set on their ability to respond or to question. The testing and examination processes also fall into this category.

For example:

> *When Margaret first began teaching at a theological college, the most worrying thing she noticed was that first year students wrote down everything she said without question and worried if they missed something. Invitations to question, explore or discuss were met with polite endorsement of what she'd said. As an experiment, she began to introduce items that were clearly nonsensical into her talk. Still there was no response. When she asked if anyone had thought her material was strange, the responses were: 'I thought it must be me', 'X said you were an expert', 'I didn't understand it anyway' and 'It was clearly rubbish and I was going to ignore it'. No one offered challenge in any form.*

Conversely, we are aware from our own teaching experiences, that some students may take advantage of a teaching style to seek to take control the learning environment and make it difficult or impossible for others to contribute effectively. This shows that everyone in teaching and learning situations needs to understand some of the issues surrounding transference and countertransference and the other unconscious dynamics that can be at play in group situations. Without some understanding of process, it is more difficult for people to develop their self-understanding and, without this, a heart for mission may be hampered by the complex dynamics of ministry situations.

For example, Michael's story:

> *I'd never had any trouble at theological college or in my first two parishes with group situations. I discovered that I could be very persuasive and people usually went along with my ideas even if initially they disagreed with me. I suppose I was quite used to getting my own*

way. Then in my third parish, at the first Parochial Church Council meeting, all the members turned out to be stubborn as mules, refusing even to discuss issues I had on the agenda. They just said 'no' to everything. I couldn't understand what was wrong with them. I was gutted and wondered why I was bothering. Later, I discovered that nearly all the members were chafing about the fact that the curate was leaving – and they took out their various feelings on me! I couldn't believe they could be so childish … I would never have worked it out if it hadn't been pointed out to me.

gaps between speaking and being heard

This story also shows us that while traditional teaching methods may be time-effective in terms of 'banking' information in education and training, students may also adopt this as the most effective teaching paradigm and transfer this into their contexts for ministry: 'the issues *I* had on the agenda'. A striking example of this can be seen in sermons and homilies where there is a tremendous gap between what is said by the preacher and what is heard by the congregation. One minister, for example, was particularly struck by the concerted hands reaching for the local newsletter as soon as she began any address, no matter on what subject. This led to a period of intense self-doubt and loss of confidence. Another place where this makes a difference to mission encounter is in the preparation of people for the occasional offices. Many people in today's society, whose knowledge of Christian theology and narrative is minimal or non-existent, say things like 'we just wanted our baby christened, not all that other stuff'.

dominator models

In any training institution, students may collude with a teacher-as-parent/ dominator model of behaviour because it avoids having to articulate doubts or deal with problems. But, transferred into the contexts for mission we have in society today, people may find complex situations impossible to deal with and retreat into a mode of behaviour which prevents their having to deal with the situation effectively. This can be either bullish dominance over the situation or refusal to engage with it without calling on someone higher in 'authority'. In some training parishes, and with the best will in the world, people who pay lip service to collaborative and partnership ministry, revert to apprenticeship models, in which 'watch me do it, then you do the same' forms the basis of continued learning.

gender

Some women ministers also have problems with gender-stereotypical roles being imposed in further ministerial deployment and training. This, naturally, has implications for mission. If we cannot build relationships that value difference on the basis of equality, we cannot witness effectively to what God has done in Jesus. Learned models of behaviour may either perpetrate a dominating model in which we present our truth as unquestionable (and incidentally represent a hierarchical and overbearing God), or we may appeal as a 'child', presenting a weak and defensive picture of our faith.

who knows best?

Consequently, in any examination of how people are equipped for mission by their theological education and training, we have to ask where these roles are being created and sustained and what styles of teaching and learning best equip people for the equality of the mission encounter. It is argued that dominator models of behaviour demand: ' be strong', 'be perfect', 'please me', 'hurry up', 'try hard', 'manage'. For some people in ministry, these demands are burdens that begin in theological training and are perpetuated by the Church. For many people in ministry, these demands are also reflected back by the congregation, for example where parishioners refuse responsibility in favour of 'Father knows best'. Where such demands are in place and the expectations cannot be countered, opportunities for mission may be seriously compromised. Moreover, dominance models in Christian ministry may become confused with the exercise of ministerial authority. Separating out what it means to be given and to exercise authority, with its responsibility to God and to the Church, and the operation of a dominance mode, is not always easy. Further, sometimes one is used to mask the other.

authority and hierarchy

This is not to say that training institutions are the sole perpetrators of dominance models. In the Church generally, such models are very often at work and are very hard to break. A pattern, based on a set of assumptions about authority, may be established at the highest level, which then filters down to other relationships. The setting up of unbreakable hierarchy, together with its attendant relationship patterns and language, may produce a cycle whereby ministers and lay workers treat congregations in the same way. Congregations then behave like this in witnessing to their faith outside the Church. People who relate as equals within these encounters get no hearing and the mission opportunities may be damaged as a result.

We can see that this is a familiar set of messages for those involved in ministry and that it is often all too difficult to disengage from the expectations perpetrated by the model. Consequently some people involved in ministry are unable to admit weakness, failure and difficulty and may struggle to fulfil impossible expectations until breaking point. This whole cycle may be set up and reinforced during the period of education and training and cannot equip people to know what to do when they cannot fulfil others' expectations.

relation to God and spiritual growth

Dominator models within Christian training and ministry matter because they have further implications for the ways we relate to God and for the development of our spiritual lives, our worship and our faith journeys. If we habitually relate to God only as a helpless child to a dominating parent, we may not be able to hear God's call to partnership in mission. If we make demands on God and require that God acts in certain ways, we may end up frustrated and isolated. Yet often in prayer and worship and in the way we relate to others, we act as if God should respond to us only in certain kinds of way. We refuse God access to our other ways of being. Yet, if we study Scripture and tradition, we can see that God calls, tests, nurtures, admonishes, protects and upholds human beings in an immense variety of ways, which allow humans the maximum space for self-discovery. This is because the foundation for every kind of relationship is always love. Fostering a heart for mission, then, requires looking at the risky business of partnership in equality, and receiving reciprocal ministry from those we would seek to serve. But is 'training', of its nature, unable to include these concepts? These are matters we will explore further.

education for transformation

what does the educational practice of the Church mean for mission?

We have argued that different styles of teaching and learning affect how people can develop a heart for mission in the world as we have it. But what has *actually* been going on in the Church? What kinds of people are produced by the education our churches currently provide and what ideas and models are sustained in the Church as a whole? In looking at this question, we started with the assumption that one of the factors that has contributed to the Church's preference for a 'pastoral' or 'maintenance' mode was the thrust of its educational praxis. In the words of Bishop Peter Price, 'in its training processes, the Church [i.e. the Church of England] seeks to mould its ordinands into good followers'.[15] Our own experience, as Christians in an ecumenical group coming from differing church backgrounds, is that Christian education such as confirmation preparation, membership courses, training for various ministerial functions and training for ordination, seems to produce people well inducted into church norms, church practice and church belief – belief both about the faith and about the world. Much Christian education, therefore, seems to have enabled people to reproduce what has been learned within the institutional context rather than to use what is learned in a transformative way: *formation* rather than *transformation*.

role of tradition in a fast-changing society

The Christian tradition has been handed down to us – it has historical continuity. This is important because it enables us to stand in the tradition and know our relationship not only to the Christians living and worshipping around us now, but those Christians long before us who have lived and died in the faith. The faith has been handed on to us as we seek to hand it on to others. Within this process is replication: we say the historic creeds, we say the Lord's Prayer and repeat other words from Scripture in our liturgies, for example. At the same time, we also have to remember that the gospel must be proclaimed afresh in every age and that Bonhoeffer's question is both challenge and critical reflection: 'Who is Jesus Christ for us *today*?' Educational practice for mission, then, depends not just on continuity and replication, but also on adaptation and understanding of new contexts and experiences. On the foundational material of the Christian faith, mission works its jazz. Without this insight, our educational praxis runs the risk of producing faithful Christians for a world that no longer exists. At this opening of the third millennium, we are very aware of how quickly global political situations can change and how our lives are affected very quickly by changes in technology. None of us can truly say that we can foresee the context of our old age. The question is therefore now very urgent: what might be the most appropriate forms for a mission-directed Christian education emerging from the tradition in such a fast-changing world?

formation

The word usually applied to describe the educational praxis of initial training in theological education is *formation*. But in trying to foster a heart for mission in a changing world, we have to go further – how does formation enable *trans*formation? In trying to get to the heart of this question we have to ask what assumptions lie behind the notion of 'formation' and how these tie in to questions such as, what is appropriate, *now*? What is education within the Church actually *for*? What are the present and future needs of the Church? What is the *Church* for? What are the relationships between the Church and the world?

transformation

These questions are in themselves missionary, but in dealing with them we must also agree how significant a factor education is in determining both the culture and the praxis of the Church. The relationship between education in the Church and its outworking in mission is often not agreed. A further question of the utmost importance for mission is: can education within the Church not only be transformative [16] of individuals but also of institutional behaviours and structures both within and beyond itself? We believe that it can. Therefore, part of the process of developing a heart for mission in theological education is to seek to encourage reflection and debate on what needs to happen within institutions, including the Church as institution. There has always been need for this, but we may have forgotten that reformation *can* be an ongoing process. We should not seek to be merely destructive, but try to find out what parts of our current education praxis are transformative and what is merely uncritical repetition. Andrew Wingate writes:

> *The question of the difference made by theological education can be seen as a double question: does it make a difference to those who undertake theological training? and does it make a difference to the church that receives them? Perhaps a prior question has to do with whether it is intended to make a difference. Some may consider that the role of education is to consolidate what people are and to prepare them to maintain a church which is happy to be where it is and has no desire for pastors who will 'make a difference' by disturbing the status quo. Students preparing for such a church are often ready to learn their craft in a way that enables them effectively to preserve what is there.*
>
> *But if we want theological education to make a difference, the question becomes 'difference in what way?' Here the answer will depend on the*

context. *For a church under persecution, it may be to enable clergy to remain faithful under extreme stress, to teach their lay people to remain firm and pass on the faith to their children. For the church in the West, it may be to bring life and renewal to declining congregations, so that they regain a sense of mission; to facilitate members to reflect biblically and theologically within the complex world of the rapidly changing secular society; to provide pastoral care to those who feel lost in such a society; to engage sensitively with that secular and multi-cultural society, witnessing to Christ by actions as much as words.* (Wingate, 1999, p. 107)

how hidebound are we?

To say that educational practice must be subject to self-awareness and critical reflection is one thing, but how do we say what we are doing in our education within the Christian community and what do we *think* we are doing? Are we *really* doing what we *think* we are doing? There is little doubt that theological education affects profoundly those who undergo it[17] but does it provide us with the tools to take that change beyond ourselves? Paulo Freire's warning about education that seeks to transform individuals and not the reality around them is quite stark:

> For the truly humanist educator and the authentic revolutionary the object of the action is the reality to be transformed by them together with other people – not other men and women themselves. The oppressors are those who act upon the people to indoctrinate them and adjust them to a reality that must remain untouched.[18]

This is not to suggest that those responsible for education within the Churches set themselves up as 'oppressors' nor that their specific aim is indoctrination. We might want to substitute, 'truly Christian educator and authentic mission partner' for Freire's 'totally humanist educator and the authentic revolutionary'. But if we accept the observation that the Churches' path of least resistance is to educate people to reproduce the current patterns and structures of the Church rather than to engage constructively with the reality beyond it, then perhaps Paulo Freire's analysis is helpful. He reflects that educational processes that act *upon* people rather than *with* people are bound to leave the reality itself untouched. If this is true, we cannot afford to become so obsessed with rearranging the deckchairs for ourselves that we forget there is a world out there to be evangelized and which must evangelize us.

good practice

While theological education seems generally to have produced people who find it easier to act in 'maintenance' mode rather than in mission mode, there are stories across our Churches about Christians managing to transform their contexts rather than remaining stuck within them. What has enabled that to happen? [19] What models and processes of learning have been employed? Examples of good practice cannot be a panacea but they can often stimulate us to think outside our boundaries.

seeing the Church as relevant

For example, one criticism of the Christian Church is that it is 'out of touch'. For some people that means, literally, that you do not see Church leaders on the streets involved in daily life. In addressing this in his missionary work on the street, the Bishop of Barking, the Rt Revd Roger Sainsbury, spoke of a Hindu woman who came up to him and touched his pectoral cross. She wanted him to know that she too loved Jesus. An act of testimony and reconciliation was enabled by being 'in touch', just as in Scripture we learn that people desired merely to touch Jesus. Bishop Roger also spoke of a Christian walk of witness on Good Friday in which he was involved, that passed by a mosque in his local area. As the worshippers emerged from Friday prayers, they stood respectfully to let the procession carrying the cross pass. Bishop Roger reported a mutual respect and recognition, which has been important in transforming the social contexts of the area. But then we also have to ask, if a bishop can be empowered to be 'in touch' in this way, who takes care of all the other responsibilities of the bishop's office? If mission is 'possible', what else becomes 'impossible'? [20]

finding out what is possible

Being aware of what we are already doing, whether it be good practice to be emulated or poor practice that needs changing, is vital but is not enough in itself. If there is a desire for change, we also need to be aware of how a process of change works in practice within our Christian communities. Asking about how things can be altered, even when there is a desire for change, is often the last nail in the coffin for overstretched church communities. What do you do if you can identify need for change, but have no resources to bring it about? Teaching and learning have to address not only the desire for transformation, but also what strategies are needed to deal with difficulty and frustration. Otherwise, people may simply fall back into a default 'maintenance' mode and be discouraged from seeing that even some forms of maintenance can be missionary. Any discussion to encourage self-awareness must also encourage debate about the realities of institutional structures both inside and outside the Church. To put it in Blairite terms, who are the stakeholders and what is it worth to them to leave things unchanged?

beyond today, working for the kingdom

Being concerned about how to enable the Church to function in 'mission' mode does not imply we should automatically make our educational practice switch attention from the Church to the world. This is no solution. As Robert Warren has pointed out,[21] 'pastoral' and 'mission' mode are not 'either/or' but 'both/and'. While we must seek the kingdom of God, the Church remains the community of our seeking. In some communities, as we suggested, maintenance can *be* mission. Furthermore, many of our educational courses have long been aimed at helping Christians relate faith to life. One of the paradoxes of some of the more successful courses, such as *Alpha*, is that they can build up transformative solidarity within the learning groups, but leave a larger question about how the life and faith of such groups then penetrate the wider community in beneficial ways.

We need to ask, rather, how to make that relationship between faith and life dynamic and effective both at the level of individual Christians working and witnessing in their own contexts and at the level of Church and society. How can educators within the Church be enabled, in Freire's words, to make 'reality', whether it be the reality of the Church or the reality of the world, 'the object of their action'? Also, how do we enable students to be partners in the learning journey and not merely the objects of the educational process? This is a methodological question, as we have seen, but it is also a content question.[22] In developing a heart for mission, which deals in the realm of the possible, not wistful dreams of mission impossible, what subject matter and what understandings of subject material help us to act upon reality transformatively? These are matters we shall now explore.

part 2 illuminations

chapter 7

mission as presence

Our conversation so far has asked how people can be generally equipped for mission through theological education and what *difference* it will make to the world in which we must witness to God's overflowing love. In the part of our work, we had to ask whether the *content* of theological education can especially contribute to this ability to make a difference. We have argued that our Christian witness is enabled by our presence in all parts of our complex culture and society. We also suggest that our prophetic viewpoint enables us to see that culture in terms of what a missionary God wants for all of creation. Our missionary impulse towards our world requires transformation to take place. How, then, does the actual content of what we may learn in theological education help to support that presence and that prophetic witness?

To answer this question, we have looked at some of the major subjects taught in theological institutions and in other courses. We have not tried to rewrite course material or modules, or to suggest that the teaching of subjects must be done in any prescribed way. Instead, we have tried to imagine what the subject material could look like if we examined it through a missiological lens. In seeing mission as a permeating element in such material we can claim that mission has a particular *presence* in the subject matter. In Part 3 we look at mission as *prophecy*, a focused look at the challenges that mission itself provides.

In doing this, we had to be clear about our own assumptions in the matter: our perspective is coloured by an understanding of mission theology as foundational to *all* theology. Through this perspective, some general questions begin to emerge which challenge all of us: teachers, students, and ourselves as people concerned for mission. We see these questions and reflection upon them as an enabling tool for both presence and prophecy in Christian lives lived out in our society. They also contain challenges to a comfortable life as Christians. For this reason, we have used these questions to underlie our exploration of how mission thinking can illuminate different subjects in theological education. In their most general form these questions are:

- **Who is God?**
  What sort of God calls us in this way?
  How can we find out what God is doing?

- **How should we respond to God?**
  What is God asking us to do?
  How do we know what is God's will?

- **Who are we?**
  What does it mean to be a Christian today?
  How does our faith relate to God's purposes?

- **How should we live before God?**
  What does our witness require of us?
  How can we make a difference by means of example?

- **Who else is desired by God?**
  Who are the people to whom we are called to witness?
  What about these people is already loved and desired by God?

- **What must we do?**
  How does mission bring about transformation?
  How do we show people the future as God intends?

The content of different subjects in the theological curriculum helps us to explore these questions in more focused ways and to begin to build a larger picture of what it means to be a missionary people. In doing this, we come to more specific questions which sharpen the christological focus of our broader mission thinking:

- **Who is Jesus Christ for us today?**

- **What does it mean to follow Christ?**

- **What does it mean to make Christ known?**

We suggest that these kinds of questions should be brought to bear on every part of the teaching and learning experience. We are aware that we often talk among ourselves as if the answers to these questions were perfectly clear, but in the complex world in which we now live, we cannot pretend that things are so straightforward. This is why we believe that theological education provides such a crucial opportunity for thinking through the issues and discovering the prophetic voice of a missionary people.

The subjects are not laid out in any particular order of importance or priority. Church history comes first because our exploration followed from some of the issues we looked at in Chapter 6. We were then able to identify themes or 'threads' in that work, which are developed further in the following subject sections, especially in relation to different kinds of narrative and our place in them, and to how we hear the voices of Christians beyond the western theological horizon. The development of these themes is reassessed in our work on mission studies where we see how our exploration of the different subjects creates challenges.

chapter 8

mission and Church history

a people without a past

When we began to ask ourselves about mission in Church history, we realized we would have to start with a broad question about what role the study of history, and particularly Church history, might have in training both clergy and laity for ministry and mission in a twenty-first-century context. What kind of content and methodology might be required? More pressingly, why should Church history be studied *at all* in a society that is preoccupied with surface and ephemera? What difference can it actually make?

It seemed to us important to start here, because in our society there are trends towards concentrating people's sense of continuity on only the recent past. We are inheritors of the twentieth century. Francis Fukuyama indeed has proclaimed the 'end of history'.[1] History becomes watchable TV drama, as in the Simon Schama series, but without any suggestion that we should feel a sense of ownership.

For example:

Imagine instead a British history in which alteration, mutation and flux, rather than continuity and bedrock solidity are the norm ... this history might be a history respectful of contingency, mistrustful of inevitability, indifferent to any pre-determined route or destination ...'[2]

This leaves us with the interesting question of how we ourselves make sense of inheriting two thousand years of Christian tradition. How can we take it into dialogue with people without a past?

For example:

the nun's story

A woman in her thirties read an article in a magazine about a man who had discovered a 'past life' under hypnosis. She came to feel that her longing for God must have had its origin in some similar 'past life' and went in search of evidence of it. She came to believe that she had in the past been a nun and that her inclination to prayer and worship stemmed from this source. This created problems as she then became concerned that she might be directly descended from the nun and thus the result of some illicit liaison which must be atoned for. The woman's attempt to construct and believe in a faith 'history' for herself, prevented her from growing in her own faith and made her relationship with God only a 'consequence' of an unsubstantiated past. After searching fruitlessly among practitioners offering access to past lives, she was helped to place her search for God in the context of the Christian tradition by a Baptist minister. After this, she was able to let go of the 'nun's story' as part of herself, but needed to keep the idea of her as a kind of 'spiritual friend'.

This story, with its interesting outcome, reminds us that we also need to decide what our assumptions in the matter are. It is easy to hear the story as a vindication for Christian common sense, sweeping away fabrications, and those practices and therapies that are supposed to deliver hidden parts of ourselves back to us. Assumptions about the rightness of our view of the matter may, however, mask important questions. *Why* was the nun's story so important, so sympathetic to the woman's own spiritual search, and *why* did she need to keep the idea of her as a spiritual friend?

People without a past, may have a definite and urgent need for us to supply that sense of memory and continuity – apostolic succession in its widest sense. But how many of us also carry around our own versions of the 'nun's story', reasons for our being Christian, and use them to justify our own sense of vocation and missionary outworking? What parts of our past and inherited traditions make us what we are? What parts of our past would we cover up or deny having? For example, for some people a powerful experience of conversion can become a dynamic marker of missionary witness. In some other people, a powerful experience of this kind can also create discontinuity with the pre-conversion self, or even become the sole permission for outreach, the *only* reason why people should hear the Good News. For this reason, we need to understand how our theological language about 'dying with Christ' or 'being born again' relates holistically to ourselves as possessing a continuous lifetime.

how we read history to suit ourselves

Examination of our personal sense of history matters if we are to engage with people in search of a past. We all carry particular assumptions, which should not prevent us asking in what ways the history of *mission* has slanted and prejudiced how we see the purpose of the whole Church. We cannot make suggestions about the role of mission perspective in Church history without considering what our own hidden interests in the matter might be. This means we have to delve into a nexus of history, missiology and education to create a web woven out of our observations, prior assumptions, and understandings in all these fields. But why is it necessary to disentangle the web?

what is the fruit?

One way of dealing with this, is to look at history in terms of outcomes, or, to use a biblical image, 'fruit'. This mitigates the picture of flux and contingency, with the suggestion that we can find God's value, meaning and purpose written into our understanding of the past. In Chapter 2, we argued that Jesus said, 'Thus you will know them by their fruits' (Matthew 7.20) and it is this perspective of the kingdom of God that Jesus 'both inaugurates and makes possible ... as a sustainable reality in the material world' (see p. 27). This offers us a benchmark against which any particular event or outcome, whether within the Church or on a wider canvas, can be assessed: 'What is this fruit, and where did it come from?' 'Is it really a fruit?' 'How can we tell?' We need to ask these kinds of question, otherwise the ways in which we can misread history, especially mission history, or pass on versions of our own 'nun's story' can mean distorted 'fruit' begin to propagate themselves in the world. The history of missions is, indeed, especially challenged by these questions and is redressed by asking people from outside North American and European contexts what their reading of mission history is. As Tom O'Loughlin has pointed out,[3] theologians can misuse as well as learn from the work of historians.

See Chapter 12, 'mission and doctrine'; Chapter 13, 'mission as prophecy'.

what use is this kind of perspective?

The challenge to those engaged in teaching and learning Church history as well as to those developing a heart for mission, is: 'what difference does it make?' In what way can the study of Church history and an awareness of historical context help us in our Christian education to act upon reality transformatively with those who come to learn? We will see how sharp this question is regarding the very foundations of our missionary understanding in the following sections on mission and the Bible. It further reminds us of the partnership between missiological understanding and ethics, which is critical in making sense of mission as an action of the Church for change.

See Chapter 6, 'styles of teaching and learning'.

See Chapter 9, 'mission and the Bible'.

'types' of history

But what sort of history are we talking about? In working through this question with our conversation partners,[4] we came to understand that the study of Church history can sharpen a missiological perspective for us because its methodology can help us understand the processes of mission better. We cannot do this, though, without considering what we mean by different 'types' of history.

First, 'history' is a flexible word and begins with an idea of 'what actually happened',[5] very little of which is accessible to us. Secondly, we use the word 'history' to mean what we can understand in the present about 'what actually happened' in the past. This is itself the raw material of the historians, whose writings are history in yet a third sense.[6] The beginning of St Luke's Gospel is an early definition of history in this third sense:

> *Since many have undertaken to set down an orderly account of the events that have been fulfilled among us, just as they were handed on to us by those who from the beginning were eyewitnesses and servants of the word, I too decided, after investigating everything carefully from the very first, to write an orderly account for you, most excellent Theophilus, so that you may know the truth concerning the things about which you have been instructed.* (Luke 1.1-4)

our story and ideology

It is readings of history in this sense that can become history in a fourth sense – the telling of a story: our story. History in the third and fourth senses can fall prey to particular ideology, a story told according to the way we want to see it, our own particular and cherished version of Christian faith, of mission history, of various kinds of hagiography. We who live out of a story grounded in events of the past need to be more aware than most of the fine line between ideology and history.[7] The ideological value of the Christian faith can produce a need to indoctrinate people into the 'right' way of thinking. This can be the foundation for all kinds of things done in the name of 'mission', not least insensitive and inappropriate evangelism. We shall explore this further in Chapter 11, 'mission and pastoral care'.

types of history and mission theology

Despite possible pitfalls and misuse we cannot sidestep issues of history in any of the four senses. Our mission theology requires we claim that the action of God is to be found in history in the first sense. When we ask 'who is God?' we discover that a missionary God acts in history in a definitive way, and supremely through the Incarnation of Jesus in our world. Our Scriptures and traditions are, for us, attempts at making that action accessible to all of us who are not contemporary with the writers and storytellers. *Transmission*, with all its inbuilt possibilities for distortion and bias, becomes the vehicle for sacred truths, themselves laden with obligation. Our faith story interweaves history in the third and fourth senses, and grows in complexity as different groups appropriate the stories of previous ones. The relation of mission theology – our knowledge of the missionary God – to history is therefore complex.

For example:

> *A wandering Aramean was my ancestor ... When the Egyptians treated us harshly and afflicted us, by imposing hard labour on us, we cried to the Lord ... the Lord heard our voice ... And he brought us into this place ...* (Deuteronomy 26.5-10)

> *... but we proclaim Christ crucified, a stumbling block to Jews and foolishness to Gentiles* (1 Corinthians 1.23)

We have argued that our understanding of mission comes from a theological understanding of a missionary God, one who acts in love towards the creation. Both the above biblical quotations are kerygmatic statements, though from different times and cultures. They refer to acts of God in history and confess God and God's deeds with no effort to prove or explain. They are expressions of our metanarrative, or foundational story, and relate us firmly to God as an eternal reality. That the acts of this God are *not* contingent or chance occurrences is fundamental to understanding both a sacred history and a forward-moving mission imperative which proclaims that more is yet to come: Christ will come again.

history in relation to eschatology

This shows how mission perspective and history are interdependent. From a mission perspective, and whether we like it or not, we are as located historically as we are geographically or culturally. The Church needs its story to live by and also to live into. This is connected to mission perspective because we need to live out of the story the Church tells of God in Christ if we are to live towards the kingdom. The past gives us the capacity to envision the future as we saw with the two biblical quotations from Deuteronomy and 1 Corinthians. We need our story – our stories – to enable us to relate, however imperfectly, with our surrounding reality, to interpret it and to situate ourselves within it. The study of history, therefore, is instrumental in teaching us how to show the presence of the living God in our culture and how to be prophetic of the future God has prepared for us.

sacred story

We have suggested that our witness takes place among a people without a past, but a people whose search for that past may reveal gaps and holes that have to be filled with conjecture or fantasy.[8] Part of our work, then, can be to give people access to the sense-making system which is provided by an eternal God, who is present in creation from the beginning, sustaining it by the power of the Holy Spirit and constantly engaged in love towards it. God is not confined to the record of human history, but enters in ways that are accessible to us. Such a God waits for us at the end of all history, giving us a way to understand meaningfulness and purpose extending through time. Beyond this stability and long view, Christian faith gives us another kind of history to offer to people who may not formerly have encountered it. Christianity gives to us a *sacred story*, re-enacted throughout the year in powerful dramatic festivals, which is a feature of our religious memory. Such memory makes possible the opening up of a transcendent reality both now and in our future. Sacred story allows us to pursue the ultimate reality that we cannot yet see – what St Paul calls the 'glory of God in the face of Jesus Christ' (2 Corinthians 4.6). Jean Vanier says that each of us is a sacred history, known entirely by God, because Jesus 'comes to us from inside'.[9]

critical tools

If we are to offer the eternal God within sacred story, which we do week by week in our worship, then we must still ask how we can carry on telling our story in ways which are accessible to non-Christians. If this way of telling our story is reinforced within churches, we risk accepting the comfortable endorsement of our dominant ideologies, thought constructions and arguments, which unconsciously legitimate our individual perspectives or church tradition.

See Chapter 10, 'mission and worship'.

It is here that perhaps we have to take the uncomfortable route and learn to see ourselves as others see us. One way to do this is to permit different kinds of theology, especially from other parts of the world, to evaluate our viewpoint. Karl Marx states that ideology can be a false vision of reality.[10] This reminds us that to live transformatively, to act upon reality, we *must* be consistently critical of our own story. Mission perspective must, therefore, see forms of historical method as critical tools helping us to guard against ideology for its own sake and against our losing sight of God. Jesus said 'the truth will make you free' (John 8.32). The story we choose to live by will only be liberating for ourselves and others if it is honest. It will only be honest if it is inclusive.

untold stories

This is another crucial facet of what we offer to other people when we reach out to them in mission. This story of God is inclusive. How does the study of history help us to show this to people? For those of us who desire to develop a heart for mission, it can help us to find different ways of telling our own faith story and to ask ourselves how the ways we tell that story change or do not change. If we can study and explore the content of Church history in a way which shows how the Christian faith has been and is being understood at differing times and places, while still remaining the historic faith, this can be helpful. Such study can lead to an appreciation of the validity of many ways of telling and retelling stories which are nourished by the history of Jesus of Nazareth, crucified and risen. Such a multiplicity of stories implies inclusiveness. How do we go about recognizing this?

Elisabeth Schüssler Fiorenza points to the example of Sojourner Truth, an African-American, born into slavery in upper New York State, and later emancipated. Sojourner Truth addressed a mostly white suffrage gathering in Akron, Ohio, in 1852 and said:

> *That man over there say*
> *a woman needs to be helped into carriages*
> *and lifted over ditches*
> *and to have the best places everywhere …*
> *That little man in black there say*
> *a woman can't have as much rights as a man*
> *'cause Christ wasn't a woman.*
> *Where did your Christ come from?*
> *From God and a woman!*
> *Man had nothing to do with him!*
> *If the first woman God ever made*
> *was strong enough to turn the world*
> *upside down, all alone*
> *together women ought to be able to turn it*
> *rightside up again.*[11]

Schüssler Fiorenza points out that Sojourner Truth does not question the story of original sin, but rather the storyteller and the theologians. Her story, one of slavery, struggle and poverty, is different. Her experience of being woman, poor and black, is different. And so she reads the foundational narrative in the light of her experience and becomes herself the teller of a new story and the singer of a different song. In twenty-first-century multicultural Britain and Ireland, it is now more important than ever to hear the histories and faith traditions of those whose cultural memory was built up in other countries.

listening to difference

This example reminds us the study of Church history is not just relevant to the training of clergy. An appreciation of historical context and how history becomes story is as relevant to lay people with other specialist ministries, such as youth workers or hospital chaplains, who need to have a realistic awareness of the many factors which influence the life choices made by the people they work with. All of us need to have an ear for the stories people tell about themselves and have the skills to judge whether the ruling narratives in people's lives and personal histories are liberating or restrictive. From the mission perspective, we need the skills to be able to help people open their stories to God's story in Christ.

See Chapter 11, 'mission and pastoral care'.

We cannot do this in Britain and Ireland without some reference to our own historical context and how different cultures and traditions have given us different means by which to express our Christian faith. We cannot act in mission without this understanding: we would not expect anyone to understand Christianity simply from observing how it is practised in Britain and Ireland today. We must also pay attention to other stories, not just sacred traditions in our study of Church history, and must pay special attention to the history of ideas.[12] Looking beyond our own traditions is instructive, because it allows us to ask what stories have been suppressed or ignored in the way we read Church history. And whose voices would the Church rather not hear today?

'untrue' stories

Many people have found in historical perspective a response to their own questions, a satisfaction of their deepest thirsts and an invitation to continue journeying. We need our stories. They tell us who we are or aspire to be. They grant us our identity and give us grounding in our location. They proclaim our uniqueness and our distinctiveness. Individuals or groups need a story to tell, to live by, and their history then becomes its raw material. Sometimes in nurturing people within the Christian faith, we can see this in action, as people make sense of their lives in the light of Christ. But loss of that history can lead to a profound lack of depth and, as we have seen, a necessary, but dangerous confabulation.

For example:

> A Jewish woman from a small French village became ill and told a doctor
> she was haunted by nightmares about her parents' deaths at the hands
> of the occupying German forces in the Second World War. She said she
> had become ill after recognizing a newcomer to her village as one of the
> collaborators who had betrayed her family to the Germans during the
> war. She feared further betrayal while at the same time seeing opportunity
> for bringing the collaborator to justice. Her doctor talked to her rabbi,
> who said with surprise that the woman's family was alive and well.
> Furthermore, it turned out that the 'newcomer' was in fact her husband
> with whom she no longer lived, but who was refusing to give her a divorce.

In this sad story the woman replaced her personal difficulties with the much
larger tragedy of the Jewish people and represented it to the doctor as a
legitimizing reason for her own suffering and illness. She did not just want
a 'cure' for her illness or her personal circumstances, but a bigger 'spiritual'
understanding of Jewish suffering, which would make sense of why she was
unhappy. This reminds us that telling the story can be liberating and can
keep significant memory alive, but it can also enslave. Stories identify. They
can also exclude, as marginalized groups know only too well and as we saw
in the words of Sojourner Truth.

distorted narratives as official discourse

We also noticed that in the study of Church history we can be alive to distorted
narratives, and our role in distorting them. This has an important practical
application because when we engage in the pastoral care of people with whom
we would share the Good News of Jesus Christ, we can also often be told
untrue stories, distorted in a way to win our sympathy. We need critical tools
to understand what is going on underneath the story. Language not only
articulates and describes reality, it also creates reality. Powerful groups will
use parts of the past or supposed past, usually idealized, to authenticate
the status quo and so prevent change. This is true also of the Church as
institution. We need to guard against a dominant interpretation that can be
raised to the dignity of being called 'official' or 'normative' or 'infallible' or
'sound'. Once raised to that status, the interpretation in its turn serves to
justify and sacralize the teaching, attitudes and structures of the institution.
Its governors can constitute themselves as the divinely appointed guardians
and stewards of the (now) sacred traditions. Once this has happened
boundaries begin to form between the institution and everything that happens
outside it. The study of Church history is instrumental in helping to
understand how this happens. Yet from the mission perspective, we

must remember that the gospel can and will cross all boundaries. Does the Church help or hinder God's unstoppable mission of love to the world?

back to the future

The appeal to history to give credibility to distorted narrative can also appear in other ways, some of which are given cachet by being described as 'missionary'. The explosion of all things Celtic is a case in point. The ancient Celtic Church (for these islands still have Celtic Christianity) has become, in the eyes of some, a blessed island, a golden repository for all the good things the Church should be but seems not to be. 'Such an entity', says Oliver Davies, 'is a fiction, and is to an extent indicative of the way that the Celtic world has been exploited by other cultures for the purposes not only of polemic but of the imagination and fantasy.'[13] Tom O'Loughlin notes that dipping into the past to legitimize the present does not proceed 'using the historians' model of enquiry but that of the lawyers citing precedents which should determine a court case' (O'Loughlin, 2001, p. 34).

Just as modern druidic religion is but an echo of pre-Christian religion in Britain and Ireland, so the espousal of Celtic Christianity as somehow more authentic of early Christian life, creates pitfalls for those who ignore the principles at stake in favour of embracing a more romantic view of what is seen as 'authentic' island Christianity. Indeed, while some forms of Celtic Christian worship do much to break down patriarchal and hierarchical modes of Christian expression, some forms of 'Celtic' Christian worship and practice are more akin to a trip to the shop Past Times. Here you can take home 'replicas of historic originals ... based on period designs'[14] (e.g. jewellery, furnishings, music) to create an 'authentic' feel of the past in your own home – notwithstanding the irony of listening to medieval music or wartime favourites on your distortion-free compact disc player. This seductive appeal to a romantic and sanitized version of the past[15] can also gain credence by appeal to its missionary possibilities. Some missionary strategies are put forward on the basis that they are creating forms of Church that are more like the first Christian communities and therefore somehow closer to what God actually wants. This uses both history and mission to identify that there is something 'wrong' with ways of being Church now, but the problems are sidestepped and ignored by going back to a time 'when all was well'. Such a process cannot be missionary, because it does not engage with the encounter between the Church and the societies in which it is immersed. It ducks out of the call to be a witnessing presence and a means of the prophetic word, calling the Church of the future into being.

ignoring history in global perspectives

In looking at mission perspectives in Church history, we realized that we also need to be aware that while some people attempt to use history to legitimize particular narratives or practices, others still prefer to ignore it altogether. Those who wish to bypass history may be no less ideologically motivated than those who press it into service. It should come as no surprise that Francis Fukuyama should proclaim 'the end of history' with the collapse of communism, seen as the only credible gainsayer to the 'free' market (Fukuyama, 1989, pp. 3–18). For this suggests that the free market has now become the secular equivalent of the *depositum fidei*, and a defining, unquestionable world view. Fukuyama's assertion implies that the study of history as the understanding and surveying of change and complexity can threaten all authorities, whether secular or ecclesial, which have investment in a 'truth' to protect and preserve. In other words, the way in which we study, understand and use history can be a dangerous weapon in terms of the radical, world-changing story we ultimately wish to convey. Our understanding of history can be used to promote mission, but it can also be used to undermine it.

rereading and recovery

Historians have long taught us that their preconceptions can colour not only their interpretation of data but its selection: 'facts' too are precarious. This is important for anyone teaching or studying Church history and it is also important for our mission perspective. The writing of history can, therefore, be a swapping of the dialogues that take place between our assumptions and the data. There is no such thing as 'pure' history: every source, every historian, every reading is particular. This means that some narratives can become persuasive and dominant and thereby seen as 'normative' and other narratives can become marginal or suppressed altogether. We have seen this in the recent 'recovery' of the perspectives of women missionaries such as Gladys Aylward whose stories have hitherto been only cursorily acknowledged[16] and of indigenous people whose conversion and outworking of Christian faith has been instrumental in the spread of the gospel in their countries. For example:

> ... the Sierra Leone missionaries, important as they are, are only a fragment of the Sierra Leone influence in the diffusion of Christianity in West Africa. As clerk, railwayman, mechanic, and above all as trader, the Sierra Leonean penetrated everywhere the British did, and often further. And wherever he went, he took his Bible, his hymn singing, and his family prayers. In area after area, well into the twentieth century, the

first contact of African immigrant people with the Christian faith was through an itinerant or immigrant Sierra Leonean. And the mission to Yorubaland, which marked a turning point in bringing about a well-grounded church in inland Africa, came about because Sierra Leoneans had made their way back as traders over hundreds of miles to the places from whence they had once been taken as slaves, and were missing their Sunday services.[17]

This recovery of different narratives from indigenous Christians rather than prominent missionaries is not enough, however. Although it provides one kind of corrective to the ruling perspective – in the above case 'assimilation to the best norms of Protestant Europe was the highest good' (Walls, 1996, p. 105) – it is not sufficient if our theological reflection does not look adequately at the consequences of our mission history. We are back again with the question of how we discern 'fruit'. Historians, including mission historians, need to be constantly reviewing and acknowledging their assumptions about what God has done among people and the assumptions of their sources. Accounts from one viewpoint enlighten accounts from another: counterpoint not harmony. Andrew Walls, for example, points to tensions between understanding an 'indigenizing principle' and a 'pilgrim principle':

> *... throughout Church history there has been another force in tension with this indigenizing principle, and this also is equally true of the Gospel. Not only does God in Christ take people as they are: He takes them in order to transform them into what He wants them to be. Along with the indigenizing principle which makes his faith a place to feel at home, the Christian inherits the pilgrim principle, which whispers to him that he has no abiding city and warns him that to be faithful to Christ will put him out of step with his society; for that society never existed, in East or West, ancient time or modern, which could absorb the word of Christ painlessly into its system.* (Walls, 1996, p. 8)

The matter of transformation and its effect on cultures becomes critical in equipping people for mission. What do such tensions mean in our own society? And further, what assumptions lie behind this vision of a converted people if the word of Christ can *never* be absorbed painlessly into cultures?

misreading and relativism

This leads us to another question about what we do if critical reflection on historical narrative shows us that distortion has taken place, for accepting the need to hear the same history from different perspectives does not do away with the need to assess each reading on its merits.

Particular kinds of narrative can be fuelled by various agenda and deliberate misreadings can take place where those agenda have to be taken forward. Further study has then to include critical re-interpretation of previous readings and we have to assess these against the new and more modern agenda of the Church. In our own times, postmodernism has been cited as an excuse to distrust making absolute choices. Instead, there are just many equal vantage points. This relativism has thus become another vantage point among many. While this keeps us alive to the way foundational stories can be changed or lost because of dominating agenda, it may also invoke in us Pilate's despairing question: 'What is truth?'

distorting mirrors

When we considered what this meant for us as Christians, we saw that the pressure of claiming our own Christian faith in a situation of religious and cultural plurality may create its own set of tensions and 'readings' of history. Consequently, in historical study, the hegemony of 'what actually happened' may prevent us asking critical questions about different kinds of truth claim. For example, teachers and students from particular church traditions may present historical (and mission) narratives as if (and only if) these traditions were 'what actually happened'. We can sometimes use perspectives of the historical Jesus to provide a validating groundwork for this view of history. Vincent Strudwick[18] points to the way in which, in the past, Church history was sometimes taught within theological colleges as a means, albeit an unconscious one, to back up a particular understanding of church tradition: *this* is how the Church came to be as it is. Here we see particular agenda being exposed, which have a consolidating influence on groups of students working together, but which become difficult or impossible to sustain in ministry out in the world. Tom O'Loughlin shows how those theological studies that use history to provide a pedigree and defence for what the writer believes to be theologically correct, can mislead the reader into thinking these studies are historical theology.

See Chapter 9.2, 'the New Testament'.

> *Many works which claim to treat topics 'historically', especially where these are matters touching present doctrine or practice in the Church should have a health warning inside the cover. 'This is a work of historical explanation of the current position, readers should not infer ipso facto that it is a work of historical theology.'* (O'Loughlin, 2001, p. 33)

many viewpoints: which help us and which do not?

Ideally, however, our use of both history and mission perspective denies neither the quest to discover 'what actually happened' nor the reality that any view is coloured by the vantage point. Accepting the validity of many viewpoints, even conflicting ones, enriches the attempt to chart and understand the past but it does not mean that we can give up a duty to reflect critically. Some viewpoints, whether primary or secondary, distort less than others; some conclusions misrepresent less than others, even though which these are is a matter for continuous and sometimes fierce debate. Discerning which help us represent the Christian faith to others, and which do not, matters.

Some forms of evidence of 'what happened', though trivial, have powerful effects on people's spiritual hopes and desires. For example the case of the 'fairies' photographic hoax apparently legitimated people's experiences of the paranormal and supernatural – the presence of an 'other' in their lives. Others have had the most profound effects on the perception and experience of a whole people such as the 2000 David Irving case, in which Irving, a British Holocaust denier, sued an American professor and her British publisher for libel, and lost the case. This debate, concerning the 'real' events of the Holocaust, showed most clearly the limits of uncritical relativism within the postmodernist project.

'what happened?' in mission history

In mission history, there are contemporary questions about the relationship between imperialism, mission activity and post-colonial rereadings of the coming of Christianity to different cultures. The myth of truth and civilization arriving with the missionaries was overturned by readings that identified missionaries with imperialism, both actual and cultural. This rereading is itself being questioned, as Brian Stanley helped us to understand.[19] These questions include asking whether everything that is laid at the door of imperialist and colonial behaviour is accurate, and whether missionary activity actually had more important roles in cultural adaptation and change. Professor Andrew Porter suggests that cultural imperialism was as much a result of 'local classes and ethnic communities turning missionary offerings to their own local advantage'.[20] This is endorsed further by a Swedish anthropologist, B. G. Karlsson, working on tribal conversion in West Bengal, who argues, that contrary to the Hindu fundamentalist view of conversion to Christianity being the result of imposition by external dominating forces, the issue must be understood as one of people *converting* rather than being *converted* (Stanley, 1999, p. 8). If we are concerned for a perspective that helps us understand our missionary role in western society, then understanding the difference in these views is fundamental. Despite such discussions, Brian Stanley does not feel this attention to Christianity outside western Christendom or western Christianity's engagement with the rest of the world has gone far enough: 'What is generally lacking is any study of Christianity as a world religion and a study of how theology has been forged and continues to be forged in the process of missionary encounters' (Stanley, 1999, p. 6). In this view, the history of mission theology and of missiology itself as an outworking of human response to God's purposes becomes important in forming critical tools for further historical study. Moreover, lack of attention to the historical development of the Christian religion in cultures other than our own can be seen to distort our understanding in a particular way.

large and small canvasses

Our understanding of mission can be helped by the fact that the study of Church history has always been both an attempt to understand the Church's past and a means of elucidating the particular versions of the Christian story we choose to live by. There are both large and small canvasses for us to study. 'History' can include works such as *The Isles*,[21] which seeks to cover the whole history of what is now the United Kingdom and Eire from prehistoric times to the present day. Other studies that concentrate on a specific subject in a specific place or time are also 'history'. Similarly, 'Church history' can mean both the broad sweep approach where an explained chronology is drawn of an entire period across a large geographical area, as well as a monograph which deals with a specific topic from a particular time and place in the Church's past. It can mean trying to explain and account for what happened in a particular period or place (i.e. Church history in the narrow sense) or demonstrate how a particular doctrine or usage has changed across the centuries (i.e. historical theology). Both these approaches can be invaluable in making sense of the Church's own mission in relation to our personal calling to be missionary ourselves, but both of these branches of the discipline can also be problematic.

creative confusion

This is because not only does Church history in the widest sense have to strive to be true to the two different disciplines to which it relates, namely theology and history, but there is a question about where exactly the boundaries lie between historical theology and Church history. Furthermore, historical theology, once a branch of intellectual history dealing specifically with religious ideas, has been opened up by new paradigm research, which rejects once and for all the idea of the neutral and objective outsider. This has sought to give voice to the unheard and unseen ones in history and gives more precedence to what had previously been seen as incidental. The notion of 'text' has also been opened up to include anything from hymns to woodcuts.[22] Schubert Ogden calls this 'confusion'[23] but acknowledges it is a 'creative confusion'.[24]

teaching in the confusion

We need to ask whether this 'creative confusion' is helpful in the relationship between mission and Church history, because it necessarily has an impact on teaching and learning styles. Our conversation partners were helpful here. Tom O'Loughlin[25] comments that 'the old Church history model'[26] is 'often taught by someone who is not a professional historian' (O'Loughlin, 1998, p. 75). Vincent Strudwick suggests that a better way than the 'old church history model' would be to give students 'a preparatory module/programme on the nature of history and an appreciation of the various settings in which Christians have prayed, studied, witnessed, cared and sometimes suffered' (Strudwick, 1999, p. 7), and then to teach all the other subjects and modules within the curriculum with 'historical theology blowing through' (Strudwick, 1999, p. 8). Brian Stanley agrees that this approach is 'fundamentally sound' (Stanley, 1999, p. 4), but adds the caveat, 'it can lead to frustration and superficiality if students are not first given an adequate grounding in historical knowledge. It can also encourage staffing policies that expect the tutor in theology (who may have little grounding in history) to turn his or her hand to the historical bits as occasion demands' (Stanley, 1999, p. 4). O'Loughlin would agree, '... in many Church-run faculties, "history of theology" is taught by systematics as background or as a subject of minor importance' (O'Loughlin, 1998, p. 75). If this takes place, what then happens to the critical tools needed for the evaluation of the history of missions and for our own mission work as we pass along our faith journey?

poor relation?

Both Stanley and O'Loughlin draw attention to the 'weak position' (Stanley, 1999, p. 4) of Church history within theological education in terms of the place sometimes given to it in the curriculum and the way in which it can be staffed. O'Loughlin refers to the Church historian as 'the poor relation within the theology department' (O'Loughlin, 1998, p. 65). In speaking of a meeting of the staffs of Anglican theological colleges and non-residential courses in 1995, Brian Stanley tells of how 'the over 100 theological educators present divided into groups according to our primary academic specialization and interest: the church history group had to be abandoned because there were not enough of us to make a viable group' (Stanley, 1999, p. 4). He concludes, 'Church history has suffered to a greater degree than other subjects from the mounting financial and pedagogical pressures on the modern theological curriculum' (Stanley, 1999, p. 4). Stanley notes the stronger position that the study of history has in Free Church colleges than in Anglican ones but sees this as a result of 'the greater need [felt by the free Churches] to shore up their creaking identity by the teaching of "tradition"' (Stanley, 1999, p. 4).

renewed interest in history

Paradoxically, this seeming dearth of Church historians occurs at a time when the academic interest in ecclesiastical history has never been so strong, 'a phenomenon of our time is the sheer quantity of history writing that has a bearing on our understanding of Christianity' (O'Loughlin, 1998, p. 65). This work is taking place in such fields as the history of ideas, anthropology, and the history of literature as well as in actual history departments. As noted earlier, Karlsson, who studied tribal conversion to Christianity in West Bengal, is an anthropologist. If we say that historical understanding is a vital tool for mission-minded Christians who wish to act transformatively, then perhaps the opportunities to explore across a number of disciplines have never been greater. Moreover, if we wish to assert that there is no mission without *ethics*, then creative interaction with anthropology and with the history of ideas helps us to place our learning about ethics in context. This is another matter that we must explore in terms of teaching and learning in Church history.

the importance of ethics

E. H. Carr claimed that history and theology are 'mutually exclusive' (O'Loughlin, 2001, p. 31). So we must also ask whether the development of a historical sense amongst those engaged in Christian ministry and mission is legitimate, or is it abusive of history as a discipline? Can history for a theologian, or indeed for a Christian, ever be anything other than a mine of ideological ammunition? In some ways, this is a question that belongs to a past age, to a 'different epistemological world' (O'Loughlin, 2001, p. 31). Of course, Christians can misuse historical research, but being committed rather than neutral is no longer a disqualification per se from doing serious history. The myth of neutrality has long since been exposed by Marxist historians and feminist historians, amongst others. This is not to underplay the difficulties O'Loughlin highlights in using historical research, but we no longer need be afraid of being partisan or committed if we also pay proper attention to issues of ethics. If we do, it will become clear that we must be honest and open about our stance.

We stand within a story, the story of the love of God in Christ, creative, crucified, risen and transforming and we are called to walk his way. Reality cannot be acted upon and transformed neutrally, but neither can it be left untouched neutrally. Someone always benefits. The questions are *who?* and *how?* Both these questions demand attention to the outworking of Christian ethics through mission in particular situations. If our aim is transformation living out of and towards the kingdom of God, a sense of how Christians have acted in the past can help us place our current praxis in context. Attention to ethics also means that historical rereading can make sense of both repentance and recovery: what have been the effects of action by Christians in the past? When and where have the Churches or individual Christians incarnated aspects of the kingdom 'as a sustainable reality in the material world?'[27] Where and when have they not? Understanding this is not just an intellectual exercise, but can lead to liturgical acts, symbols or the telling of stories that address past wrongs within Christian faith. Matching our analysis of historical actions to appropriate actions now and in the future can be a significant part of mission as transformation.

a kingdom vision

Incarnation demands a real attention to context. The kingdom of God, the real goal of our seeking, is in some sense always beyond us but always at hand as an invitation to act and live in a certain way – with compassion, with justice, with love. Jesus directs our attention directly to the 'fruit' of this. He says we shall see evidence for those that do the Father's will, empirical evidence, which will be open to testing. Historians cannot make judgements for us and may not like us judging at all; but as we are involved in an ethical project in the present, we cannot avoid making judgements. Our ethical judgements now must form part of our Christian presence and also our prophetic word. They must be informed by an understanding of the factors that have influenced how and why human communities in global, national and local contexts have come to be as they are.

range of historical contexts

Our conversation on these matters has led us to see that theological education needs to include an understanding of the broad historical contexts of the places and societies in which this mission takes place. By this means it can provide a context in which educators and learners become co-actors in the transformation towards the kingdom. Training for those engaged in cross-cultural mission has long recognized the need for such contextualization. Given that it is always easier to see the speck in another's eye, the need to understand the historical contexts of our own places and societies is just as acute. This historical understanding needs, as far as is practically possible, to embrace social, economic and political history to enable us to begin to grasp the power relationships that determine how the world now works. We need to be able to see and describe our own locatedness in time and responsibility, within it. As a matter of methodology, Freire would say that such understanding comes when educators present learners with problems rather than with answers.[28] Theological education that *enables* mission, a 'curriculum with a purpose', will see its own methodology as crucial tool. Students will not be acted upon but acted with.

Our exploration of history through a missiological lens has led us to discuss its relevance to what we can know about the past in the present and what difference its shaping by a variety of viewpoints actually makes. For us, it has become important to say that historical understanding in its widest sense opens up possibilities: it accepts and expects complexity. Ethics, the benchmark for a missionary transformation of our society, provides a rudder by which we can steer safely through. Joseph Cardijn, the founder of the Young Christian Workers Movement, used to talk about the truth of experience, the truth of faith and the truth of method. By this last he meant an ongoing critical review of life as one worked for the transformation of the world. Perhaps that is one way that makers of history, agents of transformation with a vision of the Reign, and missionaries as we all are, can situate themselves within history.

history makers

We have also learned that mission perspective gives us a view of ourselves as makers of a particular history, and that this drives ethical considerations. This is because we are working for something that is not necessarily to be realized within our lifetime. Our mission efforts are dedicated to Christians of the future who will themselves make decisions out of our present thought and actions. In this sense, Church history fuels us with a sense of responsibility.

a sense of responsibility

We saw in our work on styles of teaching and learning that just as it is important that the debate about mission-directed learning is not restricted to the education of those to be ordained, so it is important that this debate is held with others. Adult educators, working mainly with lay people, have built up a considerable expertise in how adults learn, but also, to use John Hull's phrase, in 'what prevents Christian adults from learning'.[29] A great deal of work has been done on models of education, reflecting on what enables people to use what they have learned. If we are to see the study of Church history as ultimately empowering us with a sense of responsibility for future Church, then we have to relate Church history and mission in terms of an educational praxis that can enable transformation, proper 'fruits'. To this end we suggest some questions:

- How does an appreciation of wide historical contexts help us to understand the global power relations and international situations that affect Christians in mission?

- How does the study of history help us to reconcile striving for truth with an appreciation of plurality and multiculturalism?

- How does the study of history help us to see mistakes made in 'good faith' by those before us? How do we determine what a 'mistake' is? What difference does this make to our view of mission?

- If history is seen as someone's story, how do we tell if the story is liberating or enslaving? How do we equip people to listen for the stories that are drowned out and to have tools to tell their own stories in different contexts?

- How does the study of history allow us to express our own faith without distortion (e.g. apologizing for past wrongs)?

- How does the study of history give us responsibility for the future of the Church?

- How can ethics determine directions in mission? How do we know what is or is not 'good fruit'?

mission and the Bible

1 the Hebrew Scriptures

The noise inside the synagogue poured out into the night, an
undulating, swelling and receding and thinning and growing sound.
The joy of dancing with the Torah, holding it close to you, the words
of God to Moses at Sinai. I wondered if gentiles ever danced with their
Bible. 'Hey, Tony. Do you ever dance with your Bible?'... Do you ever
read your Bible? Do you ever hold it to you and know how much you
love it? Do Christian Bible scholars write about Jesus the same way
they write about Abraham? Do they say that it's all only stories?[1]

Do we?

Our conversations with those teaching Church history helped us to see how
our witness to a missionary God who acts in history is made more complex by
competing narratives and perspectives. When we then came to look at how
we can consider the teaching of the biblical literature through a mission
lens, the question of how we make the missionary God known in a way that
is clear and accessible to people preoccupied us. We were fortunate in being
able to hold two consultations to consider the issues more deeply and to
widen the range of our conversation partners. However, in choosing a way to
approach the subject, we decided that we would look at the biblical literature
for clues to see how reading and studying the Bible, not just in theological
education but in our homes and in church, can equip us to be a missionary
people. Where do our ideas about mission come from? Biblical scholars are
divided on this question – how do we make sense of the complex arguments
in a way that undergirds our own heart for mission? And the challenge from
Chaim Potok also strikes home: do we love our Bible enough to study it
thoroughly, but also to share it with joy in our witness to the world?

So the purpose of this section is not to tell people how to teach Scripture,
nor to instruct students how to learn Scripture. Rather, this section on the
Bible is about finding perspectives which allow people to ask, and form
answers to, questions that open up perspectives and equip people to think
in a missiological way. For us, considering the questions ourselves, this
meant that certain thematic ways of looking at the material became
important. This was not only for academic study of the material, but also

for finding ways of applying what could be learned in the course of study to the contexts for mission, both in the local and in the global situation. For this reason, we have worked with Bible specialists who treat the material in this particular way[2] and have tried to bear in mind what we can learn from the way Jewish scholars do hermeneutics. We ourselves have recommended doing theology as conversation and dialogue, but how often do we bother to listen to the theological dialogues between the Jewish commentators, such as Rashi and Ibn Ezra on the Torah, which have so informed the worshipping life of Jewish communities? If we treat these holy Scriptures solely as our own possession, what does that say about our missionary intentions?[3] Further, how can we offer our Christian witness and our understanding of the New Testament to people of other faiths, unless we are willing to learn how people of other faiths themselves love and are steeped in scripture?

who is God?

Asking this question for ourselves is broken wide open by study of the Hebrew Scriptures. For it is in such study that we are first asked to consider the largest questions. What was God's purpose in bringing about creation? Also, what intention does God continue to have towards the creation? Why, after all, did God bother? And why should we? What is it about the nature of God that brings about creation and places us within it? Is the creation an expression of God's own need? Is the creation a consequence of God's being? Or is the creation an inevitable result of and testimony to the fact that there *is* God, a God whose love overflows persistently into the cosmos, which brings about creatures capable of asking questions about who, what and why we are?[4] These questions matter, because how we view the relationship between God and the creation colours our ideas about a missionary God and a missionary people.

creation and destruction

Consequently, exploration of the creation narratives together with the destruction narratives in Genesis requires us to consider God's vision, purpose and intention set against human disobedience, wilfulness, stupidity and simple failure to live up to the vision. Despite the failure of human beings to respond effectively to the overflowing of God's love into the creation, *still* we are asked to work with the Holy Spirit in reconciling the creation to God's will. The way that this is explored in Scripture provides a foundation for our understanding of a missionary God whose purposes are being worked out today in the cultures in which we live now.

However, this picture of a missionary God is sometimes overlooked in the teaching of the Hebrew Scriptures. This is because the discussion of 'mission' sometimes gets parcelled up into a sense of 'sending', which is extrapolated from the New Testament: 'as the Father has sent me, so I send you' (John 20.21). This is not merely an oversight, because the idea is also perpetuated by some mission specialists. For example, in David Bosch's large and comprehensive work, *Transforming Mission*,[5] little attention is paid to the missionary aspects of God as revealed in the Hebrew Scriptures, and even the scant few references are contained in the chapter called 'Reflections on the New Testament as a Missionary Document'. So we suggest that asking the question 'who is God?' in the context of a missionary purpose is fundamental to studying the Hebrew Scriptures with a heart for mission.

See Chapter 2, 'the world as God sees it'.

crossing barriers

See Chapter 8, 'mission and Church history'.

Yet David Bosch properly argues that mission is about crossing barriers: language, culture, geography, ethics, religion. It is easy to point to such experiences in the New Testament material: Jesus' ministry shows many such significant encounters, which become models for the preaching, teaching, witnessing, travelling apostles of the early Church and become paradigmatic of the ability of the gospel to spread 'from everywhere to everywhere'. Moreover, the Resurrection of Jesus becomes the 'ultimate energizing' experience to use Walter Brueggemann's phrase, which enables an ultimate crossing from death to life.[6] These encounters and actions, however, are rooted in the heritage of many barrier-crossing experiences in the Hebrew Scriptures which include: the liberation of the people of Israel from slavery in Exodus and its retelling in Joshua 24, the story of exile, the message of liberation in Isaiah 52, and the individual narrative of Jonah. Moreover, there are powerful explorations not only of a physical and cultural barrier crossing, but also of the turning of the human will from self-serving ideas and ambitions towards love of God and the service of other human beings, as Jonah demonstrates.[7] The conversion experience as a re-emergence of the human person oriented towards God is seen again and again in the Hebrew Scriptures and is articulated most eloquently through the psalms and in the prophetic writings. If we want to develop hearts for mission, and to evangelize others, then we need to understand such conversion experiences not just from our reading of the New Testament but also from the Hebrew Scriptures.

See Chapter 6, 'styles of teaching and learning'.

If we consider that the crossing of physical, mental and spiritual barriers is paradigmatic throughout Scripture of the relationship between human beings and God, then the question 'who is this God?' becomes more acute for us. What kind of God asks people to cross barriers if not a God with mission, agenda and purpose? This is a God who is active in human history and who has engaged the people of Israel. Nor is this merely a matter of the people being led around as instruments of the divine will, for when they cry to Yahweh, he too responds with demonstrations of power. At the call of the powerless, Yahweh can make the sea heap up for their passage (Exodus 14.21ff.) and the fire fall to consume the lone Elijah's offering against all the prophets of Baal (1 Kings 18.38). The people of Israel are, therefore, in being for a reason. This sense of ultimate purpose and, indeed, ultimate destiny underlies the New Testament sense of mission and the mission of the Church, but we need to follow the connections through. Without proper examination of this question about a missionary God of purpose, we cannot properly understand the theological underpinning to the New Testament Church.

See Chapter 8, 'mission and Church history'.

how should we respond to this God?

The question 'who is God?' cannot be answered in a vacuum. A missionary God also extends invitation, an invitation to partnership in the divine purpose for the creation. Such invitation requires response. What response can be made and what response is appropriate? If we are to have a heart for mission, we too have to ask this question and see the answer shaped by our study of Scripture. This is important because, too often, our missionary zeal and evangelistic desire are shaped in fact by our own inbuilt assumptions about what God wants and not by a reference to how the people of God have responded and what the effects have been. As in the call of Samuel, we may not know clearly what is going on at first and need our teachers to show us the way, before we can say 'Speak, Lord, for your servant is listening' (1 Samuel 3.9).

affirmation

If we start with the most basic human response, then we see that a people in partnership with a missionary God first responds with affirmation. Such a God is like no other, so the people must respond with a 'yes' to God who has given a blessing to the people as a divine 'yes' to them. Indeed the strength of such a relationship in a fallen and uncertain world is tested to the point of destruction in the book of Job. Examination of this relationship of positive promise becomes an important missiological thread, which makes sense of how people can cling on to faith in adversity, whether this be in the extreme conditions of a concentration camp, in imprisonment

See Chapter 2, 'the world as God sees it'.

in solitary confinement or under torture. This is true not only for committed Christians but for others too. For example, Brian Keenan, kidnapped and tortured in Beirut in 1985 found 'pulsating in the back of my head ... the words "Yea, though I walk through the valley of death, I will fear no evil"'.[8]

the sovereignty of God

Affirmation implies more than just acknowledgement of God and we are helped to understand this by Scripture. The faith of Israel gives affirmations about Yahweh with a polemical edge in its own context. Israel claims that Yahweh alone is God (Deuteronomy 4.35-39; Psalm 24) and is Lord over all other gods: 'he is to be revered above all gods' (Psalm 96.4). This is a proclamation that becomes part of worship, especially in the Psalms: 'The earth is the Lord's and all that is in it' (Psalm 24.1). Affirming God means that we must recognize that the whole creation belongs to, and is under, God, as for instance in 1 Chronicles 29.11, 'all that is in the heavens and on the earth is yours ...' We cannot ignore the implications of this, for they have serious consequences for proclamation. So often, claims of kingship, sovereignty and the absolute divine right of God to rule human persons, give mission a shrill, triumphalist edge, which alienates those to whom we would reach out in dialogue. After all, how offensive is it to sing '*our* God reigns'? Does this missionary God, pouring out love into the whole of creation, belong only somehow to 'us' and does this mean that in fact we compromise God's sovereignty by trying to make God relate only to ourselves. What does it now mean to say 'God is Lord of all the earth' in the context of a plural and multicultural society?

obedience to the divine will

We can explore these questions if we look at the way Israel also makes absolute claims about the *relationship* between the people and Yahweh. This is seen in the struggle against other gods. In terms of international history and politics this might be seen as mere arrogant claims for moral superiority, but the claims go beyond this. For example, in Jeremiah 27, claims are made in the context of an international Middle Eastern diplomatic conference before the ambassadors in Jerusalem, where the question is how to confront Babylon. In the midst of this, the prophet enters bearing a yoke and cords. He reminds everyone that Yahweh is God of the host nation, has made all that is and is Lord of all. If this is the case, then this God has raised up Nebuchadnezzar, so it is necessary to bow down to Babylon or otherwise answer to Yahweh. The process of events is overseen by a dynamic God, so we need to stop trying to make everything happen by ourselves and bend our human will to the divine will.

the might of God

If we consider the way that international diplomacy in today's conflicts is played out, we can see not only what an extraordinary claim this is, but also how it points us to consider the much longer term view, something which analysts now struggle to deal with in our fast-changing and politically turbulent societies. We have to look beyond this to a much larger understanding and hold on to it. Brueggemann, for example, argues that the narratives of conflict and struggle in relation to empire, to cultures and to land, are set within a vast theological drama, running from the earliest mythic background to the eschatological vision. The purpose of this drama is to show how the overflowing desire of God makes the impossible possible, miracle can and *will* take place in people's lives. The incredible power of mighty nations can be overturned by Yahweh, and, with the retelling of the story, the hope for liberation and for transformation of people's lives becomes a living promise and a permanent reality. In behaving as he does, Jeremiah dramatizes this through his propheric actions.[9] Brueggemann further argues that it is our ability to participate in this drama, through powerful memory, and through our own experience, that allows us to cope with the question: who is God? and to define our relationship with the creator.[10] Thus St Paul is able to proclaim:

> *For I am convinced that neither death, nor life, nor angels, nor rulers, nor things present, nor things to come, nor powers, nor height, nor depth, nor anything else in all creation, will be able to separate us from the love of God in Jesus Christ our Lord.* (Romans 8.38-39)

uniqueness and universality

Claims for the uniqueness and universality of Yahweh beyond all the other religious traditions therefore underlie and provide the vocabulary for the uniqueness and universality of Jesus. Such claims were also polemical in a first-century context. So here we see the origins of John 8 and the 'I am' sayings in the use of Isaiah 45. There is also the use of such affirmation in Philippians 2, with reference to the 'name above every name' as in Isaiah 43. The language of the uniqueness of Yahweh becomes the language of the lordship of Jesus. Paul, in 1 Corinthians 8.5-6, gives deliberate christological expansion of the *shema* and to the concept of one lordship over all. The phraseology shows how Christians must relate to other gods, for there is but one Lord Jesus.

This therefore fuels for us the missiological impact of biblical monotheism, but it also challenges us as to our own response. Walter Brueggemann suggests:

> *No reductionist conservative can faithfully treat evangelism as though it were only 'naming the name'. We are required to notice that behind (prior to) the announcement is an 'event' of mythic proportion to which we have no direct access. And after the proclamation comes the difficult, demanding work of reordering all of life according to the claim of the proclaimed verdict.*[11]

Mission, then, implies transformation, but we need to bear in mind that the universality and uniqueness of God apply to all of God's actions in eternity and are beyond our applications of them. God will go on working through the Holy Spirit with us or in spite of us. This is especially appreciated in the Psalms. Moreover, if we proclaim this uniqueness and universality, then we have a responsibility to live out what this means in terms of Brueggemann's 'reordering'. Evangelism as part of mission is sometimes seen as being discharged in the act of proclamation; it is not always seen as carrying a greater personal responsibility for effecting transformation. It is *costly* to be Christian.

what is our role in mission?

Putting the two questions together: who is God and how should we respond? also asks us to think further about what kind of role we are to be equipped for if we are to have a heart for mission. For example, if God chooses a people for the divine purpose, does this not tyrannically remove choice from such a people? Does the act of choosing and asking for partnership in fact enslave such a people to God's purposes?[12] What, then, makes God's partnership with human beings overwhelmingly right in the context of human history? Why do we want to say 'yes' to God and what in study of Scripture helps us to work this out? Further, what kind of people are they who are called to affirm the uniqueness and universality of this God? What form of social, political, cultural and religious contexts and customs make it possible for a people to live out an ongoing partnership faithfully? In a plural world, how does this affirmation manage not to affront, demean or shut out others, or make truth claims which do not include others? This needs to be explored, since the ethics of affirmation make a difference to how faith can be shared. For example, what do we make of the words of this hymn?

The Lord has given a land of good things,
I will press on and make them mine;
I'll know His power, I'll know His glory,
and in His kingdom I will shine.

With the high praises of God in our mouth,
and a two-edged sword in our hand,
we'll march right on to the victory side,
right into Canaan's land.

Gird up your armour, ye sons of Zion,
gird up your armour, let's go to war;
we'll win the battle with great rejoicing
and so we'll praise Him more and more.
With the high praises ...

We'll bind their kings in chains and fetters,
we'll bind their nobles tight in iron,
to execute God's written judgement –
march on to glory, sons of Zion!
With the high praises ...[13]

See Chapter 10, 'mission and worship'.

There is affirmation, certainly, but it is translated, through allusion to the Hebrew Scriptures, into a vision of overpowering and overcoming others who are not the same as us. This is a long way from the radical understanding of God's sovereignty dramatized by Jeremiah. Our understanding of universality and uniqueness has to be tempered with what this means in terms of God's desire that the whole world should be saved. The study of the particular history of the people of Israel in the context of other nations and peoples can provide us with a picture of a universal purpose, continually affirmed and restructured in the light of events, but also allowing the possibility of the whole world ultimately offering up its 'yes' to God.

who are we?

Study of the Hebrew Scriptures shows that the missionary partnership between God and the chosen people does not come to an end with mutual affirmation. There must be a sense of identity, and with this identity a sense of purpose. In the Hebrew Scriptures, affirmation of the purpose of Yahweh is seen particularly in the blessing of the nations. We can see this clearly if we set aside chronology for a canonical approach. Genesis provides a universal history: God creates humanity and the nations (1–11). But creation becomes disordered and the vision is lost. The impact of the *missio Dei* on this situation is therefore God's address to what has gone wrong, as we see in Genesis 12ff. So Genesis 12 is the beginning of the answer to the problem set out in 1–11. The stories of Noah and of the Tower of Babel ask 'is there any future for humanity?' Must all be scattered in strife and violence? In view of the number of times people in ministry are asked these questions by the people they serve, we can conclude that these are still significant missiological questions in the context of finding out who we are in God's world.

we are the blessed

For example, Genesis 12 sets out God's promise to Abraham. God will make his name great and bless the nations through him. Genesis 12.3 sets out God's intention to bless the nations and, further, God's purpose and intention is to affirm humanity. The strength of this intention to pour out blessing as a manifestation of the overflowing love from the heart of God, also feeds from here into the New Testament understanding of mission. God ceaselessly works to restore and reconcile what has become disordered so that now we are the inheritors of what God has done in Christ. If we understand what the crucifixion and Resurrection have brought about, then we are called to live and work to make that understanding available to all others. Our Christian presence in society and our prophetic word to those who live among us should be characterized by this sense of being blessed by God, by the privilege of being Christian and by gratitude to God that we can witness freely. For others, of course, especially where Christianity is a minority religion, this opportunity may be denied. We should perhaps, truly, count our blessings every day.

the Abrahamic promise

In Galatians, Paul says:

> Just as Abraham 'believed God, and it was reckoned to him as righteousness,' so, you see, those who believe are the descendants of Abraham. And the scripture, foreseeing that God would justify the Gentiles by faith, declared the gospel beforehand to Abraham, saying, 'All the Gentiles shall be blessed in you.' For this reason, those who believe are blessed with Abraham who believed. (Galatians 3.6-10)

This helps us deal with the ideas in the hymn more effectively. Paul appeals back to Abraham as justification for missionary purpose and practice. The

Gentiles are invited in and are to be given the status of being part of the people of God by faith, because of the inclusiveness of God's desire to pour out blessing. For Paul, then, the Scriptures foresaw the Gentiles being justified by God and this means that the whole human world must be exposed to the Good News. Further, in Revelation 7.9 we see the people of every nation within the picture of redeemed humanity, so there is an echo of the Abrahamic promise there also. In developing a missiological picture of the study of Scripture, we also have to determine our place in the vision of God's desire to bless the nations. Are we prepared not just to announce God's love, but help people to experience it – and what responsibility does this bring to transform contexts to make it more possible for people to experience the divine favour? The interpretation and hermeneutic employed by the first Christian communities and by the early Church help us to understand how God invests us with the responsibility for making known the divine desire to bless all the nations. Further, we should not assume that this is the only hermeneutic available; the understanding contained in the rabbinic tradition and in Jewish and Muslim scholarship about who we are in relation to the God of Abraham, should challenge our answer to the missionary question 'who are we?'

election

Another important facet of the question about who we are in relation to God is centred in the idea of election. At one level it is connected to God's intention and purpose: Yahweh's election of Israel is for the sake of blessing the nations. In Genesis, it is God's mission to bless and affirm the election of Abraham and his descendants. God's method is to use this historical route to extend the divine intention into a future and beyond the lifetime of individuals. Where the inability to bear children seems to interrupt the continuity of the elected ones, God's empowerment of women in the face of sterility and powerlessness confirms that hope and possibility for everyone is built into the idea of election. The stories of Sarah, Rebekah and Rachel are witnesses to the strength of the promise to Abraham. It is more than overcoming barrenness, for the slave girl Hagar, who has no problem conceiving, is found by the angel of the Lord after running away and receives God's promise (Genesis 16.7-16).

Hagar's response is astonishment that God has come just for her; but we also see how, in the song of Hannah, she celebrates God's empowerment of those who apparently have no human resources of their own: 'He raises up the poor from the dust; he lifts the needy from the ash heap, to make them sit with princes and inherit a seat of honour' (1 Samuel 2.8). This is the response of the mother of Samuel, liberated from her inability to conceive. The proper response to God's demonstration of such faith in the chosen people is, therefore, renewal of consecration to God's will. Samuel is brought to Eli. Naturally this lays the foundation for the virgin woman's own 'yes' to God to be celebrated in Mary's 'Magnificat': 'he has looked with favour on the lowliness of his servant … He has brought down the powerful from their thrones, and lifted up the lowly' (Luke 1.48-52), and for the bearing of Jesus as the consecrated one. Election, then, carries with it the sense that God's empowerment can become a means to override human muddle, confusion and failure. No matter what mess we make of our social processes, governance and behaviour, the fact that God has promised to be in a covenantal relationship with the beloved people means that the spiral of decline can *always* be altered and new things can happen to bring hope and promise into the world.

It follows that the concept of election is fundamental in the Hebrew Scriptures and relates to the rest of God's purposes. A problem with the concept in assessing the missiological role, however, is that the idea of 'election' can become arrogant or self-congratulatory:

> *Israel did forget sometimes that election and universality had to be held together, and felt that they had been chosen because there was something special about them. They forgot the reason why they were chosen – to be a witness to the nations, to be a light to lighten the gentiles as we sing in the Song of Simeon. Sometimes they felt that the universal significance of Yahweh was to allow Israel to wipe out all the other nations, or to achieve dominance over them, or to enslave them, to extend the frontiers of their empire. All these things have a contemporary significance. But then at other times, perhaps in a kindlier mood, they thought that God, if he is the God of all people, must have a purpose for these people, which must really be that they should become exactly like Israel. The great passages in the prophets, in Micah and in the early part of Isaiah … speak of the nations converging onto Mount Zion. Zion is the centre of the world, the culture, and everybody else comes to it and partakes of its benefits. Their model of mission was that everyone else should be like them.*[14]

ethics within the concept of election

Notwithstanding the assumptions in the Hebrew Scriptures concerning an understanding of election as the right and only model for human living, we can also see a critical stance emerging to ask the question 'what obligation does election actually set upon us?' For example, Deuteronomy 7 argues

that the 'people holy to the Lord', God's 'treasured possession'
(v. 6) must love the Lord and keep his commandments 'to a thousand
generations' (v. 9). 'If you heed these ordinances, by diligently observing
them, the Lord your God will maintain with you the covenant loyalty that he
swore to your ancestors; he will love you, bless you, and multiply you ...'
(12,13). Deuteronomy 10.14,15, relates the universal claims about
Yahweh to the concept of election: 'Although heaven and the heaven of
heavens belong to the Lord your God, the earth with all that is in it, yet the
Lord set his heart in love on your ancestors alone and chose you, their
descendants after them, out of all the peoples, as it is today.' Further, v. 19
then relates this powerfully bonded relationship to responsibility: 'You shall
also love the stranger, for you were strangers in the land of Egypt.' Election
cannot be triumphalistic in the face of such responsibility. The blessing of
our faith and of our knowledge of this missionary God must be offered to
others in a way that allows them the freedom to share our joy.

servanthood

Rather, Israel's existence in the world is related to the blessing of the
nations. Israel is required to *be* something and to show forth something.
But this has to be coupled with the discharge of responsibility. In Deutero-
Isaiah the corporate idea is of a servant of God and of the embodiment of
images of this servanthood: 'You are my servant, Israel, in whom I will be
glorified ... I will give you as a light to the nations, that my salvation may
reach to the end of the earth' (Isaiah 49 3,6). In Isaiah 61, responsibility
is related directly to recovery and redress.[15] Servanthood is also annexed
to suffering, so responsibility and obligation carry more than just the
discharge of a religious duty. The sacrifice of self for the sake of others
models God's own permanent and unstoppable self-giving. For us, then,
the question 'who are we?' in relation to God is focused by the merger of
the overflowing love from the heart of God and the responsibility of election
of the chosen people in the person of Jesus himself. Nation shrinks to one
human person, whose absolute commitment to carrying out God's intention
is reflected back to us as the absolute submission to God's own will. The
Gethsemane experience not only makes this clear, but also issues a
challenge to us as to the exhausted disciples. The end point of election
and servanthood is suffering and sacrifice on behalf of others. This itself
acts as direct criticism of the eschatological vision, cited above, in which
Israel is exalted as *the* cultural model. In the crucifixion, from the point of
view of the controlling political regime, the spurious 'king' of this ultimate
cultural model dies the ignominious death of a criminal. John V. Taylor
reflects on this:

> The servant in suffering, the Messiah who must go down rather than
> up, the self-given Son, he is God's partner. And to be called into
> partnership with him is to be called into his sonship. To those who
> have yielded him their allegiance he gave the right to become children
> of God – self-given, like him (John 1.12). We must honour all who
> share that vocation, those we know, whoever they may be, and those
> we don't know.[16]

how should we live?

the nations

If the Hebrew Scriptures give us important insights into who we are, then
this is followed by the question 'how should we live?' If election carries
with it responsibility, what behaviour is appropriate? We have seen that
Deuteronomy includes a self-critical stance, but this presupposes the
question: if Yahweh has a purpose for the nations, then it is with Israel
as a vehicle. How then does Israel relate to the nations? Are the holy
people of God over against the nations, or should there be relationship,
interaction? The relationship question is constantly on view. This is often
overlooked in studies of the Hebrew Scriptures, although Walter
Brueggemann devotes a portion of *Old Testament Theology* to 'the nations
as Yahweh's partners'. He argues that we must not forget that the 'nations
as partner' is first of all a function of the scandal of Israel's particularity,
Israel's self-preoccupation and Israel's self-serving ideology that shows
up as testimony. The nations must make their way, according to this
unsolicited testimony, in a world of Israel's preferential status with Yahweh
(Brueggemann, 1997, p. 495). This directly challenges anyone with a
mission focus to consider what our own cultural baggage might be in
witness to and proclamation of the gospel. Moreover, Brueggemann urges
us to look at the question of our understanding of God's purpose in today's
geopolitical arena. He suggests that the cultural milieu in which we now
live, with its privatizing of religion, means that we urgently need to look
at what Scripture tells us about Israel's relationship with Egypt as abuser
and oppressor, Assyria's arrogance and autonomy, Babylon and
Nebuchadnezzar, and Persia as responsive partner. If we look hard into
the relationships between Israel and the nations, he suggests, we come
out with a question which is directly relevant to the missionary question of
how we should live: 'Can that impetus for justice that Israel finds rooted in
Yahweh's own resolve be fully stopped?' and further, 'God-talk is not mere
strategic rhetoric, though it may be that. It is also an utterance of a

substantive claim that a crucial force is embedded in geopolitics that is beyond conventional manipulation' (Brueggemann, 1997, pp. 526–7).

holiness

The other side of this impetus for justice is the understanding that partnership with God through election and blessing carries with it powerful moral implications. Those whom God has chosen must consent to be an example: servanthood alone will not do. There are conditions which apply to God's community, to a holy people, and which themselves are part of preserving the distinguishing features of preferential status in God's eyes. This is also built into the argument in Deuteronomy 7. Such conditions set up positive and negative categories for the question 'how shall we live?'
 Hebrew Scriptures remind us that Israel must concern itself with being clean and holy and avoid contamination by what is unclean. The animal world becomes a mirror for this, with its categories of 'sacrificial and holy', 'clean' and 'unclean'. In Leviticus this mirrors the priestly order: the ordinary Israelites and the unclean non-Israelites. Israel is called to be holy and to resist idolatry. Israel must avoid contamination by the wickedness of other nations (and we see modern arguments in conflict theology about avoiding becoming what is hated, in both Girard[17] and Wink[18]).

For example, Israel is exhorted not to become like the Canaanites, yet Israel lives with the possibility of becoming like Canaan and therefore standing under God's judgement. There is also an important distinction between ritual purity and moral purity as exemplified in Malachi 1, which distinction Jesus brings to the fore in asking questions about defilement. The stories in Scripture about how a people must struggle to avoid becoming what it (or God) hates are instructive in our own preparation for mission, because they constantly ask the question: what does our witness look like to others? Do we ourselves properly pay attention to the distinction between ritual correctness and personal morality?

The distinction of the holy community is also an ethical distinction, for Israel is called to be distinctive from the other nations. We see this in the holiness texts, e.g. Leviticus 19.2. Genesis 18.19 sets out the story of Yahweh and two of his angels in conversation with Abraham and Sarah en route to destroy Sodom and Gomorrah. Yahweh considers holding back – 'shall I hide from Abraham ...?' (v. 17) but instead of concealing the divine purpose, Yahweh decides to lay on Abraham the charge of being chosen and it is directed that he and his household keep themselves both holy and distinctive. In this way they will be inheritors of the promise, but this does not leave Abraham feeling self-righteous, rather it encourages him to argue for the lives of the God-fearing people of the doomed city. Therefore there are links between being chosen, inheriting the promise (God's mission), blessing, and advocacy.

The fulcrum for this is the ethical demand to lead lives of righteousness and justice. Sodom and Gomorrah demonstrate the context of wickedness, oppression and outcry beyond which Abraham and his household must keep themselves pure. Righteousness, in moral and ethical contexts (as we see in the story of Lot following Abraham's plea), keeps open the possibility of salvation. God's saving purposes further charge the people to continue to be faithful and pure. God considers the purpose and links this to the demand for ethical obedience as we see in Exodus 19.4-6. 'You have seen what I did to the Egyptians, and how I bore you on eagles' wings and brought you to myself. Now therefore, if you obey my voice and keep my covenant, you shall be my treasured possession out of all the peoples. Indeed, the whole earth is mine, but you shall be for me a priestly kingdom and a holy nation.' This is not merely a cause for self-congratulation, for this holiness must be significant among the nations. Priests stand as intermediaries between the people and God, therefore Israel must stand as intermediary between God and the nations. This dual motif is linked to visible holiness of life and worship. Israel must be ethically holy. For example:

> Now the word of the Lord came to Solomon, 'Concerning this house that you are building, if you will walk in my statutes, obey my ordinances, and keep all my commandments by walking in them, then I will establish my promise with you, which I made to your father David. I will dwell among the children of Israel, and will not forsake my people Israel' (1 Kings 6.11-13).

At the same time, this distinctiveness does not mean that a holy people of God is cut off from engagement with and use of other cultural processes. In the patriarchal narratives this comes out with the stories relating to worship of Baal, but in Isaiah the Temple has the same symbols as Canaanite religion – it takes over the myths and motifs; it uses holy mountains as dramatic settings, the same poetic metres and themes. There are no great religious rifts in Genesis. In Hosea the prophet transforms the fertility cult language into a sexual metaphor for the relationship between Yahweh and Israel. In Ezekiel the Temple statuary becomes part of his vision of the glory of God. There are visual symbolic links known to the Mesopotamian world. This shows us how we can work to transform what is already in the world, and to offer this transformation to God's own restorative and reconciling work.

our own relationship to 'the nations'

This asks us to consider how mission practice and theology relate to different cultures in which the gospel is presented. What can be affirmed? What must be challenged or questioned? How do you bind together cultural relevance and Christian faith? In what way will you make sense to people operating out of another cultural frame? This is not just a modern question but also part of the New Testament themes. How do you get from a Jewish background to the Roman–Greek contexts and how did the gospel make its way into, for example, Syrian, Ethiopian, Armenian, Persian and Indian contexts? The stories of the appropriation of the gospel in the churches of these areas open up the question of how the Christian community pursues its faithfulness in the context of particular cultures.

who is desired?

If God asks us to live in particular kind of way, it makes sense to ask what this request is *for*. It is not merely a question of making a contrast between holiness and unholiness, for the ultimate purpose in view is God's desire for all creation to be reconciled to God's own self. Consequently, holy living *must* set up a longing in the hearts of others. God's desire extends past those who have already turned to the divine will. In Deuteronomy 4.6-8 there is evidence of the visibility of Israel to the nations and a motivating factor for their obedience. The argument is: you must obey – if you live like this then you will be a source of wisdom to the nations and will prompt them to ask, 'what kind of God is this, what kind of Law is this?' Israel is to be a light to the nations. In terms of a mission understanding of the question 'who is desired?', this too becomes translated to the New Testament. 1 Peter 2.9-12 picks up Exodus 19.4-6.

> But you are a chosen race, a royal priesthood, a holy nation, God's own people, in order that you may proclaim the mighty acts of him who called you out of darkness into his marvellous light. Once you were not a people, but now you are God's people; once you had not received mercy, but now you have received mercy. Beloved, I urge you as aliens and exiles to abstain from the desires of the flesh that wage war against the soul. Conduct yourselves honourably among the Gentiles, so that, though they malign you as evildoers, they may see your honourable deeds and glorify God when he comes to judge.

In answering the question 'who is desired?' we come to the conclusion: there can be no mission without ethics.

an eschatological vision

The historical promise of blessing the nations through Israel is further developed in the Hebrew Scriptures to an eschatological vision. We see this in worship, especially in the Psalms and in the prophetic eschatological visions of the future. Psalm 47 calls on the nations to applaud Yahweh for what he has done in Israel, including the conquest of them. Is this arrogant cynicism or a faith imagination that suggests that somehow, ultimately, the nations will praise Yahweh for what God has done? In Psalm 67 there is the universalizing of the Aaronic blessing of Numbers 6, so salvation is among all the nations. In Psalm 87 the nations are enlisted and enrolled. In Psalm 96 the name of God is among the nations. There is an eschatological proposition in Amos 9.11 of the restoration of the fallen tent of David with the possession of Edom and all the nations that bear the Lord's name.

> *On that day I will raise up the booth of David that is fallen, and repair its breaches, and raise up its ruins, and rebuild it as in the days of old; in order that they may possess the remnant of Edom and all the nations who are called by my name, says the Lord who does this.*

James quotes this in the Council of Jerusalem in Acts 15.16-17 in setting out the mandate for including the Gentiles under God's name.

In Isaiah 19.23-25, the description of Israel is applied to Egypt and to Assyria; the blessing is not confined to Israel. In Isaiah 56.1-8 it is personalized to the eunuch and to the foreigner. They are anxious about ever being able to be part of the sacred assembly. But there is also the promise that those who choose to believe or live the life of the Covenant will be accepted. (Luke has this in mind in Acts 8 in the context of the earliest people to congregate around the Messiah, when we read the story of Philip proclaiming the Good News to the Ethiopian eunuch.) The eschatological dimension of the place of the nations before God therefore contributes to a major missiological understanding. There is also the recognition of the eschatological hope in the intertestamental literature for an ingathering of the nations within the redemption of Israel.

centrifugal and centripetal mission

Through the Hebrew Scriptures we see this imagined in two ways that are both important for our understanding of mission. There is a centrifugal process, whereby the chosen community is 'sent' to others under an impulse to show what God is like. There is also a centripetal effect, whereby the nations are drawn towards Mount Zion by a fascination with Israel's witness to a holy life lived under God. In Isaiah 6 and 66 there is the notion of being sent out by God to do God's work and to gather the nations 'that have not heard of my fame or seen my glory' (Isaiah 66.19). But Isaiah 66 also envisages a return to the holy mountain when the task is done. If we are to imagine our own mission in an eschatological context we can see that our task does not end with going out into the world. We must also return with all that we have seen and done and offer it back to the heart of God's faithful people:

> For as the new heavens and the new earth, which I will make,
> shall remain before me, says the Lord; so shall your descendants and
>   your name remain.
> From new moon to new moon, and from sabbath to sabbath,
> all flesh shall come to worship before me,
> says the Lord. (Isaiah 66. 22-23)

what must we do?

If our missiological understanding, shaped by the study of Scripture, refines our awareness that God desires all human persons in all the nations of the world, then we must finally consider what our proper role is in relation to God's longing. What models are available to us and what perspectives can we usefully employ if we are not to fall into the trap of seeing election and blessing as superiority and divine affirmation of our particular religious ideology?

In looking at models of mission we can see events, persons and institutions that are linked to theological themes drawn from the Hebrew Scriptures. For example, the Exodus is the prime model of redemption and a metaphorical source of understanding the cross. There are further themes of redemption and deliverance that directly relate to God's land. Jubilee gives us a restorative picture: suffering, loss, slavery, depression require restoration. Individuals are called to work to the holy purpose: Moses, Samuel, Isaiah, the prophets are charged with being part of God's unstoppable work of divine reconciliation. Yet aliens and outsiders, like Rahab and Ruth, find themselves within the sphere of God's blessing.

Walter Brueggemann argues that study of the Hebrew Scriptures gives us the tools both to tell the past and dream the future. For example, he shows how Joel 2 'anticipates a terrible devastation (v v. 1-17), but then a glorious rehabilitation which is the generous, powerful, jealous work of God (v v. 18-32)'. God's Spirit will gather up all parts of the community, but at the same time this is possible because there has been long preparation in fasting, praying, being unafraid and confessing. Brueggemann suggests to us that the job of the faithful community is to trust God into the future and to conjure the future that God intends: 'A community not visited by the spirit will be unable to host the future and will be consigned to an endless present tense' (Brueggemann, 1993, pp. 122–3). He further points out that Joel 2 is the poem that is placed at the beginning of the story of the Church in Acts 2.17-21, for the Church is the community that is intruded upon by the Spirit of God, and is led out beyond the present to God's future. In answering the question 'what must we do?', we might well remark Brueggemann's conclusion that: 'This portrayal of the church as futuring God's new life is uncommonly important in a society that is increasingly in love with death, fascinated by it, and courting it at every turn' (Brueggemann, 1993, p. 124). The task we're given, in developing a heart for mission, is to develop a hope for the future that can energize others, and to make available always the promise of change and of new life.

some questions for discussion

- How does the study of the Hebrew Scriptures help us to know what God is like?
- Is there any justification for calling God 'a mad, bloodthirsty and capricious despot'?[19]
- What can it mean to be a chosen people in a multicultural society?
- What does it mean to be ethically holy in the present day?
- Does the study of the Hebrew Scriptures help us think more deeply about current international politics? Can theological perspectives inflame the issues?
- Do we love our Bible enough to dance with it?

2 the New Testament

Pushing their own expensive theological education to one side, too
many ministers foster an unthinking and naïve approach to Scripture.[1]

I suggest, with Martin Hengel, that the history and the theology of
early Christianity are, first of all, 'mission history' and 'mission theology'
(Hengel 1983b:53). Hengel applies this description in the first place to
the apostle Paul, but he certainly implies that the same is true of other
New Testament writers as well. Other New Testament scholars, such as
Heinrich Kasting and Ben Meyer, affirm this. Kasting states: 'Mission
was, in the early stages, more than a mere function; it was a
fundamental expression of the life of the church. The beginnings of
a missionary theology are therefore also the beginnings of Christian
theology as such' (1969:127 – my translation). Ben Meyer interprets:
'Christianity had never been more itself, more consistent with Jesus and
more evidently en route to its own future, than in the launching of the
world mission' (1986:206, cf. 18). In its mission, early Christianity took
an astonishing 'leap of life' from one world to another (Dix 1955:55),
since it understood itself as the vanguard of a saved humankind (Meyer
1986:92).

Contemporary New Testament scholars are thus affirming what the
systematic theologian Martin Kähler said eight decades ago: Mission is
'the mother of theology' (Kähler [1908] 1971:190; my translation).[2]

the mother of theology

This is how the missiologist David Bosch sets out his perspective on
mission in the New Testament at the beginning of *Transforming Mission*.
There are certain important features of his argument that have formed
the basis of our conversations about mission in relation to Scripture.
First, we cannot help but enter a bewildering array of other conversations
between New Testament theologians. In the passage we quote, we
already see David Bosch at work translating and rereading the perspectives
of others. More importantly, we see these conversations underlining a
particular set of assumptions about the New Testament – that there is
a dividing line between the Jewish religious world and that of the early
Church: 'an astonishing "leap of life" from one world to the other'. The
leap of life brings coherence, consistency and purpose: early Christians
knew what they were about and put it into practice. The evidence is there:

the gospel did spread. Bosch says (and his argument is predicated on this) that:

> *the New Testament witnesses to a fundamental shift when compared with the Old Testament. In surveying paradigm shifts in missionary thinking I wish to suggest that the first and cardinal paradigm change took place with the advent of Jesus of Nazareth and what followed after that.* (Bosch, 1991, p. 15)

For us, however, trying to look at mission through the whole of Scripture, this division between what we can say about God from study of the Hebrew Scriptures and what we can learn about the early Church is problematic. What do we do with the knowledge of the missionary God that emerges from the Hebrew Scriptures? Can we just assume that the Jews themselves were not interested in promulgating their own faith? Why, as a religious group, did they not see who Jesus was? Who did *they* think he was, and did it actually make good sense for them to see him in this way? Must we accept uncritically the idea that Christian mission 'started' through the faith of the early Church? We were helped by James Carleton Paget, who has reviewed the extensive literature that seems to suggest that: 'Christianity, with its aggressively proselytic tendency, introduced into the ancient world a concept that had simply not existed before',[3] and who argues that, if we are swayed by this, we are in danger of overlooking important evidence about the religious milieu of the first century. He suggests that the matter is much more complex than we may assume from our own perspective.

Apart from anything else, if we challenge and blur the distinction between the self-understanding of the people of God in the Hebrew Scriptures and that of the New Testament, we risk undermining one of the central texts of our mission theology and losing what is for us a very important idea: mission theology is in some ways a foundational theology, from which many other kinds of theological exploration flow.

our conversation partners

In order to work out how our conversation could embrace all of Scripture, we held another consultation at which New Testament scholars and teachers from colleges, courses and schemes were present. One of these was the 'link' between this and the consultation on the Hebrew Scriptures.[4] From the material emerging from this source, we were able to survey the problem. As we had seen in our work on Church history, different readings of history, each carrying its own agenda, can make a difference to the way in which we understand both the mission history and the mission purpose of the Church. In seeking to look at the teaching of New Testament studies through a missiological lens, we came up against similar questions, which are crucial for the outworking of mission. These questions concern: the 'historical' Jesus, the faith of the apostles, and the social and cultural milieu of first-century Judaism.

One of the problems, however, might be that a mission perspective in the study of the New Testament might mean just looking for evidence of things we can call 'missionary'. We would just read into our texts what we want to find. If we find such evidence in one place but not in another place, then we might well assume that the 'paradigm shift' identified by David Bosch is really there. Another way of using mission perspective, however, would be to use what we already know of mission as a hermeneutic for reading New Testament Scripture.[5] This is what we decided to do in exploring the New Testament, following Richard Bauckham's suggestion that we read the New Testament as a literature that describes:

- a movement into the ever-new future;
- a movement towards ever-new horizons;
- a movement of an ever-new people.

However, these movements take place in particular kinds of context, which we must understand. For example, there are the social and cultural settings – what did first-century Judaism look like and how did it contextualize the historical Jesus? How do we make sense of the eschatological expectation, the Great Commission and the faith of the apostles, in taking the Good News to the Gentiles?

We realize, of course, that in most theological colleges, seminaries, courses and schemes, there is simply not enough time available for in-depth study of all these issues which are of interest and concern to New Testament scholarship. What we decided to do is try to show how the mission perspective in these issues knits the questions together and generates new ideas for reflection on who we are in the light of the New Testament today, so that, however much is covered, this learning helps us to see what difference we can make in the world. Bonhoeffer's question remains: 'Who is Jesus Christ for us today?'

the 'historical' Jesus

Study of the historical Jesus – trying to discover and explain the man from Nazareth – is basic to the Christian Church's life. It is also not a matter that is purely internal to the Church, our 'property' so to speak. Joan Bakewell, the presenter who resigned over the rescheduling of *Heart of the Matter*, wrote critically:

> *Son of God ... cost a record £1.5m, scooped pages of publicity with the promise that it would unveil the face of Christ, and earned unqualified praise for its dazzling graphics. But the praise quickly faltered. What mattered about* Son of God *was that it was made by Christians and thus employed rather implausible logic in its efforts to prove their case – that Jesus really lived and the Gospel accounts are accurate. Unhappily, Jeremy Bowen ... lost journalistic credibility with his assertions that 'we can be sure ...' and 'we know for a fact ...' He must know that history and truth are elusive. It takes strong religious conviction to be so certain.*[6]

The promise to 'unveil the face of Christ' resonates with many people's desires, including our own, and is a missiological paradox. When we talk about mission as enabling people to encounter Jesus, does the notion of a historical Jesus, as a first-century Jew, complicate the way people of all nations and languages may claim him for their own? Can we too lose our credibility where people feel that truth is so elusive and are we missing mission opportunities, if we too appear 'so certain'? We decided that one way we could try to open up these questions could be to use mission as a hermeneutic for studying the historical Jesus. We chose to look at the themes explored in N. T. Wright's books *The New Testament and the People of God* and, more particularly, *Jesus and the Victory of God*.[7] These themes would be directly drawn from our understanding of mission and we would relate them to the work we had already done on the Hebrew Scriptures.

more questions

We were aware that, in the world of New Testament scholarship, Tom Wright's books have drawn considerable attention.[8] *Jesus and the Victory of God* is all centred on the historical Jesus, drawing on the work of others, but it also offers careful criticism. Yet the question for teachers and students is 'what happens then?' What can we do with knowing just a little more about the historical Jesus, how will we reflect further on how we live the Christian life, what difference does it make to how we shape the Church and serve as the people of Jesus Christ, and how can we take up his mission in the world? For his mission is our job. We are a people sent, in the name of Jesus, in and into the world he loved. How do we approach that task? How do we set priorities? How do we live as a missionary

people? What does Jesus of Nazareth, in his own mission in the name
of Israel's God, have to teach us about our mission in his name? What
are the missiological implications of a title such as 'Jesus and the Victory
of God'?

no Incarnation or Resurrection

N. T. Wright's book deals exclusively with the adult ministry of Jesus, the
period from baptism to crucifixion. This is a sharp reminder to us that the
theologies of the Incarnation and of the Resurrection, while they may
shape our faith, also weave layers around the historical Jesus. In this part
of our exploration we have to do without the Good News announced at
the Incarnation, without the Resurrection appearances and the Pentecost
experience. If this makes us feel deprived, it should be a sharp challenge
to our assumptions, including our missiological assumptions. Our
understanding of Incarnation and of Resurrection has powerful
missiological implications. When we say the creeds in our churches, we
profess and proclaim our faith precisely because God's Son was born of
a virgin, was crucified and rose again from the dead on the third day. Our
profession of these extraordinary events has great force, with the capacity
not only to capture the hearts and minds of others, but also to re-
evangelize ourselves. Saying the creeds also commits us to a certain kind
of moral outlook: belief in a God who has done these things, and in an
eschatological reality, obligates us to work for the kingdom in an explicit
way.[9] We have to ask, if we are committed to mission, how far do we *rely*
on the theologies of Incarnation and Resurrection? Wright challenges us
by pointing away from these theologies and requesting us to concentrate
on a proper doctrine of God.

history and the doctrine of God

Wright argues that a proper doctrine of God requires us to take history
seriously. Our understanding of this doctrine means that we must believe
that God can and does intersect with human history. Yet, if a particular time
and space was indeed inhabited by the very presence of God, then it
matters very much that we try to find out what was going on in that life,
in those times and in that place. The process of finding out drives certain
questions: what did Jesus do, what impact did he make, what happened
to him, and why? Jesus lived at a unique moment in history; we can
now see it as a critical moment of opportunity and judgement, and an
eschatological turning point, because he was there. Jesus brought the
presence of the kingdom into that place and time, yet that same space

and time has its own characteristics, culture and processes and these also had their reciprocal influence on Jesus' life and work.

Jesus the Jew

The historical approach, therefore, also reminds us to take seriously the Judaism of Jesus. Jesus was a man of his time, and also of his people. For example, Alan Le Grys argues that Jesus encounters and engages with Gentiles not *because* they are Gentiles but *in spite of* their being Gentiles (Le Grys, 1998, p. 54), as a by-product of the inter-cultural milieu which he encountered in the cities and towns. As we have seen clearly in our study of the Hebrew Scriptures, Israel's own self-understanding, as having a critical role in God's purposes for the world, provides a framework of perception and expectation, without which much of Jesus' ministry could not be understood. Within this framework, we can explore particular themes and ideas that help us bring a mission perspective into study of the New Testament *through* the historical Jesus.

exile

For example, the idea of exile dominates *Jesus and the Victory of God*. In Jesus' world the theme of exile was used not simply as a metaphor, but as a description of the historical context within which the people of Israel were now living. Jesus' ministry then involved speaking into that prevailing spiritual consciousness. He came to call Israel home. A good deal of theological reflection on the exile suggested that it had been Israel's own fault (Wright, 1992, pp. 272–4). The deportation was a judgement for Israel's unfaithfulness. National restoration, therefore, would fulfil the promise that the past had been forgiven. Hope of redemption would then be coupled with forgiveness as a homecoming, in which God would again commission Israel fully for a holy purpose, and the missiological strands which we identified earlier in the Hebrew Scriptures would become stronger. Israel's redemption was meant to be a blessing to the nations, who would be drawn to Israel's God[10] Yet, in Jesus' historical context, Israel was confined by Gentile power and turned inwards.

See Chapter 9.1, 'the Hebrew Scriptures'.

exile and homecoming as relevant to us

It is puzzling, then, that we do not see the theme of exile pursued or transmuted later in the self-understanding of the early Church. This is perhaps because the Jesus of faith satisfies the longing of the exiled ones.

Through submission to Christ, we find a complete sense of homecoming, and all our restlessness and sense of the temporary and contingent become grounded in an eschatology in which peace and fulfilment lie waiting for us. We wait for 'adoption' by God until we come into God's presence (Romans 8.23).

See Chapter 10, 'mission and worship'.

These twin themes of exile and homecoming, in which the figure of Jesus is significant, are still relevant to us and we can use our understanding of mission to unlock their meanings. The theme of exile, and the psychological and social reactions to it, can still make sense to Christians seeking to live out mission and ministry in today's western society. Part of being equipped for mission is that we *recognize* those who are lost and far from home. Our task is to accompany them on the way back and to receive them when, of their own will, they come into the presence of the Father. Too often, though, we can end up in the position of the obedient son in the parable of the prodigal, harping on about our own merits and really believing that the condition of separation and exile is no more than people deserve. But thinking about the contexts in which Jesus lived out his ministry helps us to recontextualize our own. Jesus calls to the house of Israel, his own people, to come home to God and so opens up a view of exile as a biblical description of the human condition. Our relational sense of being makes us long for a homecoming with an Other, so that Israel's exile can represent our own dislocation. Israel, geographically and historically, focuses and makes concrete something that is permanently true of us all. Moreover, a real return, from exile to God, brings the desire to call others and to share the sense of homecoming. To be effectively brought in by the Good News is also to be mobilized, stimulated to witness. If we use mission as a hermeneutic for these themes, we can see that this is precisely where these 'movements' in a new future, new horizons, by a new people, are generated.

inward- and outward-looking

Wright lays much emphasis on the idea that Israel's life at the time of Jesus was characterized by both introspection and defensiveness, which obscured a sense of true vocation and promise. The Temple, and the elaborate operation of the Law, served to promulgate a separate holiness bent on self-preservation in an inward-looking sense. The call to Israel to be an ethically holy people had become an introspective self-regulation and the missionary possibilities of this holy life were thereby limited. It therefore followed that the psychological context of exile, and departure from God-given destiny, must be followed by repentance. Israel must find another way of being God's people, and beyond that to live as God's people. The historical Jesus shows us that this was an urgent matter. If Israel did not do this, disaster would follow. Jesus was a person who saw most clearly that inward-looking behaviour and exhorted those around him, and indeed the whole nation, to look outwards and embrace the God-given destiny once again. This transition from inward preoccupation to outward-looking purpose is a key theme in missiological understanding in our own time and context, yet we often forget to reflect on the passion and urgency with which Jesus spoke. His sense of living in a present derived directly from God's future, meant that the slow processes of social and cultural change in response to the word of God are not enough. Hearts had to be changed too in radical and immediate ways. Asking for time to think about it would not make sense in the face of the imminent eschatological expectation with which Jesus faced people. It is a challenge to us, then, to think about what we mean when we talk about mission as bringing about transformation. Do we aim towards the gradual transformation of society to reflect a more just expression of kingdom values? Or do we want to offer people the vision of the healing miracles: that life can be changed now, and irrevocably, by encounter with the living God? The historical Jesus therefore challenges us to think again about our Christian presence in our society as leaven, salt and light and as the bearers of the prophetic word, announcing that God is not far off, but is even now here among us. Once again, our mission understanding shows how this theme sets up the need for movement out of stasis. Repentance means actively going towards God's future, embracing the end-time. The renewal it brings equips everyone to be a new people, worthy of that future.

Jesus as prophet

We can understand Jesus' challenges more clearly if we follow how Wright characterizes the ministry of the historical Jesus as prophetic. This way of looking at Jesus asks us to consider how we then view the *missio Christi*. Jesus was challenging Israel and calling the whole nation to a new way of being God's holy people. His prophetic behaviour involved constructing in himself and his followers a new community, a core group of believers who would represent a renewed Israel, remade from within. In the Sermon on the Mount, Jesus gives a picture of a new kind of community, not as something new to Israel but a re-visioning of Israel's proper life. So Jesus' 'mission' also included a critique of how things were at the time, and an address to current crises and failures. In studying the Gospel accounts of how he behaved in this respect, we can arrive at a paradigm for our modern agenda for justice and peace. To follow Jesus with a heart for mission, we need to study the contexts for our ministry and break open the human vision of affairs to alert people to God's desire. This is no easy matter: just as Jesus was attacked by people with vested interests in the status quo, so our own missionary and prophetic words can lead us to be attacked by the media, by community leaders with a 'stake' in leaving things as they are and even by those we would wish to serve.[11] Once again, using mission as a hermeneutic for Jesus' prophetic agenda helps us see how the people of God are impelled towards God's future, because here justice and peace are to be found.

critique of society

For example, Jesus criticized lovers of wealth and power (Luke 16.15; 13.32) and spoke words of judgement upon those who misused the Temple (Mark 11.17), and he described the end to which their abuse would eventually lead (Mark 13.2). Questions of 'neighbour' and 'enemy' were to be resolved. A particular attention to God's mandate for ethical behaviour and living could allow believers to be agents of transformation. To say we would follow Jesus in this way is problematic. To live out our missionary vocation standing over against aspects of culture is not easy and can be made impossible, particularly in countries where Christians are in the minority. In our own times we have seen how theologians around the world have been silenced by saying awkward things about social transformation and how sometimes the Church itself colludes with others to prevent empowerment of those who would expose our own investment in power.

If we apply this missiologically we can see how liberation theologians speak of the public and prophetic profile of Jesus. Jesus suffers and dies because he opposes corruption in public life. He willingly undergoes the revenge of those who hold the power and dies a shameful death as a criminal and enemy of the state. As he lived a prophetic life, so he died a prophetic death, a public witness against earthly power. At the same time we may recognize in Jesus' dying a paradigm of Christian obedience, and realize that the righteousness we are called to model may be controversially and painfully counter-cultural. This mission perspective on Jesus, mediated through study of the historical Jesus, may also challenge us as to how it is possible to act in our own communities, both within and without the Church, against structures of sin and misuses of power.

Moreover, attention to ethics and to modes of behaviour itself forms a new context: in the presence of Jesus the reign of God has come to Israel. Response is key, a turning back to a homecoming in God ushers in hope and promise and fulfilment. Refusal to hear will bring a time of judgement.

While engaged in mission, we often meet hardness of heart in the children of the Enlightenment, people who find their spiritual explorations baulked by our certainty. We need, not to become more aggressive in our ministry, but to see ourselves as others see us. Where do people come up against our own refusal to be open and outward-looking? If we use mission as a hermeneutic for Scripture, does that not remind us to ask whether we are seen by others as a renewed people moving towards the future others want us to describe for them?

See Chapter 1, 'the world we live in'.

moral community

Jesus called his twelve disciples as the core of a renewed Israel, which enables us to form missionary ideas about the notion of moral community. Jesus offered a model of renewal not just in theory, but in practice, a working model of what Israel's life could look like if the preoccupation with self could be turned around to focus on God once more.[12] In witness to this, he made contact with people of all kinds. His group seems to have had fairly open edges, so that others were able to find their way into his company. Further, mealtimes provided occasions for meeting new people, overcoming barriers, changing lives. We might therefore argue that we are called in our own congregations to show our local communities what it means to be truly human, to offer a model of what common life can be. Like Jesus and his core community, we have to discover what it means to be a missionary congregation in having open boundaries, and with spirituality at the heart.[13] Christian basics courses such as the *Alpha* course have rediscovered the fact that sharing of food may foster sharing of faith.

We can explore further by using Wright's three themes, which show how Jesus presented himself and which help us to use our understanding of mission to make sense of Jesus as the one who can become the centre of a universal mission. These are: vindication, kingship and suffering.

vindication

In *The New Testament and the People of God*, Wright discussed the use of apocalyptic, especially Daniel 7, in relation to the Gospels (Wright, 1992, pp. 291–7). He regards apocalyptic as a great metaphor for referring to God's work in the world, a work beyond mere description. So, when Jesus appropriates this text, he is speaking of Israel's vindication. This concept nullifies the psychological condition of exile. Israel's true destiny as children of Abraham will again be possible. Further, it is Jesus himself who is the messianic 'Man', who embodies in himself and his destiny the vindication of the nation as a whole people.[14] He takes on a representative function, submitting himself to God's restorative grace and favour. In the vindication he receives from God, Israel as nation comes home, exile is ended, and a new era begins. For us, this has direct analogy with the process of conversion and with the outworking of mission purpose. God *intends* that God's own people should come home. If we apply mission as a hermeneutic to this theme we can see that vindication becomes a *mechanism* releasing the people of God for the movement that is necessary to make God's purposes known and to describe God's kingdom.

kingship

The next theme also relates directly to understandings of kingdom. The Gospels contain much 'Son of David' language in respect to Jesus, which goes alongside his own frequent use of kingdom terminology. God's reign is expressed through God's regent. In Jesus, Israel's Davidic hope is realized. Wright finds a rich set of Davidic allusions by which means we find Jesus setting himself in the role of messianic king. The Gospels affirm, for those with ears to hear it, that the Davidic promises are devolving on Jesus, that he is taking up royal authority within Israel, and that under his leadership the true destiny of the nation will be realized. Again, we do not need to become bogged down in the arguments about 'Son of David' and 'Son of Man' language. To quote Bauckham again: 'The rule of the true God, which liberates from the human will to power, is qualitatively different from the domination of the idols, which express the human will to power.'[15] This theme then, read missiologically, says that the use of this language reminds us that we have a choice. We can follow God, which involves our movement towards fulfilment of the divine purpose, or we can follow human constructs that confine and limit us. The pursuit of idols, in whatever form they appear, limits our horizons and restricts vision to whatever we can gain selfishly this side of eternity.

suffering

Finally, Wright shows how much of the scriptural heritage in the Gospels involves the theme of suffering, in which an individual suffers pain for the good of many. Such passages are not, Wright suggests, necessarily directly applied to Jesus, but set up a framework of expectation and understanding within which his work then falls. From Jesus' own point of view, Wright stresses the role of Jesus as a prophet, both feeling the pain and distress of his community, and maintaining his stance outside the community sufficiently in order to utter judgement. We too are called to identify with the hurt in our society, but also where necessary to stand over against it. A prophet must share the life of the community in order to hear, and must know the life of God in order to speak; this is also at the heart of a missionary community.

The importance of Wright's conclusions for those with a heart for mission is that he shows us a Jesus who looked to Israel's vindication, who looked for a return from political, social and spiritual exile and who used the vision of Daniel to portray himself as the restorer of the promise. He also adopted Scriptures that spoke of suffering, one for many, in order to liberate the people for a redemptive role within the world. This means that, for Wright, Jesus has a powerful representative role, yet his work is also that of a mediator. Finally, he bears the tension between Israel's particular spiritual direction and his own perception of God's intention and this is discharged in dying in the name of Israel's stubbornness and sin, representing the nation under the judgement of its resistance to his own word. He moves beyond the office of prophet. He passes beyond prophetic lament and identification with the pain of the nation, to take on and share in that very suffering. By this means the prophetic ministry passes beyond the promise of redemption and hope and becomes actual redemption and hope.

the homecoming of the Gentiles

Our exploration of the historical Jesus through mission as hermeneutic clarifies for us missionary strands refocused through one who was himself steeped in the study of the Hebrew Scriptures. But for a missionary perspective it is also important to realize that the redemption envisaged for Israel through the themes of vindication, kingship and suffering will also signal the homecoming of the Gentiles. When Israel returns to the vision of God's purposes, the Abrahamic vision is reactivated, so that what Jesus offers the nation, he offers the world. The rebellion of Israel opens out to encompass the whole world's disobedience and wilfulness. Similarly, the redemption he offers Israel has a broader set of implications. The role of Suffering Servant calls all nations to God's reconciliation.

how did the gospel spread?

While it was helpful to focus our missiological thinking through themes associated with the actual physical presence of the living Jesus within his community, we found ourselves left with the questions of continuity we raised at the beginning of this material. Exactly how did a mission to the Gentiles emerge? Is it true that missiology only emerges from a post-

Pauline Church? We have seen that what Jesus offers the nation of Israel, he offers the world, but can this be enough to explain how the gospel spread, not only to the Roman and Greek world, but to Persia, Armenia, Ethiopia and India? What was it that enabled Christianity to become embedded in such diverse communities? Must we impose or imagine, as Bosch does, a paradigm shift in thinking and practice that formed Christian faith and expression in this way?

Jewish proselytism

One way of dealing with this is to consider whether it is a misleading assumption that the first-century Judaism in which Jesus lived was smooth and uniformly inward-looking. In our study of the major themes of the Hebrew Scriptures, it is then easier to conclude that Israel had run into stagnation and lost its will to be a light to the nations. But do we only think this because the Gospel writers presented Jesus as so radical in the context of Israel's loss of direction and purpose? Are we so amazed by Jesus' words and actions in his ministry towards Israel, admonishing his people and weeping for them, that we assume that Jews were not interested in living out their faith towards others? And what about the cultural milieu which Jews and Gentiles inhabited? There was bound to be interaction on the fringes of the Jewish religion.

James Carleton Paget suggests that we would be mistaken just to assume that this must be so (Carleton Paget, 1996, pp. 65–103). Comparing a large number of commentators, he reviews the work of Scott McKnight and uses Martin Goodman's categories of mission,[16] which may prove helpful to our own self-reflection:

> Goodman distinguishes a 'proselytic' mission from three other types of mission: an informative mission marked by a general desire to inform people about a general message without necessarily having any clear idea about the reaction they desired from their auditors; an educational mission, which seeks to change the moral disposition of the audience while not requiring that the moral behaviour of the auditors be understood as part of the belief system espoused by the missionary; and an apologetic mission, which sought to impress upon its audience the power of a particular deity without wishing the audience to devote itself to the worship of that deity. (Carleton Paget, 1996, p. 67)

We can see that our own 'marks' of mission can devolve into these categories if we do not take seriously what prophetic witness also involves. Such forms of informative, educational and apologetic mission might very properly constitute how we engage in interfaith dialogue,[17] but it might also highlight where our mission stops short of offering the Good News to others. For example, informative mission might include sharing a testimony in such a way that the listener feels this is a unique work of God available only to the one who gives testimony. Educational mission might take place in a marriage preparation course that sets out the moral expectations of Christian marriage without saying how it relates to personal Christian faith. Apologetic mission might be part of a church report on some environmental or social issue.

But Carleton Paget has an interesting observation that caught our attention:

> ... on the basis of their [McKnight's and Goodman's]) strong definition, it is only with difficulty that one can hold Christianity to be a missionary religion, especially when we consider texts outside the New Testament. Secondly, proselytic religions need not operate in an openly proselytic manner, at least as these are defined by the authors we have considered. That is, such religions need not send out missionaries, speak out violently against the prevailing cultures, or give self-conscious expression to a desire to change and convert all others (the universal dimension) outside their religion. What I am implying is that it is quite possible for a proselytic missionary consciousness to express itself in ways different from those described by McKnight and Goodman.
> (Carleton Paget, 1996, p. 67)

This suggestion leaves us with some very interesting questions. Perhaps we do not need Bosch's paradigm shift, but we can see a softening of the distinction between the Jewish world and the first-century Church. Carleton Paget himself points us to the inbuilt kerygmatic nature of the Wisdom literature, for example, and suggests that in the particular cultural climate in which Jesus lived the Jews wanted the Gentiles to understand their practices so that they could learn to appreciate, respect and tolerate them. This means that the thematic links to a mission theological understanding arising from the living out of the Hebrew Scriptures can be taken forward into New Testament literature, not read back into it. Further, it requires us to ask how a less 'strong' form of witness (in which, for example, the synagogue could be the agent of mission) could form the social background out of which hardened the Christian mission to the Gentiles of many different cultures. If we are going to continue to use our understanding of mission as a hermeneutical key, then how does the witness of God's chosen people in this more centripetal form[18] have any connection to the movement of the Christian gospel? How far did the Gentiles expect to hear news of the Messiah? What, indeed, did the Gentiles expect to hear at all in the religious marketplace of the Roman and Greek world at that time? [19]

the Great Commission

Alan Le Grys poses the problem in respect of the Great Commission:

> The post-Easter narratives ... belong to a unique category of literature. This in itself makes it difficult enough to evaluate them, but the problem is compounded by the conflicting evidence provided by the gospels. On closer inspection, it turns out that although the evangelists agree Jesus said something to his disciples about mission after his resurrection, that is about the limit of their agreement. They do not agree about what he said, when he said it, where he said it, or even to whom he said it. Further, after he has given the command, the evidence in Acts suggests the disciples completely ignored it. There is a prima facie argument to answer, therefore: where does the Great Commission come from – Jesus or the later church? (Le Grys, 1998, p. 41)

This is very interesting, because Le Grys points out (as here) that the resurrected Jesus raises all kinds of questions about how people might respond to such a unique kind of encounter. How, in fact, do we account for the faith of the apostles? What do we make of the Pentecost experience? At what point should we start to distinguish between the Jewish prophet and the Saviour of the world, if at all? If we return to Bauckham's analysis, we can see that he points to the importance of *ourselves* as readers of the post-resurrection commands. Le Grys is right to say we should be disturbed by words that come to us from a living Jesus beyond the grave, but, using mission as a hermeneutical key, we see that we need these words (in any or all of their forms) to place *anyone who believes* on the road to the universal goal. Believers are located within God's missionary purpose and the movement to the ever-new future, ever-new horizons, as an ever-new people is confirmed. We can then argue that Paul writes directly out of this perspective and his genius is to clarify what this commitment means: we are a people inexorably on the way to God. God is coming inexorably towards us. Only distraction can slow us down or turn us aside. We need to fix our eyes on this ultimate purpose.

the gospel *must* cross cultural boundaries

Our hermeneutical key tells us that Scripture offers us a vision of movement towards an eschatological reality. This means that the overflowing love of God crosses all boundaries, breaks down all barriers. Consequently, the

Good News of Jesus Christ, news of a definitive crossing from death to life, *must* cross cultural boundaries. Each such crossing carries its own momentum and creates its own form of theological and hermeneutic discussion, as we see in Acts 15. This is a text about mission and about what happens when the gospel crosses a cultural boundary. The debate that goes on here is important: not only does it have at its heart the passage from Amos 9, but it also has to determine what kind of dialogue will allow progression and what will not. The Gentiles are resident aliens, grafted on by Christian conversion. Circumcision will not solve this; rather there must be standards that have universal applicability. This is crucial for us to understand in any cross-cultural encounter, where we have to decide what are cultural impositions and what are unacceptable practices. In making such decisions, we are helped by the missiological thrust of Acts 15. We have to determine what relationship we can establish that, in the end, enables the whole people of God to move forward together. By these means, the notion of vindication is extended out through the apostles to the Gentile world.

Using mission as a hermeneutical tool therefore allows us to integrate more closely the study of both the Hebrew Scriptures and the New Testament. More than this, it enables us to use our reading of Scripture to inform the outworking of mission in our daily lives. For we are God's people similarly involved on a journey towards God. We seek to live according to his purposes. We, too, are given motivation and commission by one who is dead and risen. And, as we shall now see, we are called to earth that journey in the experience of a missionary worship.

Some questions:

- What was first-century Judaism like? How did Jesus fit into it and how was Jesus different from it?
- What were the aims of Jesus? What was he trying to do, and how? What large intentions motivated him to act in the way that he did?
- What were the reasons for his death – not just the theology, but the human influences and events, the sort of thing you might hear in a judicial enquiry?
- How and why did the early Church get started in the way it did?
- How and why did the earliest written accounts of the story of Jesus, the Gospels, take the form and content that they have?
- What might the Gentiles have expected to hear Jesus say or see him do?

chapter 10
mission and worship

O Almighty God, who alone canst order the unruly wills and affections of sinful men; Grant unto thy people, that they may love the thing which thou commandest, and desire that which thou dost promise; that so, among the sundry and manifold changes of the world, our hearts may surely there be fixed, where true joys are to be found; through Jesus Christ our Lord. Amen. (The Book of Common Prayer, *Collect for the Fourth Sunday after Easter*)

Our next exploration led us into a subject that has been at the heart of our own work as a group. Without worship together, our theological conversation could not have been earthed in a consciousness that the work we do is not just for the Churches, but for God. Also, our worship extends from our life as a group and in our Churches to our life 'among the sundry and manifold changes of the world'. Similarly, in our own theological education, worship has been more than learning about liturgy. For us, participation in the worshipping life of the community enters into and informs the teaching and learning experience.

What, then, does it mean to look at the worshipping life of Christian people through a mission lens? How does this affect teaching and learning about worship? This was the beginning of our conversation and led us to start with a comment from J. G. Davies. In his book entitled *Worship and Mission*, he comments on a passage from New Testament scholar F. V. Filson:

'Once we have recognized that in the New Testament Jesus Christ is the risen Lord, we are ready to recognize that the life of his people will stand constantly under his Lordship. This is true of the entire Christian life. We do not find life split into one area, of worship, where Christ is honoured, and another area in which man is more independent. If we are to present the New Testament position, we can make no essential distinction between worship and daily life' and, we may add, between worship and mission, since the latter takes place in daily life in the world.[1]

We see that the relationship between worship and mission is most clearly marked in the New Testament as it reflects on the life and work of Jesus Christ. In the letter to the Hebrews (3.1) Christ is described as 'apostle and high priest of our confession'. In St John's Gospel (6.51) the words, 'I am the living bread that came down from heaven. Whoever eats of this bread will live forever; and the bread that I will give for the life of the world is my flesh', indicate in cultic language the relationship between acknowledgement of Christ and the implications that this acknowledgement has for the world. The linking of mission and worship undergirds the thinking of St Paul, as can be seen in his letter to the Romans (15.15-16) where he refers to his mission to the Gentiles in terms of worship: 'because of the grace given me by God to be a minister of Christ Jesus to the Gentiles in the priestly service of the gospel of God, so that the offering of the Gentiles may be acceptable, sanctified by the Holy Spirit.'

divisions between mission and worship

Perhaps the best-known text in this area is from St Paul's first letter to the Corinthians (11.26) where missionary terminology is used of worship: 'For as often as you eat this bread and drink the cup, you proclaim the Lord's death until he comes.' Behind this selection of texts lies a variety of understandings of mission, but they emphasize the essential unity of worship and mission. Our study of Scripture, then, has given us a picture of a people whose worship of God underlies not only daily life but also every encounter with others. By this means, worship and mission become intertwined. However, there is a contemporary division between worship and mission, which has had a profound effect on the life and witness of the Church. At its most extreme, it brings a division between God and God's world: between Christians who regard their vocation as being in church getting the worship right and Christians who regard their vocation as being out in the world and getting the world right.

what our conversation covered

In our conversations about worship and mission,[2] we recognized that they are not often viewed together. Our exploration, which is reflected here, included looking at the development of the relationship between worship and mission and drawing out some consequences of the division between them. We also considered the consequences of worship that needs the limitations of its contemporary context to reach out to the transcendent, and looked at worship as a place of transformation in the meeting between God and humanity. In doing this together we formulated some questions that might help us move towards missionary worship. It is these questions (and there could be more) that attempt to focus some of the issues regarding the teaching of worship. While recognizing a need to teach the historical development of liturgy, do training institutions offer a course that truly integrates mission and worship?

In pondering how this integration might take place, we needed first to provide broad definitions of worship (recognizing the profound effect it has upon the spiritual development of the worshipper) and of mission. These definitions form the background to this chapter, and highlight the influence of the liturgical symbols used in worship.

worship: praise

We have argued that Christians respond to the overflowing love from the heart of God poured out into the creation. We have seen that response as a will to act in obedience to God, but that will to conform to God's purposes is accompanied by a desire to praise. The recognition of the reality of God's presence in the world, such as in the healing miracles or in conversion, is properly signalled by praise. For us, then, praise is at the heart of worship. Praise is a human response to God, recognizing God as God and revelling in that recognition. In their book *Praising and Knowing God*, Daniel Hardy and David Ford write:

See Chapter 2, 'the world as God sees it'.

> At the heart of ordinary Christian life is recognition of the love of God. All creation is a work of God's love. Jesus Christ is God's giving of himself in love to restore and fulfil all creation. The Holy Spirit is the pouring out of this love in endless transformation and fresh creativity. Praise of God recognizes all this and first of all enjoys and celebrates it. Praise is therefore an attempt to cope with the abundance of God's love.[3]

Praise is also a very radical activity, since in recognizing God as the ultimate source of love, meaning and creativity, the pull and force of this world are, by implication, placed in a subordinate position. The act of praise places obligations on us to view the world as God's world and to see God's presence in it. It commits us further to a moral obligation: is this the world as God wants it to be? Praise is not an end in itself, to make us feel good, but marks a spiritual orientation committing us to work for transformation so that others may have the chance to praise too. Archbishop Rowan Williams says of the Eucharist, for example:

> And what is most wonderful and terrifying in the Great Thanksgiving is that the prayer is prayed not just on behalf of a group of human beings but in the voice of God's eternal Son. The priest gives thanks to God the Father in the name of the community that is the concrete life on earth of the eternal Word, the Body of Christ. The everlasting Word has taken our flesh; standing in the middle of our human experience, bearing hellish pain and abandonment for our sakes, he gives praise and thanks to the Father, returning to the Father the glory he had with him before

the foundation of the world. Remember the three young men in the fiery furnace, praising God in the midst of the flames? And the fourth walking with them who looked like a son of God? That's the eucharistic prayer: the Son of God in the heart of the furnace stirring us and enabling us to praise. Our thanksgiving in the Eucharist is the living echo of his eternal reply to the Father.[4]

This way of seeing ourselves as living echoes of Christ commits us to being Christ's witnesses. In this perspective, our acts of praise and thanksgiving equip us to be missionary.

human need for worship

The psalmist's words 'As a deer longs for flowing streams, so my soul longs for you, O God. My soul thirsts for God, for the living God' beautifully express the human need for worship (Psalm 42.1-2). St Augustine goes further, as he says that human fulfilment can only happen when men and women and the communities they inhabit have a relationship with God in worship: 'Our hearts are restless until they find their rest in thee.'[5] Nevertheless, it would be misleading to think of worship simply as the need for human beings to be in relationship with God. The theology of the *missio Dei* tells us that God took the first step and worship is the human response to God's initiative. From the call of Abram onwards, the Hebrew Scriptures clearly indicate God's deep desire and longing to be in relationship with

See Chapter 2 'the world as God sees it'; Chapter 9.1, 'the Hebrew Scriptures'.

the people he has created. Often they turn away from God, but he does not leave them for long. As we have seen, the people of Israel struggle with what 'true' worship is as they relate their worshipping life to the rest of their life, a relationship which other religions around them did not have.[6]

transformation

Worship needs to be firmly rooted in its contemporary context and able to reflect on the historical 'saving events'[7] in order that the worshippers can pass beyond that context to meet the transcendent God. As with Jacob struggling with the angel (Genesis 32.24-32), worshippers return

See Chapter 6, 'styles of teaching and learning'.

to their own situation changed by the encounter with God. When this change happens to people inside the worshipping community, it can be transmitted outside the worshipping community. Here, then, is the significant relationship between worship and mission that is signalled by transformation. The local is a stepping stone to the transcendent, though the local with its reflection on the 'saving events' needs to be constantly reviewed and redefined in the light of the encounter with the transcendent. We need to know more about how the community gathers and what it brings with it. The question then becomes one of how we allow what we bring to worship to be transfigured by the encounter with God and how, as a transformed community, we can live out that new vision in the world.

For example:

A group of teenagers preparing for confirmation was invited to bring to a worship service a token of their life outside the church. Each could bring, if they wished, something they wanted the community to celebrate, or something they wanted to discard. After a long discussion among themselves, they told the worship leader they would bring something as a group.

At the appropriate point in the service, the group was invited to come forward. They did so, bringing with them one of their number's disabled sister in a wheelchair. The whole group then sang a worship song together. After this, the teenagers explained to the congregation that they wanted to celebrate the life and wholeness of all, but that disabled people, although loved by God, were usually left outside the church, which was not properly equipped to receive them. They said they wanted to discard the attitude that disabled people cannot contribute.

The result of the group's actions, bringing a person with disabilities into the heart of their celebration and worship, was that the congregation resolved to reach out to the housebound and disabled in the community and make changes to include them in congregational life.

how we perceive the world

St Thomas Aquinas writes that, in order to change the world, one needs to change the images through which the world is perceived.[8] Unless there is frequent reflection on the images used in worship, which are given or denied life by our contemporary context, then the historical basis of faith will become a means of holding worshippers in the past instead of liberating them for the future. In the story of the teenagers, a particular view of disabled people as non-contributing in society was challenged and changed.

See Chapter 8, 'mission and Church history'; Chapter 9.1, 'the Hebrew Scriptures'.

history of liturgy

However any attempt to define worship too precisely can be difficult because worship, as we have seen, is both partisan and political. Indeed, one storm centre in the maelstrom of the Reformation in England was the argument about the nature and purpose of worship. The Church of England struggled to maintain a pattern of worship that would order the spiritual life of the nation, following, by and large, the liturgical format inherited from the medieval Catholic Church. Through parish churches serving local communities, regular daily, weekly and yearly cycles brought the story of creation, redemption and discipleship into the lives of ordinary people. With a developing understanding that God works through and can transform the ordinary,[9] there was a recognition that a certain amount of regulation was also necessary. *The Book of Common Prayer* was developed, and priesthood and the leadership of congregations were governed by adherence to the articles of the faith and by licence. A similar pattern is found in many of the *volkskirchen* or national churches that arose in Europe out of the Reformation.

In our ecumenical group, we also had to consider that, at the same time, an entirely different type of worship arose among groups who refused to conform. The most radical of these in terms of worship were independent congregations, which gathered not for the regulation of spiritual life, but to hear the Word of God. Worship at these gatherings was essentially oral rather than written in form, and this made a very great difference in emphasis and expectation. Now, the expectation was that God would raise up leaders and preachers from the congregation, and this was the only licence they needed. The hope was not that order would be brought into people's lives, but rather that they would be disturbed, challenged by God's intervention.

Despite fierce persecution, followed by exclusion from civic life, these groups survived. We see them today as Baptist and Congregational Churches and Quaker meetings, and their essentially oral form of worship has extended into Pentecostal Churches, and many of the Black Majority Churches.

divine stories and human stories

These are two ways of bringing the divine story into contact with human stories. There is a third. Orthodox liturgy stresses continuity of tradition. While medieval liturgy, and those liturgies deriving from it, marks the passing of time by retelling the divine story through the seasons of the Christian year, Orthodox liturgy sets the worshipping congregation in the context of the eternal, unchanging worship of heaven. The two great liturgical resources, the Pentecostarion and Triodion, are seasonal, as were the Roman breviaries and liturgies. But the timeless language and constant invocation of heavenly powers subdues the human story to the divine. Of course, the pattern is far more complex than this, but these three strands may serve to indicate the diversity of expectation and underlying form in genuine and historic traditions of worship. We then needed to examine how these three divergent traditions emerging from the human response to praise and to glorify the living God translate into missionary worship.

order and spontaneity

Traces of these three can be found in the complexity of worship patterns of our own time and all the traditions have borrowed from each other. There are instances where worship that was previously strictly 'ordered' has become more spontaneous, and worship that was more spontaneous has become more ordered. In addition, liturgical practice has been influenced by churches overseas. Although Pentecostal worship is essentially an oral tradition, postmodern Rave worship, which would see itself as Spirit-filled and an offspring of the Pentecostal movement, can use multimedia presentations to create just the sense of mystery and divine presence that might be found in an Orthodox service. Often the congregation is standing, experiencing highly dramatic sights and sounds, which produce a heightened atmosphere and a vivid sense of God's majesty and power. On the other hand, Anglican prayer books from the 1970s to the present day have introduced periods of free prayer in the intercessions, and ecumenical worship often encourages participation of a kind that derives from oral traditions. In such free prayer and intercessions there is a particular opportunity to engage with the 'sundry and manifold changes of the world' and so to hold up the immediate context in which we live before the eternal and unchanging God.

effects on the individual and the community

Finally, it is important not to underestimate the power and influence that worship, and the symbols used in worship, exert upon the individual and the community.[10] Certainly in theological colleges, courses and schemes, worship can be part of a hidden curriculum, which, like the rudder of a ship, has a powerful but frequently unseen effect on students.[11] Worship permits individuals to stand in the presence of God, but it also promotes fellowship, community and a sense of common belief and purpose, which lies behind the self-understanding of a missionary Church. The experience of worship has the capacity to confirm in us the vocation to which we are called in a way that sustains and nourishes the outworking of that same call. Further, the experience of worship for those outside the Church coming into services, may provoke powerful feelings and emotions about their own relationship with God that the congregation should be aware of and ready to receive and nurture. Conversely, some forms of worship may be disturbing, off-putting or even frightening for people both inside and outside the Church who are unfamiliar with what is being offered and find its process alienating. We need to be aware that some forms of worship can be so familiar and cosy to a close-knit congregation that others can be shut out. Such worship nourishes the faithful who may have constructed its form particularly to their own ends, but it is not missionary. Control of the worship can exercise a particular form of power.[12] But then, what happens if we lose control? A heart for mission requires us to ask in what ways our worship can reach into the lives of *all* others and effect transformation. For example, this kind of question has prompted people to ask what 'fruit' have emerged from the 'Toronto Experience' in which there are different claims about whether the manifestations in churches were prompted by a 'time of refreshing' given by God in the power of the Holy Spirit or a worrying disruption of the proper worship of God.[13]

underlying meanings in worship

This means that we have to pay more careful attention to what lies behind the material we use. What are words, music, images actually conveying to people? Sometimes, familiarity with words or music can make us complacent and we cease to look for the radical energizing that worship can and should offer. We need to accept the reality that forms of worship, like the world to which they relate, are bound to promote a large number of different images, some of which are complementary, some contradictory – but are they all acceptable? For example, in today's western society some of our ritual elements of worship are commercially exploited as decorations or feel-good artefacts in people's homes. The explosion in the sale of candles (especially 'church' candles), brackets and stained glass mirrors and small decorative windows, allows people to create an artificial feel of being in church without actually being there. People also buy copies of religious icons and church music as a way of creating atmosphere.

While all these things are on sale in the shops, we have to ask further questions about the influence on worshippers of images and symbols we do use in the environment for worship. For example, what does a church filled with memorials of military exploits (such as knights' tombs and memorials and regimental flags) say about God to visitors? What does a church whose stained glass windows are filled with male saints say about women? What is an act of worship using exclusive language saying about the relationship between men and women? All too often, we accept the symbols and images in our churches without giving them proper scrutiny and without thinking what these say to people entering our churches with no Christian background. For those of us who faithfully attend church every week, we forget to wonder what our worship might look like to people encountering it for the very first time. Perhaps, then, theological education can be the place where we can create a new imagination for the power of the symbolic. But, to do this, we have to have a heart for mission: what values are we trying to promote? If we are going to conduct our worship through symbols, then we need powerful and appropriate symbolism.

For example, one of the ways in which to offer powerful symbols in worship is through the sacraments. The sacraments are both expository and performative and as such have tremendous opportunity to convey the mystery of the transcendent God and so touch people in their deepest being. It is important that the full potential of the sacraments is made apparent within the liturgy. In the occasional offices the missionary and pastoral opportunities of liturgy become very apparent: how far does the Church use these occasions?

hymns

The questions we asked ourselves about the mission opportunities provided by the sacraments also apply to what people hear when they sing hymns.

For example:

> *Jesus my Lord will love me for ever,*
> *from him no power of evil can sever,*
> *he gave his life to ransom my soul,*
> *now I belong to him.*

> Now I belong to Jesus,
> Jesus belongs to me,
> not for the years of time alone,
> but for eternity.

> *Once I was lost in sin's degradation,*
> *Jesus came down to bring me salvation,*
> *lifted me up from sorrow and shame,*
> *now I belong to him.*

> *Joy floods my soul, for Jesus has saved me,*
> *freed me from sin that long had enslaved me,*
> *his precious blood he gave to redeem,*
> *now I belong to him.*[14]

This kind of language promotes a high view of God, a low view of humanity and a strong sense of sin. This can make sense in congregations where the theological understanding of the saving power of Christ is highly developed, but what does it say to the casual visitor, seeker or enquirer? Some hymn books seem to contain a great deal of such language (such as *Mission Praise* and, to a large extent, the first editions of *Hymns Ancient and Modern*), so how can their use encourage the self-esteem of men and women, both inside and outside the worshipping community? Recognizing their power and influence, the nineteenth-century Congregational minister R. W. Dale wrote, 'Let me write the hymns of a church and I care not who writes the theology.'[15] This points up the power and influence of worship and its place as a missionary activity. We should not forget the power some forms of liturgical language have had in our history and tradition. Many people use quotations from the collects of *The Book of Common Prayer* without realizing where the phrases came from. But, equally, we rarely consider how defensive the collects are and how they, too, promote a view of ourselves as impossibly unworthy. Indeed, the collect with which we began, though outward-looking, sees us as uncontrollable, steeped in sin. These days we have learned also to emphasize the joy and freedom of renewed life in Christ.

mission

See Chapter 2, 'the world as God sees it'; Chapter 9.1, 'the Hebrew Scriptures'; Chapter 9.2, 'the New Testament'.

Just as the impulse to worship can be traced from God's initiative, so too can the impulse to mission. We have seen that mission is an activity of God (*missio Dei*) and at the same time an activity of God through Jesus Christ (*missio Christi*) where Christ is the encouraging Suffering Servant who is not defeated by death, rather than the all-powerful crusading king wanting to force people into his kingdom. Christians take part in God's activity, which aims to embody God's liberating presence in every situation. However, as every situation is different, so too the form in which this embodiment takes place will be different. Mission, then, varies according to context, and the appropriate form of mission can only be decided by people in that context. In other words, priority needs to be afforded to our situation. This is the reason why David Bosch is reluctant to give a hard and fast definition to his subject, but rather discusses mission in terms of 'mission as', and so there are sections entitled 'mission as … the Church With Others … *missio Dei* … Mediating Salvation … Evangelism' and so on.[16] Klippies Kritzinger, David Bosch's successor as Professor of Missiology at the University of South Africa, sees community as fundamental to the missionary task. He understands the mission of a religious community[17] as that dimension of its existence that is aimed at making a difference to the world, at influencing or changing society in accordance with its religious ideals.[18]

worshipping communities and transformation

We could see from our own experiences that worshipping communities move between two poles. On the one hand there is preservation, which involves holding on to a vision, and on the other hand movement and encounter, which involve sharing the vision and being willing for it to be challenged and changed in the process. Movement and encounter, then, are an essential expression of the life of every Christian community and are the only things that can prevent preservation from turning into stagnation. Both invariably involve transformation, because the 'vision', or however we would want to describe what is to be shared, has to be assimilated to be passed on. Every worshipping community that wants to survive must therefore engage in some form of mission.

Transformation is interpreted in a variety of ways: some communities argue that the transformation is one-way, namely that those entering into the community are transformed into the likeness of those already there (this is a form of proselytism); others would argue for a process of dialogue, namely that if there is to be an authentic encounter between the religious community and the world, then the religious community too has to be open to change and open to articulating afresh the Good News and the vision that it wishes to share. This process, then, involves the conversion of those within the worshipping community, which is manifested by a deeper commitment to the life of God, humanity and creation.

worship and transformation in the Hebrew Scriptures

One way in which we can look at this question more clearly is to return to Scripture. We have already shown that Israel's purpose as a chosen people was to be ethically holy, but we also have to consider what else we learn about Israel as a people constantly engaged in worship.

> *You stand assembled today, all of you, before the Lord your God ...*
> *to enter into the covenant of the Lord your God, sworn by an oath,*
> *which the Lord your God is making with you today; in order that he may*
> *establish you today as his people, and that he may be your God, as he*
> *promised you and as he swore to your ancestors, to Abraham, to Isaac*
> *and to Jacob.* (Deuteronomy 29.10-13)

Moses addresses the assembled people of Israel, revealing that God desires a relationship with his people. God promises his faithfulness in return for theirs. Unlike other religions, the Israelites' faithfulness to the God of Abraham, Isaac and Jacob, which was expressed, affirmed and enjoyed in worship, needed to be lived out in mission. This would mean a just ordering of their community and, in particular, treatment of the alien, orphan and widow that would embody God's liberating presence.[19] God's anger spilled over when there was no integration of worship and mission, can be seen in two texts coming from different but similar periods in the history of Israel. Just before the fall of the northern kingdom of Israel, and the loss of the ten tribes, Amos – a despised 'Southerner' proclaims on God's behalf: 'I hate, I despise your festivals, and I take no delight in your solemn assemblies ... Take away from me the noise of your songs ... But let justice roll down like waters, and righteousness like an everflowing stream' (Amos 5.21-24). The people are complacent and their rulers corrupt. They have turned 'justice to wormwood' (5.7), but they continue to carry out the rituals of worship – which, in this context, God hates.

Speaking to an equally complacent and equally doomed southern kingdom of Judah, Isaiah lets rip: 'I cannot endure solemn assemblies with iniquity. Your new moons and your appointed festivals my soul hates; they have become a burden to me ... even though you make many prayers, I will not listen; your hands are full of blood ... seek justice, rescue the oppressed, defend the orphan, plead for the widow' (Isaiah 1.13-15,17).

There are many more examples. Jeremiah satirizes the people's empty confidence in the 'Temple of the Lord', when there are no fair dealings, no justice in the land. Much later, the prophet cries out in a now famous passage against empty fasting: 'Is not this the fast that I choose: to loose the bonds of injustice, to undo the thongs of the yoke, to let the oppressed go free, and to break every yoke?' (Isaiah 58.6) What binds the contexts of these words of hatred and anger is a recognition of the emptiness of worship where nothing is being done to change an unjust and corrupt society. Stagnation had occurred. The relationship between mission and worship has been broken.

need for reinterpretation and action

Although the historical situations of these examples are different, they all share a requirement to take their context seriously, to take God seriously and to allow an interaction (a movement and encounter) between God and their local situation, which will bring about transformation. In other words, as a people, the Israelites were constantly on the move in their understanding of God and therefore of themselves. The old ways of understanding had to be revisited and reinterpreted and updated constantly, otherwise there would be a danger that they would become the object of worship instead of God. For example, both Ezekiel and Jeremiah make the discovery that the present generation is responsible for its own righteousness. Both challenge the received wisdom that a person could die for his predecessors' sins, expressed in the proverb, 'The parents have eaten sour grapes and the children's teeth are set on edge.' Ezekiel 18 contains a highly analytical exploration of the proverb, which comes to the conclusion that each person will live or die for his own righteousness or sin, with no reference to the righteousness or sin of his forebears. A view of the world's events as the consequences of the actions of others, becomes a view in which personal responsibility assumes more importance.

See Chapter 6, 'styles of teaching and learning'; Chapter 8, 'mission and Church history'.

repentance

Twice in the chapter, God expresses his desire: 'Have I any pleasure in the death of the wicked, says the Lord God, and not rather that they should turn from their ways and live?' (v. 23) and, more forcibly, 'Repent and turn from all your transgressions ... Cast away from you all the transgressions that you have committed against me, and get yourselves a new heart and a new spirit! ... For I have no pleasure in the death of anyone.' (v v. 30-32). What God desires is the transformation of the individual within the community from a sinner, weighed down with the iniquity of ages, to a righteous person who can live and, in living, offer true praise.

sacrifice

We see that the ritual pattern for achieving transformation from judgement to forgiveness, that is, the restoration of the individual's and the community's relationship with God, was the cult of sacrifice. A complex web of sacrifices, guilt offerings and sin offerings acknowledged sin and achieved restoration. For example, Leviticus records one grand set of offerings, which overcome the accumulated mass of witting and unwitting wrong, in the Day of Atonement. However, there exists, alongside the sacrificial cult, a critique of bare ritual: that sacrifice on its own does not achieve God's desire. That is, what is required is not the offsetting of just retribution, but commitment to change, to make something new: transformation. This is explored in a number of writings. Psalm 51, the great psalm of penitence, expresses the singer's longing for a total cleansing from sin and restoration of the broken relationship with God. The words are intensely moving, but the psalmist recognizes that the heart's desire is not to be found through ritual sacrifices. 'For you have no delight in sacrifice; if I were to give a burnt offering, you would not be pleased. The

sacrifice acceptable to God is a broken spirit; a broken and contrite heart,
O God, you will not despise' (v v. 16-17).

It is important to establish the relationship between worship and mission
in the Hebrew Scriptures in order to understand the relationship in the
New Testament which, as we have seen, has become so much part of the
intellectual climate that the imagery articulating this is both natural and
sophisticated. What is apparent is that when the two are separated there
is a serious breakdown in a community's relationship with God and often
within itself.

worship and mission: a place of meeting and transformation

We recalled that William Temple, former Archbishop of Canterbury, wrote:

> *People are always thinking that conduct is supremely important and
> that because prayer helps it, therefore prayer is good. That is true
> as far as it goes; still truer is it to say that worship is of supreme
> importance and conduct tests it. Conduct tells how much of yourself
> was in the worship you gave to God.*[20]

Temple is highlighting the relationship between worship and mission,
which is so central to Scripture. The conduct and relationships within
worshipping communities are inextricably linked with conduct and
relationships outside those communities. But, having established that
there is a relationship between worship and mission, a question facing
twenty-first-century Britain and Ireland is the nature of that relationship.
When we are in the world of worship, do we turn our backs on the
everyday world we inhabit most of our time? Is worship an opportunity
to leave behind the 'problems' of the world and rest awhile with God with
a group of like-minded people? Is worship, for some, a form of therapy?
To put it another way, is worship a way of preparing us for mission, yet
done away from the hurly-burly of ordinary life: or are we in mission while
we are in worship? Is worship part of mission and mission part of worship?
Does the prayer '… we thank you for feeding us … Send us out in the
power of your Spirit to live and work to your praise and glory'[21] suggest
that one is prepared for mission in worship but one actually is in mission
outside worship?

Church and world focus

If we regard worship as a *preparation* for mission (in other words worship and mission are separate) there can be two consequences. For the 'church-focused' worship and the pastoral care of worshippers come to be seen as the primary role of the Church. For the 'world-focused' it will be important to get out into the world to show God's love. Worship, especially using services and singing hymns that can appear so archaic in churches which are shrinking in numbers and growing in age profile, can come to seem a distraction from this.

exclusivity

The first attitude can result in a form of sectarianism where the Church cuts itself off from the world, seeing the world as basically evil and corrupt and regarding only those attending church as God's 'chosen'. Among extreme examples of this are 'exclusive brethren' churches and the Movement for the Restoration of the Ten Commandments of God, a new religious movement in Uganda, whose members either committed suicide or were massacred in April 2000. The second outcome can result in the Church being regarded as an irrelevance because it has nothing to say to the world.

As a result of this, some clergy have regarded the worship of the Church as a hindrance to God's mission and so have seen it as something to be tolerated while the real work is outside in the community. Some have left the ministry to become therapists, social workers or community workers, which seems more real in meeting needs. Of these two positions, one results in a Church without a world and the other in a world without a Church. It is important, therefore, to distinguish between worship that is also missionary and worship that is a preparation for mission.

The Orthodox Church views the liturgy as an act of mission expressing this concept in the phrase 'liturgy after the liturgy'. For the Orthodox, the liturgy of the Eucharist is the very heart of worship, and the worship of God that is centred at the Eucharist continues after the formal liturgy has finished (hence the term 'liturgy after the liturgy'). Orthodox theologian Anastasios Yannoulatos, formerly professor at the University of Athens wrote:

> Each of the faithful is called upon to continue a personal 'liturgy' on the secret altar of his own heart, to realize a living proclamation of the good news 'for the sake of the whole world'. Without this continuation the liturgy remains incomplete ... The sacrifice of the eucharist must be extended in personal sacrifices for the people in need, the brothers for

> whom Christ died ....The continuation of the liturgy in life means a
> continuous liberation from the powers of evil that are working inside
> us, a continual reorientation and openness to insights and efforts aimed
> at liberating human persons from all demonic structures of injustice,
> exploitation, agony, loneliness, and at creating real communion of
> persons in love.[22]

This concept is also reflected in the wider Church. In some parts of the
world, simply celebrating the sacrament is dangerous, thus doing so is
itself an act of mission and evangelism:

> We hear of those who come together at great risk, and whose courage
> reveals to those around them how precious is this sacrament. In other
> situations the eucharist may be an open-air witness so planned that
> many may see it. Such a joyful celebration as this may offer fresh hope
> in cynical secular societies. There is, at the Lord's table, a vision of God
> which draws the human heart to the Lord.[23]

The seventh Assembly in Canberra (1991) raised another challenge by
asking how far the worshipping community actually modelled the inclusive
community it was preaching:

> Worship space needs to be designed so that all people are able to
> participate fully. A lively ministry of hospitality, welcoming all in the name
> of the Lord, is most important. The plea of young people for forms of
> worship and celebration which fit their culture must be taken seriously.[24]

If we accept this relationship between worship and mission, then it also
follows that the way one community articulates its worship is affected by
the world in which that community is situated. The words, images and
symbols used by the worshippers need to express their world outside the
church in order that it can be offered to God inside the church. Worship
needs to express its contemporary context and therefore needs to be
reviewed and changed in order that it speaks to the contemporary condition
of the worshipper. Worship needs to be able to use words and symbols
which speak to the twenty-first century, although this needs to be done in
such a way as to enable people to encounter the very deepest mystery of
God's being. At the same time, worshipping communities are part of a
history ('saving events'), which, through different traditions, goes back to
Jesus Christ himself. These traditions (such as Orthodox, Roman Catholic,
Reformed and Anglican) have nurtured adherents through the ages and
have provided vehicles through which the Good News of Jesus Christ has
always been carried and expressed. But, too often, denominational labels
have hindered mission and, instead of encouraging people out into the

contemporary world, have forced them to look inwards to the preservation of the Church (including what is perceived as its particular worship tradition). Too often Churches have become slaves to their past rather than inheritors of it. By taking mission seriously in worship, a dialogue takes place between ecclesiology and the contemporary context and this may bring about change.

where changing society begins

So, in our picture of a missionary worship, different streams combine in order that the community can offer itself as it really is to God and, in the offering, be transformed into what God wants that community to be. It is an environment of both social and personal transformation. It is, to follow the reasoning of St Thomas Aquinas,[25] a place where the work of changing society begins. If the worship of the Church takes place through Christ as our great high priest, then it follows that we cannot confine Christ's action to our sacred spaces. Indeed, it is through worship that these images can penetrate deep into our being. It is at worship that mission meets ministry and they become one, thereby enabling the insights gained from mission to encounter and challenge our ecclesiology.

intercession

Walter Wink argues that 'history belongs to the intercessors, who believe the future into being'.[26] In making this statement, he points to the possibility for times of intercession to be so much more than a ritual mention of current events, and the names of the sick and bereaved. He argues that intercession is an intense and dynamic process in which we are not controlled by time, but able to use the power of Christian hope to change the world. He says:

> *Hope envisages its future and then acts as if that future is now irresistible, thus helping to create the reality for which it longs. The future is not closed ... Even a small number of people, firmly committed to the new inevitability on which they have fixed their imaginations, can decisively affect the shape the future takes. These shapers of the future are the intercessors, who call out of the future the longed-for new present. In the New Testament, the name and texture and aura of that future is God's domination-free order, the reign of God.* (Wink, 1992, p. 299)

The question we must then ask is whether theological education takes account of the importance of intercession and its important role in witnessing to Christian hope? The intercessions in the liturgy can be the one place where the congregation is reminded of the world outside the church walls. Are clergy and lay people trained to make public intercession inspiring for the whole congregation's participation and response, and is the responsibility for intercessory prayer felt to continue beyond formal liturgy?

modern and traditional liturgies

If history belongs to the intercessors, how can the past illuminate and feed the present and open up ways into the future? How can the present in which we live help us view the past and make it a living reality? How can the worshipper be in the past, present and future and maintain the integrity of them all? These kinds of questions show that we cannot make assumptions about the attractiveness or effectiveness of modern over traditional liturgies, since the former can be less missionary than the latter.[27] Some churches and cathedrals using ancient liturgies can attract people by their preaching and music. Liturgist Don Saliers provides an important caveat:

> ... it is possible to be relevant and yet inadequate to the mystery of faith. It is also possible to set forth dogmatic truths which do not elicit a living faithfulness in worship or in common life.[28]

towards a missionary worship

It is clear from the foregoing that the form of liturgy itself does not make worship missionary, but rather it is the way that the congregation relates to God and God's world. The role of the liturgy is to provide the framework for the nurture of this relationship. If the liturgy is not able to do this, a congregation will either change the liturgy or introduce hymns, prayers or readings that will be effective vehicles of worship, and that congregation will place its energies into these parts of the service. Beyond this, we have to ask in what ways worship carries on in people's lives outside the church environment.[29] How does this worship of God which goes on in our hearts and minds when we pray as individuals or as families, as groups, or even as a Mission Theological Advisory Group, undergird our hearts for mission and make us more aware of the need to make a difference in the world? Any form of theological education can help to reflect on this. Does what goes on in the chapel permeate daily life and shape our Christian witness? If we are called to be a Christian presence in our community, how does worship become a witness? For example, if we are able to feel comfortable praying with others at work or in other aspects of our daily lives, can this not make a great difference? Given how many people access prayer sites on the Internet, such as the Jesuit-run *Sacred Space*,[30] perhaps more opportunity for others to stand in the presence of worship in non-church environments could make all the difference. When public figures, such as Diana, Princess of Wales die, crowds of people will stand in the street and try to join in saying the Lord's Prayer. Many simply do not know or have forgotten the words. Who will remind them? How much trouble do we take to pray the Lord's Prayer in non-church situations? What might it mean to meditate on a Bible passage or to pray the rosary on a crowded train?

Teaching and learning about worship in theological education can help us to think through the issues and look at the mission possibilities. Equally it can confirm a sense that the worship of the Church belongs in the church building. The missionary God asks us to make Christ known everywhere. Can we take our songs of praise to where the people are?

Here are some questions we can put to ourselves. These might help discover the extent to which worship is, or is not, missionary.

- Is there an enthusiasm for God and for God's world?
- Is there a love and concern for each other that is reflected in a love and concern for God's world? How does the worshipping community affect the wider community?
- Is there a concern for the marginalized, both inside and outside the worshipping community?
- Is there a willingness to look with a critical eye at understandings of God and God's world in order to see them afresh? Is the community open to change?
- How is the relationship between the 'saving acts of God', the contemporary context and the worship of God (that is, the relationship between ecclesiology and missiology) negotiated?
- What understandings of God and humanity are being promoted in the worship building, hymns, prayers and other symbols used in worship? What values does the community really wish to promote in worship?
- Does the liturgy enable worship?
- Sometimes the 'liturgy after the liturgy' is coffee at the back of church! Are visitors made to feel welcome and given the opportunity to worship?
- If a church is for the local community, does its membership reflect the demographic trends of the local community?
- What *difference* does it make to say or sing, for example, the Lord's Prayer in worship?

chapter 11

mission and pastoral care

In approaching this subject, we were aware of a number of contemporary debates on the subject of pastoral theology and its relation to mission. In our conversations so far, we have been very much aware that the desire of a missionary God is transformation and, consequently, our mission under God should actively seek this transformation. However, writers such as Stephen Pattison have suggested that although we might think that pastoral care provides ministers with many opportunities for transformation, people often do not see a natural link between pastoral care and mission.

He says:

> Pastoral care should be aware of structures of injustice. Ministry has social and political implications. It is important to be aware of differences of power, wealth, status, and the identification of 'the poor' in any pastoral situation. It is necessary to analyse how pastoral practice fits into the wider social order and the ways in which it challenges or affirms structures of injustice. It should be recognised that pastoral care has helped to make the poor invisible and has been complicit in maintaining injustice. Pastoral care should be open to the voices of the powerless on the margins, recognise its own implicit and explicit biases, and adopt a preferential option or bias towards the poor and marginalised with a view to helping them attain their own liberation. If fundamental social change is required to ameliorate a situation, then pastoral care must work towards this. It must commit itself to action and develop a prophetic, challenging dimension oriented towards social and political liberation against oppression. In all this, pastoral care needs to use the mediation of some of the insights and methods of the social and political sciences to understand the nature of the present human social context and appropriate social action for liberation.[1]

In order to see how mission, which includes working for the transformation of unjust structures, can be mediated through pastoral care, we looked at the issues in two ways. First, we considered how the matter has been debated in theological education, through the development of the Oxford Bachelor of Theology rubric.

We also decided to extend our conversational method to a number of experts in the pastoral theology and pastoral care fields, whose books form the background to much teaching in pastoral care, asking them what 'mission' means to them. We did this in order to understand the divisions better and to see whether our own prejudices and vulnerability on the question of 'mission' were distorting our perspectives. This helped us to see whether the missionary integration Stephen Pattison envisions is possible or whether there are differences in approach and understanding which theological education could help to address.

the Oxford BTh

The Oxford University Bachelor of Theology is a vocational degree available to those studying at registered theological colleges and seminaries. The colleges and seminaries cover a whole range of denominations and traditions including Anglicans, Roman Catholics, Baptists, United Reformed Church and Unitarians. Accordingly, the rubrics need to cover topics appropriate to them all. Until the latest revision of the rubrics (September 2000) the pastoral and missionary were seen as distinct, with the rubrics on the mission paper placed in the 'Further Subjects' section of the rubrics, which means that it is optional. Until the latest revision, the pastoral paper (a three-hour examination) had been in the section headed 'Pastoral Theology and Human Studies', which also contained papers on: 'Introduction to Sociology', 'A Field Study or Programme approved by the Supervisor Committee' (which was a theological reflection on a placement) and 'Theology and the Social Sciences'. The Anglican Colleges required their students to opt for the pastoral paper and the Field Study. The pastoral paper had to be accompanied by a declaration by the candidate's college that the candidate had satisfactorily undertaken pastoral placements during the course of the degree that pointed to a hope that reflection on pastoral experiences would form part of the preparation for this paper. It is worth underlining that mission was seen as distinct from pastoral care. The BTh degree enabled papers to be taken at the end of each of its three years and both the pastoral paper and the Field Study would usually be taken in the candidate's final year.

In 1990 the rubrics to the subject 'Pastoral Psychology and Pastoral Care' were:

Introduction to Pastoral Psychology:
human growth and development; the major determinants of human behaviour; social psychology and small group behaviour; psychological and psychiatric problems and their pastoral presentation; treatment methods and resources, including systematic approaches to pastoral counselling.

Pastoral Care:
the role of the pastor in counselling and confession; in special pastoral functions, e.g. baptisms, weddings, funerals; in visiting and congregational leadership; in group training and therapy; the role of the pastor as teacher.[2]

The rubrics show a sharp distinction between pastoral psychology and pastoral care and the examination paper reflected this distinction requiring the candidate to answer questions from both sections.

In 1996 the rubric was changed to:

Introduction to pastoral theology and pastoral psychology. An exploration of concepts of personhood; human growth and development; marriage, family and the single life; small group behaviour. This study will employ approaches from both theology and psychology and will encourage a mutual critique between them.

Psychological and psychiatric problems and their implications for pastoral care. The pastoral counselling movement, including a theological and psychological assessment of it. Resources for healing and caring in the Church and in society. The role of the pastor in pastoral relationships, including the promotion of maturity, preventative care, counselling and confession; in the rites of passage, e.g. baptism, weddings, and funerals; in the pastoral care of the bereaved; in visiting and congregational leadership; in small group work.

The role of the pastor in training and teaching. Ministerial lifestyle, including stress and time management.

In addition to the change of rubrics, the division of the questions, requiring candidates to answer some questions on psychology and some on pastoral care, was removed. The key shift was to bring pastoral theology into the rubric and to require a critique between theology and psychology. Behind this shift lay two key struggles.

First, there was the provision of academic respectability to the subject by referring to pastoral theology. For a long time, the pastoral side of training had been viewed as the practical aspect of ministry and the relationship with other academic disciplines had been non-existent: it had been regarded as an 'add-on'. However, with the development of pastoral theology as an academic discipline in its own right and a very slow recognition by the academic world of the intellectual and emotional rigours associated with pastoral theology and care, the need to integrate reflection on pastoral experience into the theological kaleidoscope was gradually recognized.

Secondly, the mutual critique between theology and psychology challenged the times when the psychological tail had wagged the theological dog. The consequence of seeing pastoral care as a practical and not theological discipline had meant that it had not been rooted in theology. Since the 1960s, pastoral care had been regarded as pastoral counselling and the prevailing psychotherapeutic climate had provided the tools and the philosophical background to pastoral care. In the Christian tradition pastoral care has always been clothed in contemporary understandings of human relationships, and the behavioural sciences provide that clothing today. However, the behavioural sciences have understandings of humanity and human relating which need to be challenged by theology and so there needs to be a critique between them. To phrase the issue differently: does the Church want pastors or counsellors?

The 2000 revision of the rubrics accompanied a radical revision of the whole degree. To prepare men and women for ministry in the twenty-first century it was recognized that mission had to be a key element in that ministry. 'Christian Witness and the Contemporary World' is now one of the foundation papers:

> *Candidates will study the relationship between the Christian faith and contemporary culture, including religious and secular understandings of society, environment, personhood and faith. Candidates will be expected to reflect on the practice of mission and pastoral care.*

Tutors from the variety of colleges mentioned above had many meetings before agreeing the rubric. The paper can be assessed by a three-hour examination or submitted as a 5,000-word essay (with four internal, college-assessed pieces of work). In part two of the degree, candidates have to do an examination entitled 'Mission and Ministry' in a section entitled 'Practical Theology'. 'Mission and Ministry' is assessed by a 7,000-word essay (there also have to be four internal, college-assessed pieces of work) and the rubric is:

> *Candidates will study and reflect on issues of mission and ministry. College-assessed essays should demonstrate knowledge of contributory disciplines. The long essay must be based on a supervised placement of at least 21 days in a church or secular setting in which the candidate shares in the experiences of those involved, and should contain theological reflection on the situation.*

These two rubrics indicate a number of important shifts. First, Christian ministry is not defined exclusively in terms of pastoral care, but in relationship with contemporary culture and all that influences it. Secondly,

mission has a pivotal role to play in this new understanding. Thirdly –
and this is apparent from the last rubric – the subject is now clearly a
theological discipline.

Clearly, then, there is a form of theological conversation that can enable a
closer dialogue between mission and pastoral care in which one influences
the other. In such a picture, we might assume that theological education
could answer Stephen Pattison's challenge. But we discovered that, even if
the framework for this close interaction and mutual enrichment exists in the
structure of theological education, the content may not support it in the
same way.

a chasm that need not exist

When we involved experts in the fields of pastoral care, spiritual direction
and counselling in our conversation, we noticed at once a gulf between
their perceived ideas about mission and about pastoral care. There was
an artificial distinction arising out of the idea of mission as something
which is done 'out there' and pastoral care which takes place 'here, on our
doorstep'. There then seemed to be a division between energy spent on
outreach and time given to pastoral care. For us, as we have suggested,
we would not intend that this should mean that less time is devoted to
pastoral care, but rather that pastoral care is of its nature missionary.
Notwithstanding, the responses from our conversation partners particularly
challenged our own thinking about who and what we say we are when we
proclaim ourselves to be people with a heart for mission. In our study of the
Oxford BTh, our underlying presuppositions could be that Pattison's
arguments were *obviously* correct. The responses from experts in pastoral
care challenged us to look again at our assumptions about transformation,
especially about the way we can unwittingly try to control people's lives.

directive and non-directive approaches

The non-directive approach often draws on casework, counselling and the
methodology of psychotherapy. Those who espouse the directive approach
– however qualified and sophisticated – can be seen by some adherents of
the non-directive approach as bullies, colonialists and even rapists, whilst
the advocates of the directive approach tend to say that the others have no
gospel to share, or otherwise share it in a mass of equivocation and lack of
commitment. There is for both approaches the snare set by those whose
personalities determine the approach: some people have a *need* to be told
what to do, or to be commanded. Thus some people can be powerfully

attracted to some more 'closed' churches where public repentance and/or giving testimony are a condition of entry. Conversely, some people set the agenda by fiercely determining the terms on which they will accept the Christian gospel. Sometimes, such people have a powerful need to hover on the periphery until they have set up the conditions under which entry is possible. For those of us with a heart for mission, interaction with people whose evangelization is driven by their own needs can lead us ourselves to begin to make divisions between 'mission' and 'pastoral care', irrespective of whether we think our ministry should be directive or non-directive in stance.

We offered our conversation partners a simple eight-point questionnaire. In this questionnaire we asked questions which tried to discover what kinds of understandings of mission the pastoral care specialists had, and to find out what kind of separation there might be between notions of pastoral care and mission. Although we, as representing those who have a primary interest in mission, were asking the questions and reflecting on the answers, we were clear that we shouldn't assume that we ourselves were in possession of some 'perfect' answers. In constructing the questions, we tried to choose ideas that we felt would make a difference to how people might see pastoral care related to mission. This is what we learned.

what pictures come into your mind when you hear the word 'mission'?

The responses to this question showed that the very word 'mission' triggers a wide variety of pictures in people's minds when they are encouraged to give an immediate response to its use. The images used were very interesting and were a challenge to us and to all who care about mission: pith helmets, Bible and rifle, street-corner speakers, hell-fire denunciations, dualistic theology, colonialization, deceit and disingenuous advertising methods are just a selection of the negative images offered by the respondents. Others saw mission as unconsidered activism: 'busyness, telling … bringing into church'.

Yet, there were also positive images to be shared. The workers in pastoral care and counselling and spiritual direction also wrote of a mission of love that all people deserve to receive. They pointed out to us that, by specializing in pastoral care, their work has a consciously *redemptive* side – repairing and recompensing people who, for whatever reasons, have been the victims of bad parents, harsh teachers, dominating pastors, spiritual workers or other Christians, or who have been victims of self-proclaimed

Christians who have misrepresented God because of a mixture of prejudice, heresies, sin, error or a desire to find people to dominate. Mention was made of breaking barriers and prejudices to do with all kinds of injustices, evils and divisions. One very vivid comparison between healthy and unhealthy mission was to liken the first to loving intercourse and the second to rape. It is unsurprising, then, that a division occurs between mission and pastoral care, where pastoring people has to repair damage done by inappropriate evangelism. On reflection, we were able to find evidence of this ourselves. For example:

> *Jennifer joined a Methodist youth group which some of her friends attended. Her initial interest in the group was not to become a Christian but to play her guitar with her friends and to meet boys. After she had attended two sessions, she became very uncomfortable when the leader suggested they have a time of open 'confession' of sins. The young people were especially enjoined to confess sins of a sexual nature, for example thoughts about other people in the group. Jennifer became upset and refused to contribute, especially as she had an interest in one of the boys. The leader of the group, a man in his forties, later offered to take her home, but instead drove her to a local beauty spot and pressured her to 'release the sin'. She refused, but he would not take her home until she had 'given way'. He kept insisting that she must become a Christian and that confessing was the only way to accomplish it. Jennifer left the group and kept well away from anything to do with church. Two years later she went with a friend to a Roman Catholic church to sing in the choir. The friend mentioned in passing that she was going out with one of the altar servers and Jennifer burst into tears. The parish priest talked to her and the whole story came out. He explained to her that she had been harmed by her experience and that what had happened to her was not acceptable Christian behaviour. Gradually Jennifer was able to overcome her experiences and turn towards Christian faith once more.*

This story demonstrates what problems can ensue when evangelism is fostered on the back of a misuse of power. Moreover, in this case, healing through sensitive pastoral care has to take place before outreach can become meaningful and it is interesting that this took place across a denominational divide. In asking what kind of mission makes sense in today's world it is as well to remember that many people outside the Church have been hurt by the unthinking or insensitive behaviour of others inside the Church, and that these wounds are often never given the opportunity to heal. In such cases evangelistic effort may simply make matters worse. For this reason pastoral care, counselling and spiritual direction may be invaluable in remaking the context in which evangelism may again take place. Anyone desiring to develop a heart for mission therefore needs to be aware of the relationship between the mission and pastoral care in ministry.

When thinking about mission, some respondents simply listed verbs: to look outwards, to seek, to move, to forage, to love, to pray, to engage actively with society; mission is to participate in all life rather than to react to evil by denunciation; and a 'first aid plus preaching' approach.

The confusions of the present day surrounding ideas of mission were put revealingly by one respondent who reported his reaction to the word 'mission' as stirring, but guilt-generating at the same time. One person simply said that mission is 'to be the love inside ... history', but another said mission implied simply, to be 'people with purpose'.

The respondents also showed that, today, the very word 'mission' may be as likely to mislead as it is to enlighten. It is rarely seen as *missio Dei*, but far more it is seen as the imperial ambitions of churches of varying and competing brands and blends. This is aggravated by management jargon, which likes to use the idea of mission in its training work. If mission permeation is to spread healthily in ordination training and beyond, much re-evaluation and repair still needs to be done to offset these negative perspectives. Also the idea of 'mission' as a sexy concept to be hijacked to cover up a bullying attitude to evangelism needs to be challenged. Nonetheless the fundamental concept of 'being sent by God' is essential to Christian faith and, in any case, too deeply rooted in Christian experience for the idea of mission simply to be erased from the vocabulary of churches that find the idea of mission difficult. This places a burden on all of us, however, to be even more careful how we use the word 'mission' and especially what we do in its name. Moreover, we should not assume that those who report negative feelings about it are simply misinformed. Much of the arrogance that people may perceive in Christians stems from our own assumption sometimes that because we all *agree* that we know what we are talking about, we are necessarily right. Teaching and learning in pastoral care should, perhaps more than in any other discipline, alert us to the importance of the perception of the 'other' and the importance of allowing that perception to challenge and change us.

All this trouble over the word 'mission' also sends us a strong signal that a constant return to the doctrine of the triune God is the only and the necessary precursor to arriving at useful thinking, let alone action, of mission of a missionary kind. If we are to grasp the nature of the Church and its mission, we cannot proceed by picking out a series of practices and policies which we then call 'mission'. The prior question must always be 'what does the eternal loving nature of God, Creator, Saviour, Spirit lead us to think, pray, plan and do?' As David Bosch put it well in *Transforming Mission*, 'mission is not primarily an activity of the church, but an attribute of God'.[3] It was noticeable that our respondents dealt with mission as if it were primarily an activity of human beings rather than a response to the prior activity of a God whose love overflows constantly into the world.

For this reason, developing a heart for mission may require increased contemplation of God's own missionary nature as an antidote to skewed ideas of mission which may be based on such long legitimated but confused reasons as, for example, national prestige, the desire to make a church organization survive and flourish or, more subtly, the projection on to other people of painful memories and unsatisfied needs in the missioners. Nor is this a simple cure, for *missio Dei* itself creates difficulties as we shall show. If we are truly called to be in partnership with God, then we need to ask where that partnership has been let down by our own self-serving ambitions, distorting mission *through* misuse of our pastoral care and generating negative images which destroy the relationship between the different parts of ministry. We see this especially in the recovery of Christian integrity for indigenous peoples in post-colonial literature. This requires an examination of mission practice and rereading of our inherited stories to see where the Church has actually damaged its own commitment to mission.

See Chapter 13, 'mission as prophecy'.

Theological education, therefore, has an opportunity to re-evaluate our pictures and understanding of mission. These must be God-centred with all the sacrifice, prayer, self-examination and repentance that this implies. If we do this, we have the basis to show that it is precisely this response to a missionary God which lies at the heart of pastoral care, counselling and spiritual direction, for *to respond to human need by loving service* is indeed one of the five marks of mission.

what do you make of the phrase 'the Church's mission'?

The distortions surrounding the word 'mission' did not prevent respondents from speaking sensitively about the mission of the Church in reply to this second question. Here, the caricatures tended to be set aside as people thought about an institution that was clearly capable of holding their affection as well as exasperating them at times. Mission was seen by one respondent as the total task of the Church and this was echoed in different ways across the spectrum by the various pastoral carers and counsellors and spiritual directors. Suspicion of any tendency for the Church to seek to replace God was expressed in various ways, together with the view that the Church must exist to witness to the kingdom of God as given in Christ, bringing hope to a world of dashed hopes and schemes. This echoes the finding of David Hay and Kate Hunt in *Understanding the Spirituality of People Who Don't Go to Church*, that people outside the Church, no matter how critical of the institution, also may long for the hope that is within Christians.[4] The Church was seen by one respondent as prone to having its 'little' agenda for itself at the expense of God's agenda for the Church. It is a pertinent question for all involved in mission to ask if we think *missio ecclesiae* rather than *missio Dei* is really what we are about. From the point of view of those specializing in pastoral care, such a priority was seen as deeply undesirable.

These reflections underline the suspicion among some pastoral care and counselling and spiritual direction workers that mission can become a battle cry of ecclesiastical pretension and expansion rather than a response to the love flowing from God. A view was expressed that the so-called 'new' churches are especially prone to this temptation. Above all, the respondents expressed sorrow and anger on behalf of people who have been mauled and injured by church policies and especially by the preaching of a vengeful and merciless God who demands doormats rather than disciples. This also demonstrates that having an impetus to and a heart for mission can be challenged and changed by the repeated experience of having to care for those who have been hurt by the Church. How can a minister encourage those in a church to become a missionary congregation if those outside the church have first to be healed of various hurts, old wounds and prejudices?[5]

how do you define the Church's purpose for existing?

Asked about the purpose of the Church's existence, a wide variety of answers arose with a broad theme of making God and God's love plain and accessible: 'To love and make Love loved.' Depending on the respondent, this was expressed as proclamation or revelation or activity relating to worship and the service of God. One respondent who was very critical of the Church's tendency to distort individual people's personal gifts by institutional and doctrinal demands, replied that the Church should increase love and harmony and not 'propagate belief'. In a global context in which suspicion of 'fundamentalist' polemic carries extravagant concern and fear, such a view deserves further analysis. Another respondent emphasized that the Church should work, where possible, with other organizations – a reminder of mission to the structures of society as well as to the people within them. In the current international context, this too should prevent us from becoming complacent about mission.

The most frequent common theme was eschatological in tone, referring to the Church as the place where people should be able to receive foretastes of the kingdom. Over half the answers mentioned this, and they offered a wide spectrum of self-interrogation for the Churches to carry out vis-à-vis their worship, teaching and corporate life, as well as to define what is meant by mission and outreach. 'Is this church and its life a true gateway to heaven?' is not a whimsical question, but a serious question to put to Churches and church congregations everywhere. Again these answers direct us to ask what we think both mission and pastoral care are actually *for*? If all our ministry and mission have this eschatological dimension, then surely there should not be a gulf between them? Indeed, we might argue that the missionary possibilities of all pastoral care, counselling and spiritual direction are to make the eschatological dimension real and present in people's lives. The giving of hope, and the sense of value, meaning and purpose beyond the immediate and the contingent, may be the most important missiological thrust that pastoral care brings into people's lives.

For example, John V. Taylor argues that this is precisely the way Jesus brought the healing ministry of God's love directly into the path of God's asking us to be partners in the eschatological enterprise. He says:

> *When Jesus saw him lying there and was aware that he had been ill a long time, he asked him, 'Do you want to recover?'* That was a devastatingly perceptive question. For like so many people in deep depression the man believes he is the victim of other people's indifference. *'Sir,'* he replied, *'I have no one to put me in the pool when the water is disturbed, but while I am moving, someone else is in the pool before me ... Jesus answered, 'rise to your feet, take up your pallet bed and walk'.* By commanding the impossible – 'Stand up' – Jesus simply defied the man's inveterate, sulky dependence and released in him a new responsibility for his own life. *The man recovered instantly, took up his pallet, and began to walk.*[6]

John V. Taylor's choice of illustration here points up the whole question about how pastoral care and mission, working together, can break through institutional perspectives that create a chasm between the two. In teaching pastoral care with a heart for mission, it is necessary to work through the issues further, as Taylor does. He points out that later in the story 'we meet the kind of religion that works against God by frustrating that purpose through making people dependent upon the guardians and the interpreters of a tradition'. The man is told that he should not be carrying his bed on the Sabbath. He blames Jesus but, later, when Jesus encounters him again in the Temple:

> 'Now that you are well again, leave your sinful ways, *(yes, sulky despair and passivity can be a besetting sin)* or you may suffer something worse' – *very stern advice, but loving.* The man went away and told the Jews that it was Jesus who had cured him – *not that it was Jesus who had made him carry his bed. The man was not transferring the blame this time, but giving credit where it belonged. It was Jesus who had cured him. That begged all their questions.* (Taylor, 1998, pp. 13–14)

What has happened in the working out of this story is that care for the man has opened out new possibilities which go beyond the religion's restriction and refusal. The man now has a new vision of God's desire for creation, which creates the context for acknowledgement, confession and proclamation. In his new wholeness, the man stands as witness to the reality of the kingdom. This is radical pastoral care indeed, in which healing is not just a local event but also one that has a transformative effect on the whole religious community, stirring it up and provoking new questions.

does God have a mission?

The answers we received to this apparently simple, but in fact very complex, question here clearly displayed a feeling that purpose is part of God's fundamental nature, expressed in creation, resurrection and in the work of the Holy Spirit. Further, it was largely felt that the Church exists to reflect and to participate in God's mission. Here, pastoral carers and counsellors and spiritual directors displayed an almost unanimous sense of a mission in which they play an effective part. Warnings were given about the danger of using the word 'mission' ('sent') in respect of God in God's self, but a belief that God is concerned, loving and has a purpose for the creation was strong in all the respondents.

What was interesting about this perception of God was the suggestion that workers in pastoral care and counselling and in spiritual direction have something of a priority in their work to protect people from the overlaying of the gospel by the pressures of working for a 'successful' Church. Again, the interface between mission and pastoral care challenges those of us who desire to develop hearts for mission to guard against appropriating God for the cause of our own 'right'. Mission theology suggests that God asks us to be partners, but our partnership with God does not give us special privileges over others. Pastoral Studies can show us directly how ministering to others in loving service can teach us humility. Too often the gulf between pastoral care and mission has pointed up the difference between Jesus, stripping off his outer garment to wash the disciples' feet, and Peter, astonished and discomfited by the Lord's humbling of himself to serve his friends. Or it has made some in the Church into Marthas, running around all day and others into Marys, waiting quietly and chided by the 'doers' for not contributing enough to the success of the enterprise. This gulf is directly addressed by refocusing the issues through the understanding of a missionary God, who goes forward among us in pursuit of an ultimate purpose, but who yet has been among us as one who serves. The twinning of both roles in God's own self points to the necessary relationship between mission and pastoral care in Christian ministry.

what do you think of the phrase 'a missionary God'?

This question was designed to discover the extent to which workers in pastoral care, counselling and spiritual direction might be put off by bringing the old 'pith helmet' image alongside the word 'God'. The answers showed a coolness but not a complete rejection, except by one respondent. The major stress was upon a God who loves and waits, who reaches out to all creation and draws creation on by love. There was a desire to show how God is already present ('a secret presence' as one respondent put it) waiting to be recognized, rather than needing to be brought in from elsewhere as a fait accompli. Mission seen in this way is a process of attending to people in whom God is already present. This means that in learning about pastoral care we have an important opportunity to discover and develop the missionary understanding that there is no human person whom God has not already disturbed and in whom a spiritual search is not inevitably to be found. Each encounter provides mission opportunity, not necessarily to convert or claim for the Church, but to create relationship within which the Holy Spirit can work. Pastoral care, counselling and spiritual direction of their nature require person-to-person contact as a means of exercising ministry and, in each of these relationships, the mission of the Church, under a missionary God whose essence is overflowing love, can work. The question then, is what *difference* this awareness of the closeness of mission and pastoral care makes in terms of praxis and outworking in each unique situation.

Further, this matter of God's presence, in the double form of active, loving God and Suffering Servant, is sharply elucidated by David Ford, when he speaks of his encounter with Antonio, a dying disabled person at Jean Vanier's L'Arche community.

> *All these regular disciplines in the service of the handicapped have their testing and their fulfilment in facing the overwhelming mystery of death ... So part of the provocative witness of L'Arche is its following Jesus by living vibrantly in the face of death. The household sang daily as Antonio lay there. He regularly took communion. The way of Jesus to crucifixion and resurrection enabled facing death and disability in a certain spirit, blending utter realism with hope and joy.*[7]

David Ford finds at L'Arche a 'provocative witness' and it is this that knits together the missionary impact of pastoral care. Even in situations of death and dying, God's presence, purpose and intention can be made manifest as a witness to others, so that they too can perceive what is called 'the awaited beauty'.

This theme of 'mission as discovering God who is already there' also chimes in with much thinking in industrial mission, which includes concern about the environment and the proper struggle that Christians have at all times to remain clear-headed in the ocean swell of the knowledge explosion. Pastoral care in many ministerial and indeed other roles, therefore, has the capacity to reveal in unexpected ways where God is and what God is doing. The missionary edge, however, may be to enable people to explore what this means for themselves. In this way, many people in caring professions may also serve to open up this sense of presence. It is further our missionary task to discern, acknowledge and make sense of the opportunity such ministry outside the Church also provides.

Our respondents had very largely moved beyond a fear of the word 'mission' to an ability to use it creatively in appropriate places, although warnings about the damage that the word can do to those outside the Churches continued to be given. One respondent summed it up: 'A missionary God ... an apt phrase ... often misunderstood to mean a "pushy" God.'

how can mission relate to your specialist work?

Seeking to press further into the usefulness of the idea of mission in pastoral care and counselling and spiritual direction work, our respondents were asked to relate the word 'mission' to their specialist work either in pastoral care and counselling or in spiritual direction or, in some cases, in both. This brought some very perceptive answers and, in their differing ways, each respondent, however critical of mission language, made clear a sense of purpose – a sense of mission to enable people to find God and God's kingdom for themselves. One made the helpful observation that in today's 'postmodern' search for meaning in life, more people would respond to Christianity if their innate spirituality were taken more seriously as a preparation for considering the faith in depth. This links with the important research by David Hay and Rebecca Nye in *The Spirit of the Child*[8] and emphasizes the reverence that those engaged in mission must always have for people and their personal histories.

One respondent talked of pastoral care as bringing theology to the marketplace and emphasized that pastoring work must be dictated by the person pastored, who must have complete intellectual freedom, be kept clear of all manipulation and deceitful pressures, while being enabled to make well-informed choices. Only then can a missionary purpose be free of contaminations such as manipulative use of emotions and preaching the love of God in a way that provokes fear and anxiety.

A second respondent saw mission as a process of liberating another person from the factors in their lives that hold them prisoners of the past. This was put another way by a third respondent who saw the pastor/counsellor/ spiritual guide as one person supporting another person in their search for salvation, renewal and their own style of prayer and spirituality. A fourth answer talked of the need for counsellors 'to be people imbued with divine love who recognize that the Spirit of God might mediate the love of God through the work of pastoral care and counselling'.

Other respondents defined pastoral caring as 'helping people to worship God', a thought echoed by others who stressed the eschatological and eternal aims of spiritual direction and the need to keep the focus of pastoral counselling on the care and the love of God.

These answers show a remarkably powerful grasp of the realities of mission and evangelism in the present day. On the evidence of this small sample, the pastoral carers and counsellors and spiritual directors seem to have a more sensitive and aptly tuned approach to mission than many who urge that mission today is a matter of refurbishing styles and practices that have been used in the past. One thing that we who are involved in mission can learn from this is that mission perspective can be helpfully filtered through the understanding of pastoral care to expose hidden motivations and inherited assumptions. Similarly, using a mission perspective in teaching and learning about pastoral care can help to sharpen its focus and set clear parameters. For example:

> *Ken, a minister for many years, had always adopted a policy of making his home available to anyone in need. Ellen, his wife, a marriage counsellor, found this difficult, since she would be expected to care and cook for anyone whom Ken determined was in need of shelter and help. Such people could arrive on her doorstep unexpectedly and stay for an indefinite period. Ellen was used to dealing with people within controlled situations and with defined expectations and outcomes and soon found Ken's open-ended desire to help anyone an intolerable burden on her own life and that of her small children. Things came to a crisis when Ken took a woman whose marriage was in crisis into the home. Ellen could see clearly that Ken was reacting to the woman's emotional dependence and that he was soon feeding his own needs. Soon after, Ken asked Ellen for a divorce, having transferred the woman's intense feelings of confusion and dependency to his own situation. Ellen, recognizing that Ken's understanding of pastoral care was now compromising their marriage, swiftly asked for help. She noted that: 'Ken never asked what he was helping these people for.'*

Our respondents were particularly alive to this need to be clear about what pastoral care is for. High standards of non-manipulative attention were reflected in the answers received, indicating an integrity of approach that compares very well with the misuse of 'counselling' of which the Churches are sometimes, with justice, accused. Yet sometimes this misuse comes not as an open-ended expression of care, as with Ken, but as an overt agenda. For example:

> *A minister was seeking to advocate the setting up of a Samaritan telephone service in an outer London Borough. He was pleased when he found there was support for the project, but was dismayed when he was asked to present statistics demonstrating how many people became Christians as a result of Samaritan work. He agreed that the kind of distressed and desperate people using the service may urgently need God's unconditional love and Christian service, but that the implication that love and service should necessarily lead to conversion was*

inappropriate. The matter could not be resolved and the phone line was set up elsewhere.

This last illustration demonstrates how counselling, in its true client-centred focus, can even seem 'anti-mission' to some sections of the Churches. This was the unfortunate impression given when the Church Army drastically reduced its counselling service in 1995. The action was taken because of a need to reorganize, and because of a belief that the Church Army could not cover all aspects of mission and evangelism, given its necessarily limited resources. Without disputing the financial and organizational considerations, it can still be said that for one of the Church of England's most prominent evangelistic bodies to make such a move increased in a small but significant way the chasm of misunderstanding between those working in pastoral care and evangelists.

does traditional eschatology have any grip on you and on the way you go about your work?

To be asked whether traditional eschatology had any grip on them gave the respondents an invitation to comment on the hell-fire traditions often associated with mission and evangelism, enough to put anyone in a 'blue funk'.[9] All the answers received were along the lines of inaugurated and realized eschatology and one described the Church as the place where an eschatological, indeed heavenly, lifestyle should be the hallmark of its worship and its mission. One respondent explicitly avoided answering the heaven and hell question, one stated that they had never believed in it, but all stated in various ways that Christian living puts us in the context of eternity now in this present life. Only one respondent saw a specific future moment of final consummation, but this was firmly in a context of God completing God's purposes, rather than an interventionist view of the end of the world. Each respondent had a vision of 'ultimate things' to be preserved amid the mundane and practical.

There is a question here for us if we want to develop a heart for mission. Do the particular tools and gifts, which enable us to engage in pastoral care, counselling and spiritual direction, relate to these expressed eschatological understandings? The implication is that what God wants for us is to 'have life, and have it abundantly' (John 10.10), and achieving this becomes a priority rather than being focused from the point of an ultimate destiny. The difficulty here, and one which forces another gap between mission and pastoral care, is an ethical one. Pastoral care may become caught up in seeing the present situation of a person only as the result of antecedent causes, whereas, as John V. Taylor has pointed out, we stand in a present that is offered to us as a gift from the future God has prepared for us if we are willing to accept it.[10] The missionary perspective, then, speaks of hope and possibility permanently in a person's present situation, which appropriate pastoral care can make it possible for that person to accept. However, the responses from our correspondents encourage us to spend more time rethinking the use of traditional imagery to do with the four last things: death, judgement, heaven and hell. They point up by implication the Churches' frequent failure to restate their doctrines of human accountability to God in terms which can avoid the 'music hall' distortions and jokes but preserve a proper element of clarity in the balance between justice and mercy, which are to do with divine and human truth and dignity, rather than wrath and condemnation. What this especially asks us to consider is whether the theological understanding of, and the treatment of, *sin* are different in the outworking of pastoral care and in missiological discourse. Again, the answer to this question suggests that ethics must be the theological glue that binds mission and pastoral studies together, since we cannot offer people divergent eschatological understandings of what God wants and intends of us in the fulfilment of the divine purpose. This is a reminder to all who would develop a heart for mission, that our mission-theological approach to other disciplines has to be very clear about its relation to an eschatological vision.

See Chapter 9.1, 'the Hebrew Scriptures'; Chapter 13, 'mission as prophecy'.

how do you think that the word 'mission' relates to the word 'evangelism'?

This final question we asked was intended to seek out the views of the respondents about the words 'mission' and 'evangelism' and where they may overlap or not. One respondent felt that both words mean what each user chooses them to mean and are, therefore, approaching meaninglessness. Another respondent thought both words arrogant in the way that they are commonly used, and a third felt that 'evangelism' carries overtones of violation and coercion.

However, the other respondents who dealt with the question saw evangelism as mission made explicit, 'the naming the name', the personal end of the mission spectrum. One respondent drew no distinction between mission and evangelism but pointed to the interpretative role of the pastor of explaining God to the person, of introducing the person to God, and helping the person to understand themselves.

One respondent added, at the end of the questionnaire, the following general comment which became an appeal for understanding:

> *Mission and pastoral care can, should and must be deeply related to one another. However, the reality is that, in my experience, they are usually these days deeply polarized along the doing (mission)/being dimension. Pastoral care isn't sexy; mission is! Pastoral care is seen to be inward-looking (though it isn't), mission outward-looking and related to the latest agenda of making the organization work. (Yet) pastoral care (i.e. giving and receiving of love) is the object of mission in that the purpose of spreading the good news is to enable others to experience love – the love of God – the love of the Christian fellowship ...*

The warm urgency and the eirenic nature of these words leads us on to ask what lessons can be drawn for those who train others for ministry of whatever kind.

some implications and conclusions

Although the investigation was limited in size, we had great respect for the people we consulted as published authors and acknowledged practitioners in their various aspects of pastoral care, counselling and spiritual direction. As a result, the interaction we have had with these people has opened up particular challenges regarding how we keep the perspectives of mission and pastoral care together. However, we now summarize some points that are especially pertinent in considering the place of a mission perspective in teaching and learning in Pastoral Studies.

- We have been challenged to consider that the relationship between all forms of ministry, pastoral care and mission can only be truly healthy if we are ready to share in a theological, biblical and prayerful dialogue as well as in debate about missiology.

- We must underline how the standards of non-manipulation, together with respect of others' dignity and freedom of choice must be a hallmark equally of pastoral care, mission and evangelistic outreach in all their various words and actions. 'Spiritual rape' must be anathema, and the damage caused to many by the pride and imperialism that can invade Church life is a form of sin from which we ourselves can suffer and will suffer in our ministry and mission until it is entirely rooted out. To do this we need to examine and understand our own motives. How does mission suit and feed our own needs as missionary people? How willing are we to face up to what this might say about ourselves? Similar questions need to be asked about the motives of pastoral care. The question 'whose need am I meeting?' should surround every pastoral encounter.

• It is as dangerous to over-focus on individuals to bring them to decisions for faith as it is to lose any vestige of a gospel message in a desire to be objective and non-coercive. Pastoral carers cannot pretend to be devoid of personal opinions and convictions. All forms of pastoral care, counselling and spiritual direction have their inbuilt purposes and a priori values, and it is important to be frank about these, treading a line of integrity which respects the other person, the congregation or group whilst preserving the integrity of the carers who inevitably have their own convictions and beliefs. What would happen if we applied the same analysis to ourselves in mission? Mission cannot be allowed to justify itself just because it *is* mission. If we are rigorous about the way in which we undertake pastoral care, how can we ensure the same rigour is applied to our missionary motives? What ethics do we need to bind mission and pastoral care together in this way?

• Issues of right and wrong, of justice, poverty, peace and reconciliation are as essential in 'outreach' as they are in pastoral care, counselling and spiritual direction, where they tend to be focused into individual people. Indeed, it is worth observing that pastoral carers have had to learn this essential feature of their work and reject any tendency to think that their work is simply to adjust people to bear what ought to be changed because of its unfairness and cruelty. It is a factor that has sometimes been forgotten in a desire to help others to find stability and peace in believing. People who feel offended against are as likely as not to be right about the matter. It is here that pastoral care and counselling and spiritual direction may have a continuing mission towards the 'secular', helping disciplines which can be politically blocked or ideologically blind to some moral issues. David Ford points to a condition of 'compassionate attention', which combines response to those who cry out to us, solidarity with a person's need or pain and an urge to act appropriately, which set of acts, when reflected upon, show how mission has not only taken place, but changed the world:

> In experiencing acts of compassion we are touching what is really important in world history. Before God, compassion is what matters most. At our point of need we recognize this. It is accidental whether

> these acts become widely known. Most are done by ordinary people
> in unspectacular situations. The 'last judgement' is perhaps best
> pictured as showing and confirming God's judgement on this sort of
> history. Matthew chapter 25 gives a list of the sort of events that will
> prove to have been most significant: feeding the hungry, giving drink
> to the thirsty, welcoming strangers, clothing the naked, visiting prisoners
> and caring for the sick. The story graphically shows a glimpse of the
> 'alternative history', which is woven into our lives by those people
> who, at our point of deepest need, have paid us compassionate
> attention. It is also an invitation to take our bearings from those
> events and, in our public as well as our private lives, to play our
> role in the ongoing drama of compassion. (Ford, 1997, p. 144)

- Work needs to be done on the language barriers between the 'mission'
  and the 'carer' sides. It will never be possible to end the process of
  making and remaking terminology, but an attempt to work on key terms,
  such as 'evangelism', 'conversion', 'self-determination', 'discipline'
  and others, could only be of benefit and a uniting force in the Church.
  Problems with the semantics of mission (or indeed pastoral care) need
  to be addressed by further dialogue and interchange between those
  actively engaged in mission and those in pastoral care, counselling
  and spiritual direction.

While it seems clear that a gap does still exist between 'pastoral carers'
and 'missioners', the gap may be less serious than it was some years ago,
now that the Church as a whole has to face up to the fact that the picture
of Church life in our contemporary society is fast changing. There are still
those who seek large-scale missionary initiatives and those who believe
that this is the very opposite of mission. There are still those who
believe that to deal with individuals and small groups can never be called
mission. It is most important for there to be a maintained dialogue between
the 'pastoral' and the 'mission' sides of the metaphorical chasm between
them, to address questions of purpose, value and meaning in the light of a
God of overflowing love. This is essential as a continuing feature of ministry
and mission and cannot be limited to initial training. It is a lifelong learning
need, which needs to be maintained in continuing ministerial education,
and all other similar learning environments.

What is most important is that teaching and learning in Pastoral Studies
provide a particular opportunity to reconcile differences of philosophy and
approach. It is no longer necessary to feel that mission and pastoral care
represent either/or choices, but that there is mutual enrichment between
them. Loving service not only generates mission opportunities but is

mission. It is a context of Christian ministry that gives the Holy Spirit full rein to work. Here are some questions to enable further discussion about this.

- 'The congregational member with natural gifts as a pastor who is asked to be a member of a pastoral team should first be given training in theology rather than counselling skills.' Is this true and why?
- Does pastoral care really bring 'good news to the poor' or does it help them become content with their plight?
- How can a recognition of the 'stages of grief' help the pastoral care of the bereaved?
- 'The practical exercise of Christian vocation towards others.' Is this an adequate definition of Christian ministry?
- 'Christian ministry's practical implementation will include: preaching and worship, pastoral duties, and Christian community, but also socialization, democratization, education toward self-reliance and political life.' Would you agree with this definition of ministry?
- Would you agree with Grace Davie's description of contemporary society as wishing to 'believe' but not 'belong'?
- Do you think that twenty-first-century Britain and Ireland are secular or pluralist?
- What challenges does the public response to the deaths of Diana, Princess of Wales and of the Queen Mother bring to the Church?
- Is the primary purpose of pastoral care to bring people to Church?
- What is the relationship between mission and pastoral care?
- Think about some people you have met over the last year and indicate what you have learned from them about mission and pastoral care.

chapter 12

mission and doctrine

whose theology?

In the December 1989 edition of the evangelical journal *Third Way*, the following letter was published.[1] The editor gave it the headline, 'Whose Theology?'

> *We were surprised to read on the back cover of* Third Way *that you have chosen to be the exclusive UK distributors for* The Best In Theology.
>
> *It seems to us that a more accurate title would be* A Digest of Some North American and European Evangelical Theologies. *The present title is an extraordinarily extravagant claim.*
>
> *Our criticism is threefold. Firstly, geographical isolation. Your advertising selection of 10 out of 34 contributors is exclusively from North America and Europe: your advert gives no indication that the other 24 may come from other parts of the world. In our view no selection of 'the best in theology' can possibly justify such a name without voices from all six continents. Exciting new light is breaking out from God's word in continents with little economic power.*
>
> *An important African theologian, John Mbiti, poses the question to American and European theologians:*
>
> *'We know you theologically. The question is "Do you know us theologically? Would you like to know us theologically? And how can there be true theological reciprocity and mutuality if only one side knows the other fairly well, while the other side either does not know or does not want to know the first side?"'* [2]
>
> *Secondly, ecclesiastical isolation. In using the blanket term 'theology' instead of 'evangelical theology', the worlds of Conciliar, Catholic and Orthodox thinking are ignored.*
>
> *Thirdly, linguistic isolation. 'Il n'y a pas aucune indication dans la publicité qu'elle existe la réflection théologique en autres langues'.* [3]

There were four signatories to the letter: Graham and Alison Kings (St Andrew's Institute, Kabare, Kenya) and Jeremy and Carrie Pemberton (Institut Supérieur Théologique Anglican, Bunia, Zaire).

the dominant western paradigm

The thrust of our explorations through the content of subjects in theological education has produced a particular perspective that is critical to mission understanding. One of biggest problems in becoming equipped for mission is that we have inherited and are called by God to live within a particular western paradigm. Most of the time we never think very much about this. Yet our typical theological discourse and understanding is framed by a white, male, western mode of ideas. When we talk about our faith, it is in these terms. When we talk about mission or about theology, we work out of this frame of reference. Yet we have seen increasingly that Christianity speaks to us out of the encounter between every kind of human person and feeds back to us in many ways. In studying Scripture we have seen how the Christian faith spread to all parts of the globe, carrying with it a history of encounter between many different tribes, peoples, cultures and faiths. But how far are we willing to be involved in reciprocal learning? When people of other countries become Christian do we really expect them only to speak of Christ thereafter among their own people? In the twenty-first century, Christians of all countries and cultures offer to us their stories of God. Are we ready or willing to accept them? Are we going to be changed by their insights and different images and metaphors for God's overflowing heart of love?

In looking at mission and doctrine, then, we have to start once more with Bosch's assertion that missiology is the 'mother of theology'. If this is so, then missiological thinking should be at the forefront of receiving, affirming and making known the theologies beyond our western context, challenging the dominant forms of theological discourse and opening up new ways of making Christ known.

who else has theology?

The question 'whose theology?' is a mission question of the profoundest importance. We are ourselves acutely aware that the discourse we employ in our own discussions, writings, reflections and meditations, is the result of our living and thinking in western society and in the context of a western theological discourse, which is both sophisticated and patriarchal. We have been challenged to think outside this particular box and to see our mission discourse as one capable of improvisation, a subversive jazz for people stuck with humming the same old tune. As mission specialists, we have also been aware, however, that many world theologians, seeking to engage in dialogue with us, find themselves required to adopt western styles of speaking and writing in order to gain a hearing and to command credibility. Their improvisations are suppressed unless they can sing our particular song. This means that the way we both teach and learn our theology, despite its intent, can limit the ways we seek to know, understand and speak about God to others. Learning about Christian doctrine can, in fact, limit our mission horizons, because we may miss what other people, in their very different ways, are trying to tell us about their experience of God. When we study systematic theology, we can forget that there are many other voices, and many other perspectives, coming to us from theologians whose ways of showing God to us are fresh, real and exciting, but who have not been born, nurtured and trained into the western tradition we tend to regard as the norm. Consequently, the study of Christian doctrine has potentially a great deal to challenge, disturb and revitalize our ways of thinking, if only we will allow some of those voices to penetrate our consciousness and to overturn our set ideas.

In order to approach the matter of teaching and learning in courses on 'doctrine' or 'systematic theology' we have included three different angles, which reflect the titles we have given to the three parts of this book. The first examines the relationships between theology and mission ('settings'), the second looks at some current issues in western academic theology in a missiological light ('illuminations'), and we end by trying to answer the question 'what would theology be like with mission at its centre?' ('heartenings'). In order to do this, however, we have engaged with David Ford as a dialogue partner, using his own different writings on matters of Christian doctrine and asking him to comment.

settings

We begin with David Ford's *Theology: A Very Short Introduction*. Here, he describes academic theology as 'a subject which deals with questions of meaning, truth, beauty and practice raised in relation to religions and pursued through a range of academic disciplines'.[4] How can we make sure that this meaning, truth and beauty is expressed in its full range and that we are ever alive to receiving it in new forms?

Our own 'setting' for this in our meetings and conversations is missiology as *missio quaerens intellectum* (mission seeking understanding).[5] It stresses the foundational starting point of engagement in mission and the exciting movement of enquiry, which rejoices in ever-widening horizons. The study of mission organically develops into the study of world Christianity and these two have their own integrating dynamic of 'movement' and 'horizons'. Mission and world Christianity relate not only chronologically – in that the present worldwide Church is historically the fruit of various missionary movements (including significant indigenous movements) – but also creatively today – in that people in mission are being sent 'from everywhere to everywhere'.[6]

As we have seen through our work, authentic mission involves an interweaving and outworking of evangelism, compassion and justice. Mission implies transformation. These three are one and interpenetrate: there is no grasping for priority but only mutual reflections of God's glory. Moltmann and others have reillumined the doctrine of the Trinity by developing Basil of Caesarea's and John of Damascus' doctrine of *perichoresis* or co-inherence. There are both indwelling and mutual relationship within the Father, Son and Holy Spirit and we see this too as inherent in mission. There is also mutuality between mission and the doctrine of God, for, as we have seen, mission comes from heart of God.[7] We can further argue that mission and doctrine, or more specifically, the theology of mission and systematic theology, interweave and interpenetrate more than is usually appreciated. Mission is the river that waters gardens of theology:[8] when it is blocked the gardens become a desert.

See Chapter 2, 'the world as God sees it'.

We showed in *The Search for Faith and the Witness of the Church* how Christian doctrine has been shaped by reaction to 'heretical' thought. We said:

> *Alternative ideas about what God has done and is doing arise to challenge neglect of aspects of the faith. In early times, this sometimes happened as a consequence of a political or power struggle, but also meant that dialogue, resulting in redefinition of belief, made sure that Christianity did not stagnate. Because of a continuing dialectic, our understanding of Christianity has accumulated. This is fundamentally important to mission, for as we explore more ways of understanding God's story, so the missionary task becomes better described. Today, for example, the contribution of liberation theologies and, in particular, Third World theologies, challenges us in the west not to be complacent about what we think we know about God. It is most often a fresh perspective arising from different contexts, or outwardly an alternative or complementary view which can become the prophetic word.[9]*

Different strands of thinking feed into and shape Christian doctrine over time. Similarly, biblical theology feeds into systematic theology and current systematic theology has had to take into account various features from around the world. Eurocentric theology has been named as such and now African, Asian, Latin American and Pacific theologies bring biblical perspectives and correctives. We have had to extend our view into different settings.

For example:

> The era of African theological literature as reaction to Western
> misrepresentation is past. What lies ahead is a critical theological
> construction which will relate more fully the widespread African
> confidence in the Christian faith to the actual and ongoing Christian
> responses to the life experiences of Africans. Here, academic theological
> discourse will need to connect with the less academic but fundamental
> reality of the predominantly oral theologies found at the grassroots of
> many African Christian communities, where in the words of John Mbiti,
> 'much of the theological activity in Africa today is being done as oral
> theology, from the living experiences of Christians ... theology in the
> open, from the pulpit, in the marketplace, in the home as people pray
> or read and discuss the Scriptures ....' As, through the very process of
> Scripture translation, the central categories of Christian theology –
> God, Jesus Christ, creation, history – were transposed into their local
> equivalents, suggesting that 'Christianity had been adequately
> anticipated', they created, in indigenous languages, resonances
> far beyond what the missionary transmission conceived.
>
> Through these local equivalents, Jesus Christ the Lord had shouldered
> his way into the African religious world, and could be discovered there
> through faith by all those who 'approach the spiritual world with requests
> for guidance and help us in difficulties' even where these requests are
> 'formulated in traditional terms'. This process is entirely consistent with
> what is reported to have taken place in New Testament times as in Acts
> 14:15-18. For the centrality of Scripture translation points to the
> significance of African pre-Christian religious cultures, as a valid carriage
> not only for the divine revelation, but also for providing the medium of
> Christian apprehension. Thus the possession of the Christian Scriptures
> in African languages, probably the single most important element of the
> Western missionary legacy, ensured that an effectual rooting of the
> Christian faith in African consciousness took place. This is turn provided
> the conditions in which an authentic dialogue would ensue between the
> Christian faith and African tradition, authentic insofar as it would take
> place, not in the terms of a foreign language or of an alien culture, but
> in the categories of the local language, idioms and worldview.[10]

There is a delightful irony in this piece of text, for it is written to us in *our*
language as a piece of carefully argued and insightful discussion.[11] We read
words in English written on paper, yet it speaks to us of the power of oral
theologies and of the way in which people can and will speak and learn
more about the doctrine of God outside the academic institution and

outside of theological textbooks. It is a challenge back to us to be reminded that this is true *here*. People do indeed both teach and learn through talking and praying together, reading and discussing the Bible and wondering and dreaming about who God is, what God is like and what God is really doing in the world. If we are to have a heart for mission, will our mission theology teach us to listen to every bereaved person, every child's question, every scribbled prayer request as entry points to the discussion of Christian doctrine as a meaningful part of every person's life. Or will we assume that we are the privileged possessors of difficult concepts and ideas to be meted out in parcelled doses in sermons and seminars?

a multiplicity of settings

If we choose to be challenged by theological thinking, living and sharing from the six continents, we can begin to see that there are a huge number of settings. In each setting there are opportunities to learn something new and significant about God. Our understanding of the doctrine we have received expands in each different setting. Moreover, settings have different modes of transmission. For example, some theologians spend their lifetime writing to each other, carrying on a conversation in letters, sharing different experiences. Our mission partners and exchange groups mutually inform and feed not only information about practical necessity but new images for familiar things returned to us in a fresh and vital way.

But if we want to be enriched by theological discourse in this way we have to go and find it. This, too, has to be part of our motivation, our heart for mission. But if God's overflowing love pours out into the communities of every ethnic group, then should not our response be to go and find out what God has been saying and celebrate it?

the settings of mission theology

If we look at the settings of mission theology we can see that both 'permeation' and 'focus' are needed. Without the focus of 'theology of mission', mission is too often ignored in theology: without a multiplicity of mission insights 'permeating' all theology, mission often becomes merely an 'added' extra, rather than mothering theology into what it is called to be – 'theology *ad extra*'.

missiological illuminations

In this second angle of our enquiry, we decided to look at four aspects of current academic theological enquiry in the West under a missiological light. These are: typology, the 'audience' of theology in the public arenas in which such discourse is heard, the relation of the 'self' and the 'other', and how we know and understand things. The aim of shining the light of 'mission' onto these subjects is to see what new ideas emerge and further to see what our knowledge of mission theology and mission theologians adds to the study of Christian doctrine.

the types of theologian and theology

In both *Modern Theologians* and *Theology: A Very Short Introduction*, David Ford effectively utilizes Hans Frei's fivefold theological typology to sketch how modern theologians have related to 'modernity'.[12] In what follows we use Ford's summary of these types, give their examples for the three mainstream types – all German theologians[13] – and then for each type add what seem to us to be missiologically equivalent examples.[14] This helps us to 'place' different kinds of missiologically thinking within the spectrum of theological range, but also asks us to cross refer to other important forms of theological thinking. Ford summarizes:

> Intellectually, the field is not best described by the labels conservative, liberal and radical. Instead, a different map of Christian theologies was sketched to show the main options. The key axis for distinguishing the types was the way in which the past is related to the present and future. At one extreme (Type 1) theology is assessed from the outside according to whether or not it agreed with some modern framework or agenda.[15] At the other extreme (Type 5) theology is a repetition of some past expression of Christian faith and so is completely internal to it.

No examples are given for these two extreme types.

> In between are the three types of most concern in this book. Type 2 tries to do justice to what is distinctive in Christianity while choosing one modern framework through which to show its relevance.

Frei and Ford offer Ruldolf Bultmann's existentialist framework as an example of an external philosophy being given a priority in theology. Ford also mentions Pannenberg and 'some leading representatives of theologies which propose issues of gender, race, political liberation, or interreligious dialogue as the decisive integrators'.[16] We could suggest Raimundo Panikkar as a missiological example. Born in Barcelona, the son of a Hindu father and a Spanish Roman Catholic mother, he was brought up in a Hindu-Catholic environment, learning the Hindu scriptures alongside the Bible and taught in India and the USA. His classic book is *The Unknown Christ of Hinduism*[17] in which he seeks to 'uncover' the Christ present and hidden in Hinduism.

Type 3 does without any overall integration and engages in continual correlation between Christian faith and various questions, philosophies, symbols, disciplines, and worldviews.

Frei and Ford offer Paul Tillich as a typical example of this correlation between faith and culture: Ford also mentions that Schillebeeckx and Küng could be linked in here. Amongst missiologists, Robert Schreiter, the contextual theoretician and Louis Luzbetak the cultural anthropologist, both of Chicago, could be listed. We could also refer to Kwame Bediako, whose work has already been quoted, the leading African cultural theologian from Ghana, who dynamically relates biblical and patristic theology to his own African Traditional Religion.[18]

Type 4 gives priority to Christian self-description and is best summed up as 'faith seeking understanding'.

Frei and Ford offer Karl Barth as an example of this type, which insists that Christian identity is primary and that all other reality needs to be construed in relation to it. This is where we could locate David Bosch, the South African mission theologian whose *Transforming Mission* has been constantly in our minds. This book contains fascinating insights into the subject of Christian doctrine in the section 'From a theology of mission to a missionary theology'.[19]

Ford makes the important point that 'such a scheme is too neat to fit the whole of any major theology, but it helps in mapping some of the major possibilities in relation to a central and unavoidable matter, the interaction of Christianity with modernity'. Here we see that he points out that Karl Rahner, in particular, who never produced one big work of theology and whose favourite form was the essay or paper (gathered in over twenty volumes of *Theological Investigations*) does not neatly fit any of the types, but goes beyond them (Ford, 1999, pp. 30–31). Maybe Max Warren's and John V. Taylor's perceptive and prophetic *CMS Newsletters* were a form of 'Missiological Investigations'?[20]

the public forums of our knowledge

David Tracy, in chapter 1 of *The Analogical Imagination*[21] outlined the three 'publics' of theology, which David Ford developed intriguingly in his inaugural lecture *A Long Rumour of Wisdom: Redescribing Theology.*[22] These are the 'academy', 'the churches' and 'society'. But could we not extend this to include a fourth 'public,' which would be that of 'other faiths'? It could be argued that they are included in 'academy' or even in 'society'. This is certainly important in the former, 'the academy', particularly in view of Ford's desire to hold the integrating balance between 'theology' and 'religious studies' and his definition of theology quoted above refers specifically to questions raised in relation to religions. The latter, 'society', is usually taken to involve politics, economics and cultural matters. We could include 'other faiths' here, but 'society' is too often seen (though not by Ford) as 'secular society', a plurality of cultures but not of religions.

the contribution of other faiths

The case for adding a fourth 'public' comes from our shared mission experience and can be extrapolated from two key missiological books, Kenneth Cragg's *Troubled By Truth: Life-Studies in Inter-Faith Concern* [23] and Vincent Donovan's *Christianity Rediscovered: An Epistle from the Maasai*. [24] Theology that engages in mission (as well as dialogue) with people of other faiths is forced to rethink issues in a way that returns the resourceful theologian *ad fontes*, back to the sources. Missionary encounter with people of other faiths brings about a re-evaluation and rediscovery of Christian sources. If the fourth public of 'other faiths' is specifically included, then theological reflection can be vitally renewed.

'Other faiths' as a fourth 'public' for theology inevitably involves translation. Ford describes movingly how in an earlier book on 2 Corinthians, co-authored with Frances Young, it was through the rigours of translating Paul's letter afresh from the Greek into English that key insights into Paul's theology were rediscovered. [25] This theological impact of translating increases when languages other than the vernacular of the translators are involved. We can learn from the way the pioneer missionary scholar and translator Henry Martyn (1781–1812) engaged in 'theology-in-philology' in his Hindustani and Persian translations of the New Testament. Kenneth Cragg describes his learning curve:

> [H]is brief career in missionary translation is as telling as any concerning the problematics of words and terms in the transactions of faith. Martyn encountered the 'x into y will-not-go' situation and faced it with a strong equipment of scholarship sustained by steady anguish of spirit ... 'Grace', 'truth', redemption', 'church', 'hope', and other vital words in his New Testament currency struggled to fulfil themselves in Indian idiom. It is evident in Martyn how he was more vitally in encounter with theology-in-philology than any academic professor. For he was made to feel, via his robust munshis, or local scholar-aids, the full strain, and even the venom, of the resistance to meaning implicit in the otherness of words. (Cragg, 1992, p. 7)

Ford also develops Tracy's concept of 'journeys of intensification' to illuminate various metaphors for salvation. The context of the following passage implies that it refers to different Christian theological positions but, if 'other faiths' were a fourth 'public', it could also refer to 'mission'.

> *One cannot travel more than one journey, and one's intellectual outlook is, like all other aspects of life, shaped by travelling. Yet theology has to study and discuss all of them, and might be seen as the place where those who travel different journeys can meet, be hospitable, argue and even at times persuade each other to alter their route, welcome new companions and redraw their maps.* (Ford, 1999, p. 123)

how we relate: the self and the other

In David Ford's book *Self and Salvation: Being Transformed*,[26] he plays variations on the theme of 'face' and develops the concept of a 'worshipping self'.[27] The book combines 'Dialogues' in Part 1 (with Levinas, Jungel and Ricoeur) and 'Flourishings' in Part 2 (which include expositions of Ephesians, the Eucharist, Jesus Christ, the cross, and intensive studies of two modern saints, Thérèse of Lisieux[28] and Dietrich Bonhoeffer).

In the chapter on the Lithuanian Jewish philosopher, Emmanuel Levinas, who settled in France, the important 'difference' of letting the 'other' be herself or himself without imposing in a totalitarian way your own categories on that other, is stressed.[29] This is surely significant for our understanding of the mission encounter. In the chapter on the French Reformed philosopher and theologian, Paul Ricoeur, his theme of 'testimony' is highlighted. Ford quotes:

> *Testimonies are real events whose depths no reflection can plumb. Testimony even divides itself, outside of reflection. There is first the testimony rendered by real acts of devotion up to death. Next, there is the testimony rendered to this testimony by witnesses to its witnesses ... A dialogic structure of testimony is indicated here between testimony as act and testimony as narrative.*[30]

This analysis of the nature of testimony can shape our attitude to mission. Our speaking and listening becomes an unbroken process by which meaning is conveyed to anyone capable of receiving it. But equally, casting theological discourse in terms of 'self' and 'other' ties us down to the transaction between ourselves and our interlocutor. From our point of view is there not a further way of reimagining the relationship between self and not-self? Testimony to someone is usually about someone else, so it is not just a 'dialectical' self/other, but rather a self/other/yet another. God enters into all our discourse about God's own self, informing and shaping it, disturbing us and urging us to get beyond reflexive relationships.

For example:

> *Who is the third who walks always beside you?*
> *When I count, there are only you and I together*
> *But when I look ahead up the white road*
> *There is always another one walking beside you*
> *Gliding wrapt in a brown mantle, hooded*
> *I do not know whether a man or a woman*
> *– But who is that on the other side of you?* [31]

This is T. S. Eliot's reimagining of the Emmaus Road experience. As yet unrecognized, the two are aware of the hidden, half-glimpsed presence of the third, who yet, because they are talking and wondering about what God is doing, appears with them and shares their journey. This presence of the hidden third who is God helps us to imagine God's involvement in our teaching and learning, discussing and dreaming, as part of our study of Christian doctrine.

We see this trend in the thinking and reflection of mission theologians. For example, John V. Taylor's description of traditional religion in Africa and of 'two' becoming 'three'. After discussing whether one religion would have to cede to another, he went on:

> *Ruthlessness has had a long run in Africa, and so long as the missionary encounter is conceived of as a duologue one will have to 'cede to the other'. But may it not be truer to see it as a meeting of three, in which Christ has drawn together the witness who proclaims him and the other who does not know his name, so that in their slow discovery of one another each may discover more of him?* [32]

In a similar vein, Max Warren wrote in *A Theology of Attention*:

> *When you and I venture to listen to another person 'in the name of Jesus Christ' there is an unseen listener present, Jesus himself. We have to listen to him listening. We have to know Jesus and be ready to learn all his meanings too. And in the context of this listening it may be that he will have something new to say, something we have never heard before. And if we listen very carefully, with concentrated attention, it is likely that we will hear him speaking through the lips of a Hindu, a Muslim, a Buddhist, a Jew, a man or woman of some tribal religion – or perhaps a Marxist or humanist. Jesus, now as always, is very full of surprises.* [33]

Thus missiological thinking has the capacity to add to the study of Christian doctrine a further dimension. It can reimagine the study of Christian doctrine as an Emmaus journey in itself, as we share our learning with others until we recognize finally the third who walks beside us.

how we know things: four structures of understanding

Bernard Lonergan's long career in teaching philosophy and theology in Canada and Rome bore fruit in two seminal books. *Insight: A Study of Human Understanding* focused on epistemology, a theory of knowing, which he later applied to theological method in *Method in Theology*.[34]

Lonergan's four levels of 'knowing' are: experience, understanding, judging, and deciding. David Ford illustrates these levels in a simple but profound way by discussing an apple – before going on to discuss 'knowing God'. You can see an apple in a bowl (experience); an earlier learning links with present experience and you have an insight – this is an apple! (understanding); but the insight may be wrong (plastic apple?), so further questions are needed and you can touch or bite the apple, which can lead to a new insight into your first insight: I was right! (judgement). Judgement is the level of tested insight. Ford summarizes:

> *Knowing is experiencing plus understanding plus judging and the dynamism of that movement to knowledge is in questioning.* (Ford, 1999, p. 159)

However there is a fourth level, which is deciding to act. This relates to the future and requestions the present. In terms of the apple, Ford's suggestions run wild: 'Will you eat it? Cook it? Plant it? Sell it? Paint it? Throw it at someone? Contemplate it? Experiment on it?'

> *If we want to know its future we need to recognize that the answers may be affected by our decisions. In fact there is always a future horizon in our knowing – we have some aim or interest in view in pursuing questions. So orientation to the future enters into our present knowing and it can be a crucial factor in how we question and what we find out.* (Ford, 1999, p. 165)

Lonergan went on to develop four matching 'precepts': be attentive (experiencing), be intelligent (understanding), be reasonable (judging) and be responsible (deciding).

For us, however, these levels and precepts, even with the fourth 'deciding – be responsible' may be inadequate when you consider how you 'understand' in mission (and in other ways too). It seems that a fifth level of 'communicating' is also needed, for it is only when you try to communicate what you think you know (especially to 'outsiders') that knowledge is clarified in your own mind (as any lecturer should testify!) and/or challenged by the questions of the other person or people. This questioning then returns you *ad fontes* – to the sources for reconsideration.[35] Authentic mission work produces this dialogical movement. Perhaps the precept to match 'communicating' is 'be generous'?

In terms of the apple, communicating to others your delight, etc. in it focuses and thereby *intensifies* your understanding of it. Praise and worship focus and *intensify* your delight and growing understanding of God. When others are invited to join in the joy of this praise, then the 'worshipping-understanding-self' becomes also the 'sharing-understanding-self'.

heartenings: theological heart searchings

In our final section, we attempt to outline some answers to the question 'What would theology be like with mission at its centre or at its heart?' In 1995 Daniel Hardy gave a paper that relates to this question, at the inaugural consultation of the Centre for Advanced Religious and Theological Studies (CARTS) in Cambridge. This consultation, chaired by David Ford, was extraordinarily 'heartening' in that it gathered together theologians, historians, anthropologists and missiologists from Europe and Africa (including two Muslim scholars from Nigeria) to consider the central theme 'Searching for God in Europe and Africa: the Interplay of Mission, Theology and Religious Studies'. Hardy's paper was entitled 'Reshaping Faculties of Theology in Europe':[36]

> Mission is better treated as 'inter-mission', a 'sending between' of religious studies and theology, and between them and wider spheres of life and understanding. For example, mission can take the understanding of religions which is provided in religious studies and generate interaction with theology, and vice versa. But more is involved: the 'sending between' religious studies and theology is not only for the mutual interaction of two disciplines, but one which invests this interaction with the vitalities of life and understanding found more widely in the world. It is from these 'refractions' that new understanding of the purposes of God for religious studies, theology and mission will arise. (Hardy, 1996, p. 326)

So seeing mission as a form of 'inter-mission' may be helpful in forming a dynamic centre for theology which looks outwards.[37] Theology with mission at its centre or heart would recognize the double dynamic of 'movement' and 'horizon' (mentioned earlier concerning the study of mission and world Christianity) in relationship to its memory of the past, its attentiveness in the present and its expectation of the future. Again, what would this theology look like? Here are a few tentative sketches at a portrait:

It could be:

- **engaging in mission**, locally or in another culture, through prayer, experience, regular information. We can find this in expositions of Christian doctrine: it has been suggested that there is evidence that Aquinas' first magnum opus, *Summa Contra Gentiles* is a missionary apologetic engaging with Islam and written at the request of his Spanish Dominican superior, who saw a bright young theologian who would be able to counter the resurgent Muslim philosophers.[38]

- **communicating with non-theologians, non-believers and 'other believers'**, thereby pushing through to the crucial fifth level of understanding (communication – especially to 'outsiders') and to the fourth public outlined above (people of other faiths).

- **open to the insights of the cultural shapings of theology**, thereby being self-aware of its own culture as well as the contextual effects of other cultures: in addition to involving genuine doctrinal differences, Bosch has raised the question whether the Protestant Reformation can also be seen as an inculturation of the rediscovered gospel amongst the Germanic and related peoples. (Bosch, 1991, p. 453)

- **delighting in surprising sources from 'elsewhere'**, using unpublished or ephemeral material from around the world in the form of sermons, reports, poems, videos – libraries should be open to collecting these.

- **enjoying the breathtaking raising of horizons**, sometimes through geographical relocations (however temporary), sometimes through seeing a period of history from a wider perspective: an international planning consultation sponsored jointly by the International Association for Mission Studies and CARTS proposed a project 'Mission in the First Millennium'. This aims to consider, with insights from contemporary mission and world Christianity, the theological and historical movement of the gospel to the East (into Persia and China) and to the South (into Nubia and Ethiopia), as well as the (well-known) movement to the West into the Roman Empire.[39] We need to look at these living traditions as they are today, for example in India.

- **working collaboratively and dialogically with the 'unlike'** in other Christian traditions and contexts, in other faiths and other disciplines. John Mbiti, one of the fathers of African Christian Theology, with whose challenge to European and American theologians we began this chapter, went on to prophesy, 'It is utterly scandalous for so many Christian scholars in older Christendom to know so much about heretical movements in the second and third centuries, when so few of them know anything about Christian movements in areas of the younger churches. We feel deeply affronted and wonder whether it is more meaningful theologically to have academic fellowship with heretics long dead than with the living brethren of the Church today in the so-called Third World.'[40]

In these different ways the study of Christian doctrine can enrich our missiological thinking, but equally mission perspective can add a new dimension to the ways we think about doctrine. Further, we have to ask in what ways study of Christian doctrine helps us to act transformatively upon the world. How do we take what we have learned and make it the foundation of our further spiritual journey, seeking, with others, always to know more of God? How do we offer the doctrine of God as the structure for our Good News? These are particularly matters which theological education can address in the way it offers the study of Christian doctrine. Here are some questions to help focus the issues:

- How does studying the 'types of theology' help us to engage more effectively in missionary dialogue?
- How do the insights of other theologians help us re-evaluate western theological concepts?
- What sort of theology do we encounter beyond the written, academic studies?
- In what ways do people ordinarily encounter Christian doctrine? How do we hear *their* theological discourse? What difference does it make to mission?
- How do people of other faiths help us to think more deeply about our Christian theology?
- How can we develop our understanding of God through a mission perspective?

part 3 heartenings

chapter 13

mission as prophecy

mission as a defined subject within the curriculum

Throughout this work our extended conversation has been about considering what particular subjects in the theological curriculum could look like if permeated by mission thinking. We suggest this is how both teachers and students in all kinds of theological education can develop a heart for mission. Such permeation should exist, not for its own sake, or because 'mission' is a fashionable word to use, but because it can encourage the growth of personal faith and understanding in ways that equip people in ministry to transform the contexts in which we live.

why have mission as a separate subject?

However, mission is also taught as a subject in its own right in the curriculum; but would this be relevant in a curriculum permeated with missiological thinking and reflection? Moreover, does having mission as a 'subject' muddy our argument about mission as a way of looking at things that is catalysed by the study of other subjects? We have argued, for example, that we will not treat ethics as a separate 'subject' but indicate how ethics underlies the materials for study and becomes intertwined with mission: no mission without ethics. How then will we argue that 'mission' itself deserves separate and focused study?

For us, the answer to this lies in the challenges we have received in the process of doing this work. Just as so many people use the word 'mission' in different ways, so mission thinking is continually under revision. This means that the mission perspectives that permeate other disciplines must also challenge and change set materials for mission studies. In this section, then, we do not attempt to produce a paradigmatic content for the ultimate mission module, but discuss some of the issues that our dialogue with other disciplines has provoked us to explore.

The different questions that have arisen about mission also demonstrate that it is necessary to have a specific place for mission studies within the curriculum. If we rely merely on permeation and make everything mission, we can end up with nothing to call 'mission' as a particular discipline. Some of the issues we have encountered in the course of this work have required us to revise our thinking as people with expertise in mission theology and practice, and this has been an uncomfortable but exciting experience. We have had to listen to a jazz that subverts even our most dearly held ideas.

We should not be surprised by this, because we have argued that effective theological education has the capacity to disturb and surprise us, so the process of doing this work has also been an educational experience whose fruits we seek to share. For this reason, this particular chapter looks at the challenges that doing this work has set before us and we address these in the context of mission studies. We have placed this chapter in a section called 'heartenings' because engagement with other disciplines has led us to renewed vigour, vision and hope and has confirmed in us anew the heart for mission which we have sought to share. The challenges we have particularly identified come under these headings: mission theology, conversion, creation theology and eschatology, the history of missions, relations with people of other faiths, questions of practicality in relation to evangelism and the relation of mission perspective to concepts of wisdom and hope.

mission theology

what is God *really* doing?

See Chapter 2, 'the world as God sees it'.

In our work on the contexts for mission we stated that mission theology flows from an understanding of a missionary God. We have a theological language and a description of such a missionary God, which underpins the way we talk about mission. But these concepts may be too familiar and become all too easily bandied about if they remain unchallenged. We have to address the fact that criticism of the term *missio Dei* prompts us to revisit prior questions about the nature and doctrine of God. We speak of God as being continually at work in the creation; we speak of the crucified and risen Christ in our lives; and we speak of the power of the Holy Spirit; but what is God *actually* doing? We have noticed that the presupposition that God is, of God's own nature, missionary, is *not* sufficient to assume that all ministry is predicated on this understanding or follows naturally from it. What an examination of focused mission *can* do is to ask again why the concept of a missionary God, a God whose love overflows into creation and demands response, further generates a rationale for our own commitment to mission action in the world. Interaction with other disciplines in the theological curriculum therefore challenges anyone with a heart for mission to question what the outworking of mission theology must be. What *difference* does it make to be in relationship with a missionary God and what evidence of transformation will we look for as evidence of the dynamism of such a relationship? Without answering the challenge posed by this kind of question, we cannot argue effectively that we are called to be present as Christian witness in our society and to speak the prophetic word in a description of what God desires.

For example, here is a difficult and disturbing story:

> *A successful businessman suffered a serious breakdown while on a foreign business trip. One manifestation of his breakdown was a feeling of terror and the idea that he was likely to be harmed. He felt increasingly unsafe in his hotel room and fled to the streets where he rapidly became confused and ended up among other broken people, completely without resources.*

> *Once home, he told an extraordinary story of reaching a point of total disintegration out on the streets in which he felt there was nothing to hold on to and nothing to protect him. At this point of desolation, he cried out 'who will help me?' and heard clearly in his mind the words 'I will'. From that moment and in despite of his disordered thoughts and jumbled feelings, he felt that he was completely safe and had been rescued by God. Back home he began attending Church and became deeply committed to its life in the desire to share this story of being lost and then found.*

This story may polarize the question for us: is this the kind of God who generates our rationale for mission? For, on the one hand, this is a picture of an active God, searching out those who are broken, hurt, destitute and in despair. This is a God who saves by acting directly upon the creation and without reference either to the Church or to bearers of the faith. Yet there has been fruit, there is a transformation. On the other hand, are we deluding ourselves, by falsely recognizing 'God' in the way this story works itself out? How do we respond when healthcare professionals argue that the sick man's transformative experience is merely a by-product of his breakdown? The story contains 'definable units' which make sense to us (see Hoedemaker below). How do we determine what constitutes the proper action of a missionary God and how does this relationship shape our own feelings and reactions? We have argued that God sends a divine 'yes!' to the world and we respond 'yes!' to God if we have a heart for mission, but how do we ensure that we do not affirm what is *not* of the missionary God in our zeal to respond? Or, in what ways might we fail to affirm divine activity? Discernment, dialogue with others with different theological perspectives and maintaining critical reflection may be ever more important tools in a coherent mission theology in the complex world in which we now live.

conversion

The story about the businessman further asks us to consider what role we think conversion plays in the self-legitimizing of the missionary enterprise. Much of our description of mission through the five marks of mission suggests that conversion resides at the heart of our purpose and intention. Conversion and transformation are therefore markers of missionary success. Our missionary understanding is sometimes easily identified with a particular christological emphasis that reinforces the rightness (and perhaps inevitability) of conversion. Yet a global picture can demonstrate that sometimes people convert to Christianity for reasons other than a personal response to evangelism. There may be political or social reasons for the adoption of Christianity as an overt faith. What happens to our christologies then? Who is Jesus Christ for us today in a welter of complex motives and transactions? Is it less honourable to be turned around by Christ in a different way from the one we expect? The results of 'mission' may seem very different to an anthropologist or a sociologist studying the same phenomena and we have to ask what we can learn from interaction with these disciplines.[1]

conversion from Christianity

Where we are challenged to rethink what part conversion plays in our theological construction of mission, we must also take account of the reasons why people also convert *from* Christianity to other faiths, and see this as significant to our understanding. If Schreiter's argument that the

See Chapter 1, 'the world we live in'.

refusal to hear another's story in encounter causes us to witness to a 'narrative of the lie', then the wilful refusal to be challenged and changed by stories of conversion away from Christianity must similarly damage our authentic witness. Are we strong enough to respond to such rejection, or is mission only for those who respond favourably towards our presence and prophetic witness? This kind of question also challenges some of the ways in which we teach mission as a specific subject, in that we can sometimes assume that we are only learning about these things because the world out there is waiting for us. How can we carry mission into times of exile, into situations where people may listen politely and then ask us to leave? How often do we bother to listen to the faith stories of those Christians who live in countries where Christians are in a minority? The testimony of some Sudanese or Pakistani Christians, for example, can cut across forms of western mission-theological discourse in which *our* God reigns. Moreover, how do we listen to those among us whose experience of living in a multicultural society leads them to question what they believe and how they belong?

For example:

> *Amrit was brought up in a Christian household and was a member of a Christian fellowship for many years. Eventually she confided to the minister of her fellowship that her faith had 'gaps' in it which could not be filled by the life of the fellowship. These 'gaps' became more acute and caused her much distress until an aunt came to visit her family and offered to take Amrit to a Hindu temple. Amrit was impressed by the experience and, as she learned more about Hinduism, gradually began to feel that her 'gaps' (some of which were cultural) were being filled. Her parents and her Christian friends were dismayed by Amrit's warmth towards her aunt's religion and reacted with hostility. Amrit remained nominally Christian until she went to university, where she renounced Christianity and turned to Hinduism. She told her tutor that she now felt at peace and the sense of disquiet with which Christian faith had filled her had been put to rest. At the end of the university term, her family refused to receive her and she had to go and live with her aunt.*

This kind of story challenges us to think about what the 'end' of mission is. Is it to see sheep safely within the fold and then to forget about them, or does mission require a continuous dialogue with all people, Christian and non-Christian alike, in order to give encouragement and accompaniment on the spiritual journey? Theological education can provide a resource in which to look at our own 'gaps' and ask why they are there and what should be done with them. What provision does specific mission make for the assessment and critique of 'failure' in the evangelistic enterprise? This question is important because people entering ministry with a heart for mission can become profoundly discouraged when the people they serve repeatedly show indifference to sensitive evangelism and even turn away from the Church. In some cases lay people and clergy either give up or work harder and harder until they burn out. Equipping people for mission in today's world requires acknowledgement of how planting seeds and small achievements can mean a great deal. God can work with even the smallest and most insignificant of our deeds.

mission and creation theology

We have set out the case for a mission-theological understanding of ministry in Chapter 2, but in looking at specific mission we have another task to perform. We must attempt to understand with clarity how the *missio Dei* relates not only to human vocation but also to the purpose and outworking of the creation. One area which mission theology does not always properly address is the nature of value, purpose and meaning in relation to the created order. Mission is assumed to function in a *disordered* universe (as in the story about the businessman) and to concern itself with transformation for restoration. So does our definition of mission depend on our living in a fallen world? What sense do we make of God's loving action towards the creation before the Fall in the creation narratives? The missionary God has a purpose beyond merely restoring order to disorder. For this reason, we often have a very incomplete or inconsistent creation theology and with it diverse ways of thinking about both ethics and theodicy. Yet mission theology has an input here, if only we allow notions of grace, blessing, goodness, rightness and the theologies of kingdom and eschaton to interact creatively with our missionary agenda for liberation, justice and peace. Other disciplines have made clear to us that we can sometimes be lax about dealing with this effectively and this is something that mission as a focused subject can address.

mission in relation to the beginning and the end

However, if we understand mission in a very fundamental sense as the effort to hold on to a real connection between 'eschaton' and 'world' – bypassing the intermediary structures of Christianization and modernization – there might still be some room for redefinition. Of course, this fundamental theological understanding of mission was already developed to some extent in the ecumenical missionary movement: the missio Dei *formula was invented to express just that understanding. Yet* missio Dei *thinking retains a measure of modern containment. It tends to ignore the locality, plurality and ambiguity of human struggles with the humankind perspective. It remains loyal to the project of modernity in its focus on a worldwide church, and especially in its persistent use of modern concepts of culture and religion. Even terms such as inter-cultural communication and interreligious dialogue presuppose these modern concepts: cultures and religions are conceived as definable units that can be brought into relation with each other.*

How to break out of this captivity? Perhaps by reminding ourselves that the most fundamental polarity with which mission deals is not the polarity between human beings and church or Christianity, but between contextual struggles for meaning and direction on the one hand and the vision of divine judgement and reconciliation on the other. Mission is the effort to localize and actualize the promise that God is constructing one heaven and earth for a diverse and pluriform humanity; it is the reflection of the dual movement of gathering and multiplying. It is,

*to put it differently, upholding the metanarrative of human suffering
and final redemption that takes its clue in Jesus Christ.*[2]

Bert Hoedemaker directs us to an important point about the way we can
treat mission as a set of theological 'givens' or as 'strong' theology, without
engaging effectively with either the prophetic nature of mission or the
messiness of our own relationships with the multicultural world we find
around us. It is a challenge to us, to allow mission modules in theological
education to demonstrate the open-endedness of the learning process. The
study of mission can show that there are no predetermined responses to a
rapidly changing world, and in the light of Scripture and tradition we have to
respond to what we find happening around us. This is a world that *demands*
our jazz, our creative response within God's purposes. Perhaps it should be
impossible to set examination questions on the study of mission, for the
answers take not an hour, but a lifetime.

differing theologies, differing 'spirits'

the activity of the Holy Spirit

We argued throughout our work on mission and doctrine that we should
dialogue with both diverse and unfamiliar theologies. The study of mission
should therefore seek to learn from the experience of others whose contact
with different parts of the world and different outworkings of mission has
led them to see differently a world flooded by the activity of the Holy Spirit.
Cross-cultural encounter is the best way to do this and perhaps the
experience of Christians from other countries, or indeed people of other
faiths, coming into our theological institutions and living among us there,
could do much to facilitate this. In our own work we were challenged by
Kirsteen and Sebastian Kim, whose experience of teaching and learning in
British, American, Indian and Korean theological education has created for
them a complex and multifaceted view of mission. In their learning journey
they have reacted to thematic statements adopted by theological education
institutions such as 'from all nations to all nations', 'witness to the world',
'all things to all men', 'speaking the truth in love' or 'sharing life', to realize
that these are only partial descriptions of what mission can be about in
terms of a creation theology and an eschatological understanding. Indeed,
the Kims' work challenges us to ask the paradoxical question whether to be
truly a reflection of God's intention, mission must sometimes take place
outside theology.

the work of the Holy Spirit

One area in which this question becomes acute is in the missiological understanding of the work of the Holy Spirit. A western view of pneumatology can be limiting and ineffective in the context of other theological dialogues in which 'spirits' are actively doing God's work. There are problems of language and perception in receiving insights from different parts of the globe, and these can lead to serious misunderstandings that distort dialogue with other Christian thinkers. We can be so suspicious of ideas of pagan and shamanistic practice, that we can overlook the various ways in which people perceive, aid and celebrate the work of the Holy Spirit. We read pagan practice into people's testimony because our own ruling paradigm of what the Holy Spirit can and will do can be so rigid.

For example, what might we make of this?

> In the reading of the coca leaves ritual, the Yatiri or Paqu (Andean priest) invites the client to take in his hands a good portion of coca leaves, to be offered to the Yatiri. The Yatiri then will make the sign of the cross on the leaves and cross himself too. He will place a small crucifix at the top and middle of the Inkuna (ritual linen cloth), and will select perfect coca leaves to make a cross with them.

> After this preparatory procedure and in an attitude of prayer, he will proceed to invoke God the Father, Jesus Christ, the Saints, and the protective Apus for help to discover whether there is anything maleficent in the house and belongings of his client that may be causing personal or family problems. So, all during the prayerful reading of the coca leaves, he will continue to examine the signs for messages and continue to talk to his clients in an effort to verify these.[3]

In this example, we may see acts of divination and superstition glossed by Christian language and symbols. It is no better than shamanistic practice. In many such examples, we might be right to question and to critique practices which have the outward appearance of Christian trappings, or which have become idolatrous.

But our critical perception must not lead us into making only surface readings, which may prevent us from deeper understanding. In the article from which this example is taken, Domingo Llanque Chana, an Aymara theologian, argues that for these people, the whole of life is lived under the cross, their entire existence is christologically defined in a way in which our life manifestly is not. There is a challenge in this. Do we ourselves live a life in Christ that equips us to 'test the spirits'? 1 John 4.1-3a reminds us:

'Beloved, do not believe every spirit, but test the spirits to see whether they are from God; for many false prophets have gone out into the world. By this you know the Spirit of God: every spirit that confesses that Jesus Christ has come in the flesh is from God, and every spirit that does not confess Jesus is not from God.' Domingo Llanque Chana therefore suggests to us that we do not have the right to conclude that what happens in this ritual is purely shamanistic, because the transaction between the priest and the client is one in which the Holy Spirit can and will act to bring peace into their lives. This can only happen because both priest and client live out of the same christological existential understanding: Christ is all in all. The challenge for us is to get beyond simple judgements of what is and what is not the work of the Holy Spirit and to seek to discover appropriate tools for discernment. In this, cross-cultural encounter and the experience of our partners in the world Church is of great benefit, but the challenge to us remains: will it ever be possible for our own society to live out of an existential reality in which Christ is indeed this present?

Further, we may also overlook the insights of people of other faiths. Our own versions of mission thinking can sometimes produce an imperialist notion that we somehow 'own' the work of the Holy Spirit. How can we get beyond this to 'test the spirits' in a way that allows the enrichment of the world through the Spirit to become manifest? John 16.8-11 says: 'And when he [the Holy Spirit] comes, he will prove the world wrong about sin and righteousness and judgment: about sin, because they do not believe in me; about righteousness, because I am going to the Father and you will see me no longer; about judgment, because the ruler of this world has been condemned.' These words tell us that the Spirit bears witness to Christ in the world. It is *our* task to recognize and make known that witness, for we are reminded by John 16.13: 'When the Spirit of truth comes, he will guide you into all the truth.'

history of missions

Another way in which a specific mission subject can deal with challenge is to consider carefully the pluriform stories of the way the gospel has become a global reality. It is a mistake to suppose that western Christianity holds principal ownership of the missionary enterprise, rather Christianity has spread from 'everywhere to everywhere' from its apostolic beginnings and continues to be fed back to us as other cultures offer us re-evangelization. This requires us to look carefully at the political, cultural and social contexts of the missionary movement and of the history of missions, in order to understand what these do to mission thinking and practice and what they are still doing to us today in terms of what Andrew Walls calls 'the gospel as prisoner and liberator of cultures'.[4]

For example, we may take Vincent Donovan's description of the evangelistic imperative in his *Christianity Rediscovered*:

> *At that moment facing me was that vast, sprawling, all pervasive complex of customs and traditions and values and dictates of human behaviour which was the Masai [Maasai] culture, a nation in the biblical sense, to whom I had to bring the gospel. At this point I had to make the humiliating admission that I did not know what the gospel was. During those days I spent long hours thinking long, difficult thoughts, and sometimes frightening ones, about the momentous task that faced me – the bringing together of a culture and the gospel.*[5]

Beyond this sense of doubt and the notion of the missionary not as personality but as *agency*, Donovan also describes mission as 'lack' of assumptions and pre-formed intentions: 'I have no theory, no plan, no strategy, no gimmicks – no idea of what will come. I feel rather naked. I will begin as soon as possible.'[6] This directly challenges other assumptions we may have of what we have asserted all along is the necessity of being 'equipped' for mission. In Donovan's description, the missionary becomes transparent and moves aside so that God can be seen more clearly.[7] Moreover, this refusal to 'be' the missionary in the engagement between the gospel and culture gives us back a new story of what God has done – it is an epistle *from* the Maasai.

other factors

If we can grapple with this as a challenge to our received notions of mission then we must look for others. For example, Professor Andrew Porter[8] has suggested that we need to look again at the notions of missions as agents of cultural imperialism.[9] He suggests that '"cultural imperialism" associated with missionary efforts and linguistic change was not that of the expanding metropole, but of local classes and ethnic communities turning missionary offerings to their own local advantage'. He further suggests that the 'cultural imperialism' which Christianity has been judged to bring requires 'perhaps more than any other form of control – a significant measure of collaboration, compliance, and freedom to choose on the part of the colonized, something in its turn inconceivable apart from considerable flexibility and forbearance on the part of the expanding power'. He further argues that the reluctance of missions to relinquish control to indigenous peoples in terms of the management of their Christian faith, means that actual attempts to dominate and control were *not* successful.

What this means is that missiology has to look at the entire issue of complicity and at the interplay of power, control, authority and integrity in the sharing and commending of Christian faith. We saw in Chapter 8 that the matter of understanding history is highly complex, but it is tempting to read the history of missions in a simplistic way. This is *not* just a matter of setting the record straight or having a more complex and interesting view of the history of missions, but of learning real lessons about sharing the faith with others in our own society. For example, issues of complicity and the trade-off between getting what you want in exchange for some form of evangelistic encounter, are often at work in the occasional offices and even within some congregations. Is marriage preparation a form of cultural imperialism? And is the fact that we so often make people jump through strict hoops an indication of our failure? These are challenging mission questions that perhaps only focused mission studies can address.

Further, the Canadian historian, Jane Samson, has studied missionary and humanitarian imperialism in the south Pacific in the nineteenth century.[10] Here she suggests that we should look beyond the 'imperialist' notion to discover how humanitarian intervention made indigenous peoples vulnerable to exploitation by traders and others looking to capitalize on people exposed by western contacts. Brian Stanley suggests that:

> *Samson thus implies that the evangelical paternalism of the nineteenth century was not so very different from the well-meaning liberal humanitarianism of today. It is a point which today's theological educators, operating with a Christian global conscience that can too easily invest 'development' with the same absolute and self-justifying value which previous Christian generations tended to give to 'civilization' would do well to ponder.*[11]

This means that we must look again at the 'mark' of mission that enjoins us to 'respond to human need by loving service'. If such missionary service and pastoral care can make others vulnerable to exploitation, then we also have to consider what place *protection* has in the missionary enterprise. For example, if elderly people are served by the Christian community and readily open their doors to people dressed as clergy or to people who say they are Christians, perhaps we also have a missionary duty to make sure they also check for identification or ring a trusted Christian friend before allowing people in or giving money to people they do not know.

relations with people of other faiths

A specific study of the history of missions necessarily requires us to look at relations with people of other faiths and to assess what in our own contexts is possible in the contemporary mission enterprise. We live in a pluriform and multicultural society and may encounter not only people belonging to the other major world religions but also adherents of New Age practices of new religious movements, some of which are 'Christian' in origin. Again, the understanding of 'mission' in this context has to be coupled with rigorous attention to Christian ethics: it is not just a question of right action, but also of right behaviour. It is sometimes the case that theological positions in relation to interfaith matters are taught without further examination of the pastoral, social and cultural issues that face students as soon as they take up a placement or a job. Sophie Gilliatt-Ray has shown that there is a gap between teaching and practice in this respect in theological education and that the provision for such teaching varies widely.[12] Moreover, Ann Davison has shown that diverse approaches to interfaith matters across the spectrum of theological education often leave people with no further wish to explore other faiths, even if large other faith communities exist in their ministerial situations.[13] In a dedicated mission course, it may be possible to get beyond 'inclusivist' and 'exclusivist' intellectual positions and begin to make sense of living among people of other faiths and none. Making visits to places of worship belonging to people of other faiths and understanding their religious custom, observance and practice, can help to contextualize mere intellectual knowledge and make sense of the lived life of the other faith community. Further, as with 'placement', being among people of other faiths in their places of worship can challenge any sense we may have of 'rightness' and 'superiority' and ask us what mission really means when the territory is not our own.

See Chapter 6, 'styles of teaching and learning'.

faith sharing

If we desire to develop a heart for mission, we first have to discover what it is within ourselves that makes us want to share our faith with others. Where does this drive, the imperative to speak and share the Good News of Jesus Christ, actually come from? We need to understand this fully first and to know what it is about individual personality, spirituality and spiritual journey in the Christian faith that makes us people who want to share. The integrity and authenticity of our own Christian faith and hope have to be established before we can begin to listen to the faith stories and experiences of others with patience and respect.

right behaviour

Understanding ourselves as religious people should help us to respect the faith of other people and understand why they hold the traditions and beliefs that they do. Moreover, this should help us further, in studying the texts, prayers, traditions and worship of different faiths, to discriminate properly between those who follow their faith with integrity and those who abuse people in the name of that faith. Often adherents of different faiths are distressed and appalled by what others are doing in the name of that same faith in some countries and require from us not condemnation, but sympathy, support and mutual understanding. At the same time, we need to be aware of the suffering of Christians and other groups in relation to some countries in the world and to hold up this suffering before others. However, some Christians also behave badly in the name of Christ. We also need to look at what kind of repentance and forgiveness we should seek from our fellow human beings. One of the serious issues facing anyone with a heart for God's mission, is the potential for the abuse of power within the Church.

interfaith encounter as witness to others

In encounter with people of other faiths, we need to explore the possibilities inherent in every situation. Sharing of story does not automatically have to be an exposition of Christian apologetics; but exploration of similarity and difference can open up the way to enriching relationships. This having been said, encounter with deeply religious people from another faith may actually provide more opportunity for similar sharing of deeply held religious convictions than with people who do not share a similar faith vocabulary or sense of religious tradition.

For example:

> A member of the Baha'i faith, and a Christian, spent a long evening discussing how the Baha'i had coped with problems in his personal life. His wife had left him taking his children with her and he had been offered an excellent job in another country. He told his Christian friend that he had been helped and inspired by intense reading and reflection on the parable of the Good Samaritan, which convinced him that Scripture could help him, as the outsider, and by deep immersion in the parable of the Prodigal Son which helped him to envision his love for his family continuing to reach out to them no matter what the physical distance between them. Beyond the dialogue between the two of them, another person present, who remained silent and without making contribution, and who subscribed to no faith, was so moved by the

description of how the outsider could be touched and changed by Christ that her hostility to the Christian Church and her refusal to allow her family to be involved were completely changed. She remains outside the Church, but her husband has been confirmed and her children are now committed members of the local church.

This story recalls the point in Chapter 12 about the presence of Christ in every encounter, whose availability is not restricted just to the participants.

We need to explore how relations with people of other faiths should allow us to pursue agenda for common issues of interest such as justice, peace and reconciliation. People of other faiths often look to Christian communities for partnership or advocacy, and we need to explore this as a missionary task in which this trust should not be squandered or abused. Beyond this, there are also important situations in which Christian pastoral care is required for people from other faiths crossing boundaries, in, for example, interfaith marriages. This again is a powerful mission challenge in order to determine what is appropriate in each pastoral situation for nurture of the whole family. We also need to look at how the building up of a 'missionary congregation' can include a sensitive understanding of relations with people of other faiths. Sometimes Christians who are sensitive and sharing with others at church functions and events, display a quite different and unacceptable way of behaving in the workplace where people of other faiths are present. Peer pressure and work relationships can make it difficult for people to stand up for the rights of others and to stand alongside them against the abuse they may suffer. As people with a heart for mission, our first task may well be to address a history of community and cultural hostilities and to effect reconciliation and respect for people of other faiths.

Focusing the study of mission precisely through encounter, dialogue and relationships with people of other faiths can break open a whole range of issues that commonly make mission precepts and the 'marks' of mission difficult in practice. Careful exploration of what makes us want to share our faith and the ways in which it is possible to do so can help us unpack the questions of appropriate evangelism.

evangelism

Although evangelism often forms a major component of mission studies, there are particular challenges here to which we must respond, especially in the relation of evangelistic practice to ethics. A specific mission course permits attention to be paid to the particular matter of evangelism and its outworking in practical applications. For us, it is not helpful merely to rehearse all the arguments for particular methods and ideas in evangelism, but to approach this through the mechanism of *analogy*. That is to say, our efforts in evangelism successfully reach out to others when they present a picture of what life *could* be like if lived in Christ. It is the difference that offering of change makes in people's lives that allows the Holy Spirit to work. Again, presenting the evangelistic witness as another person's possibility, brings up the matter of attention to ethics. The way we live and behave has a direct bearing on our ability to evangelize, but at the same time, if not attended to, tars us with the brush of hypocrisy.

proclamation

Proclamation, as acts of testimony, conviction or witness, makes powerful statement and sense in a context where the personal integrity of the one who proclaims, perhaps with visibly changed life, is accepted and understood by the hearers. Acts of testimony, whether in church, on the street, in the workplace or on a programme like *Songs of Praise* can evoke responses of sympathy and spiritual resonance, which help others to see the possibility of a similar commitment.

For example:

> On Sunday evening of 8 July 1962 ... I was confronted by another gospel evangelist, preaching the same gospel of certainty ... I stayed on after the preacher was finished and walked with him to the bus station. I said that I knew (intellectually) the particular passages about new birth and 'God so loved the world, etc.' but I was still troubled in my heart. I knew that I must surrender my self-centred will to His will but had not yet done so. The evangelist did not attempt to 'argue' me into the kingdom but said that we should bow our heads and he would pray for me. As they say 'you could have knocked me over with a feather'. I was 'defeated' by this. The Holy Spirit shifted the 'centre of gravity' from my will being done to accepting that the sovereign will of the Lord Jesus Christ was to be the primary guiding principle in my life.[14]

For some people, analogy is the sense-making apparatus: my life is as that life was; my life could be as that life now is. In others, the evangelist is the midwife for a new birth, permitting the self to discover a new orientation of the will as in the above story. Acts of giving life over to Christ therefore impose a particular burden of ethical responsibility on the Christian community, since it is done in the hope and expectation that the same life has the possibility of henceforth being filled with promise and hope.

Transformation is at the heart of the gift. Many people fall away from faith after the first heady flush of conversion, because they discover that little seems to have changed and the Christian community has turned its attention to others; responsibility has been abnegated in terms of evangelism as an end in itself.

sharing and accompanying

Similarly, helpful emphases in evangelistic technique, such as *Telling Your Faith Story*,[15] allow the sharing of stories to become the basis for faith sharing. There is important responsibility here, too, because many people have sequencing problems with storytelling and get lost if narratives are too complex, too long or filled up with too many issues. Yet theological education itself may equip students with very sophisticated abilities, especially in enabling people to deal with text and with narrative. This may leave us more liable to leave people struggling to cope with our sermons, homilies, addresses, talks, explanations and simple faith sharing. Many people articulate the desire for faith sharing that comes down to the articulation of a promise that *all will be well* as is demonstrated by the popularity of certain kinds of memorial verses in local papers.

For example:

> *Please treasure her God,*
> *in your garden of rest*
> *For on earth our Mags*
> *was one of the best.*

The people who use this kind of language give us important clues to their heartfelt desire for God in a discourse quite different from our sophisticated theological language. Yet here is the desire for the investment of our love for others to be found in God, the promise made to us that God's love is indeed a redeeming love. Who, if not us, will help people to reach out for and take hold of that promise for themselves. Again, evangelism in the story-sharing context may require a simple analogical process: what I am looking for is a life *like this*.

Another matter arising from a consideration of evangelism in theological education is that theological education itself often equips us to deal effectively with *words*, so that this means of communication becomes the most favoured and the most used. In writing this report we are ourselves deeply conscious of our dependence on words for theological discourse and that is why we have tried to introduce reflection on other kinds of media into our own times of sharing and prayer.[16] Yet, *Telling your Faith Story* and faith-sharing of all kinds, can be fostered by use of images, video presentations, drawings, storyboards, music and role-play. The memorizing and retelling of stories in different ways can be an important missionary act.

hospitality and embassy

Evangelism as a result of the relationship between hospitality and embassy can also be explored as an appropriate means of sharing the gospel in many different contexts. *Alpha* is one obvious example where meals are used to precisely this effect, but there is no reason why a church fete or social should not offer precisely the same opportunities. Similarly, meals in residential courses of theological education can be just as significant a part of theological education as learning information. Hospitality means breaking down boundaries and allowing others into personal territory. It also works reciprocally – we should also be prepared to accept the hospitality of others in an appropriate way. This is so often overlooked by those lay and ordained people in ministry who visit people in their homes. Refusing people's hospitality, or misuse of the space they make to accommodate people who enter their homes (even in tiny ways) can make a big difference to the way those we visit come to view Christian people and their behaviour.

For example:

> Monica, a lay worker on an urban estate, visited Jenny, a very houseproud elderly widow, after a stroke in which Jenny lost the use of one of her arms. Monica was very kind and caring, but announced that the house was now dusty and dirty and that she would find Jenny someone to clean her house. A cleaning lady arrived and upset Jenny by 'doing it her way'. Meanwhile, Dorothy, a friend from church, came to see Jenny and saw how upset she was about her house being made 'different' though more 'hospitable'. Without discussing it, she said to Jenny she remembered how lovingly she would take care of her collection of brass ornaments and held each one for Jenny while she gave them a wipe with her good hand. In this way, Jenny was able to 'repossess' her things and make the house pleasant and welcoming again for visitors.

how practical are mission and evangelism in today's climate?

The story above is included in order to show how little things are as important as large evangelistic enterprises and may indeed be all that is actually possible in today's western society. Although we have spent much of this work discussing how a heart for mission may be fostered in theological education, there is another matter to be considered alongside the contexts for mission, which is the context of the Church itself in this country. What use is it, developing a vision of the kingdom, powerful desire for justice and transformation, and a heart for mission, when the scant resources available may make the task of doing mission impossible?

lack of resources

Mission as a discrete subject in the curriculum may focus on strategies such as church planting, the establishment of *Alpha* and *Emmaus* courses,[17] other Christian basics courses, housegroups and other means of faith sharing in ministry, but in practical terms, these matters may be simply items on a wish list. Maintenance, in the face of financial stringency, may absorb all human resources. Just keeping the set-up going may take every fragment of a minister's time and more. In certain ministry situations, there may seem to be no mission possibility whatsoever and, for those who have spent time in theological education developing a heart for mission, this may be depressing, frustrating and a challenge to faith.

dealing with failure and frustration

Consequently, mission as a separate subject also needs to deal with the possibilities of failure and frustration and look for sources of encouragement and hope which people in ministry in today's churches may find. One such source of hope is that small things matter to God. Maintenance can be mission. Transformation can be effected by the sowing of a few tiny seeds. Every encounter contains a possibility and opens up a new relationship. The biggest problem is perhaps in accepting that there may not be *rewards*, so that, for many people in ministry, faith is sapped, strength dwindles, energy levels fall and relationships falter. Clergy stress is not necessarily all due to overburdening, but can include the consequence of so little feedback and so few opportunities for refreshment and energizing. There is an urgent mission question then, which asks: *what do we expect to get out of mission and ministry?* If students emerge from their theological college or course 'placement' full of enthusiasm and excitement, then the reality of a frustrating ministry may hit them hard if strategies and resources are not adequately offered. The hope that people want from us also needs to be offered to ourselves.

the coming of wisdom

Where does this hope come from? This is an important question for a
specific mission studies course because it can cross the gap between
learning about mission and the experience of *being in* mission. In this way
it is a vital part of equipping for mission. In his address to the Primates'
meeting in Kanuga, North Carolina, on 5 March 2001, Professor Daniel
Hardy suggested that:

> *God gives their truth and holiness to all things, and opens the possibility
> of truth and holiness to all insofar as they receive them. That is why we
> need to be shaped in this truth and holiness; as they are given to the
> world and to us, we need in some very fundamental sense to be
> conformed to them.*[18]

Again here, there is the assertion that there is no mission without ethics,
but this time with the sense that mission, ethical understanding and
theological education are profoundly linked with God's desire for us to grow
in wisdom and stature as Jesus did. Further, Professor Hardy argues that
there are a number of implications relating directly to the way we perceive
hope in the missiological enterprise through theological education. Learning
wisdom is inherent in Christian faith and manifests itself as a deeply felt
need in us. We need to respond appropriately and this lays a particular kind
of responsibility upon us. Moreover, all forms of learning are ways in which
human beings can be shaped in truth and holiness by God. Our faith and
our theology give us the means by which to recognize this. Theological
reflection allows us to reach a deepening sense of the movement of God's
life and purposes in the world.

We have spoken of the need to have a heart for mission, but Professor
Hardy spoke further of the scriptural descriptions of the transformation
of the heart, a transformation which is at the centre of Christian hope and
which energizes the possibility of transformation in the world. Nor should
we ever expect to complete our learning, for 'patient, long-term formation
of human beings in God's truth and holiness, compassion and love, is
all that is available to us who struggle with what it is right to do in our
situations' (Hardy, 2002, pp. 172–3). This means that all who teach
and all who study can be free from the burden that they must somehow
encompass all of a subject, including mission; rather, all of us can
recognize the desire and need to learn which a period of theological
education can freshly awaken in us.

the long view

Therefore we end this section on the challenges to learning mission as a particular subject by turning to this prayer from Archbishop Oscar Romero, martyred on 24 March 1980, which articulates this hope in the context of both presence and prophecy.

*It helps, now and then, to step back
and take the long view.
The kingdom is not only beyond our efforts,
it is beyond our vision.*

*We accomplish in our lifetime only a tiny fraction of
the magnificent enterprise that is God's work.
Nothing we do is complete,
which is another way of saying
that the kingdom always lies beyond us.*

*No statement says all that could be said.
No prayer fully expresses our faith.
No confession brings perfection.
No pastoral visit brings wholeness.
No programme accomplishes the church's mission.
No set of goals and objectives includes everything.*

*This is what we are about:
We plant seeds that one day will grow.
We water seeds already planted, knowing that they hold future promise.
We lay foundations that will need further development.
We provide yeast that produces effects beyond our capabilities.*

*We cannot do everything
and there is a sense of liberation in realizing that.
This enables us to do something,
and to do it very well.
It may be incomplete, but it is a beginning, a step along the way,
an opportunity for God's grace to enter and do the rest.*

*We may never see the end results,
but that is the difference between the master builder and the worker.
We are workers, not master builders,
ministers, not messiahs.
We are prophets of a future not our own.*[19]

Here are some questions for discussion on the challenges to
mission thinking:

- In what way is the *missio Dei* an unhelpful theological concept?
- Is mission only really possible in a disordered world?
- How does mission thinking which affects the here and now relate
  to eschatology?
- How do we avoid simplistic notions of conversion?
- Where and how do we perceive the activity of the Holy Spirit in
  our world?
- How does mission history help us to act transformatively in our
  own situations?
- How does the study of mission help us make good relationships
  with people of other faiths?
- What do you see as the difference between evangelism and mission?
- What is the role of hospitality in evangelism?
- In what ways is it practical for today's Christians to be involved
  in mission?
- How can we find hope for ourselves and offer it to others?

chapter 14

conclusion

Mission is one and it's God's Mission. We are invited to share in his work
of reconciliation, and that reconciliation was achieved through the blood
of the cross. We come therefore as Christ's Ambassadors, delivering the
message of the King in the language of those to whom we are sent. It is
therefore about moving on from where we are, or even sometimes going
back to the community from which we came. It's worth remembering the
confused and angry young man who called himself Legion when Jesus
asked his name. After the Bay of Pigs incident, the local farmers found him
sitting at Jesus' feet, clothed and in his right mind. When Jesus is leaving
he asks to go with him but Jesus says, 'No, go back to the city and tell
them what God has done for you'. And the wonder is that, restored and
made whole, he can go back ... Mission and evangelism flow naturally
from worship, the overflowing of a grateful heart. And that reminds us
yet again of one of the themes I would want us to hold on to, which is
about abundance, hospitality, courtesy, which is modelled for us by the
Trinity, that loving interdependent community to which through the cross
Christ is taking us back. One of the liturgy tutors here warns some of his
more evangelical students that liturgy is important – there's a lot of
worship in heaven. I believe that eternity will be about worshipping the
Father and laughing with the Son and dancing in the Spirit.[1]

See
'introduction'.

This was Marion Mort's reminder to the participants at the *Making Christ*
Known conference, that the end of all our theological education resides in
this Trinitarian vision of God's overflowing love. Without the knowledge and
experience of this love, there is no mission and no transformation. At the
end of our teaching and learning together, no matter how much study and
effort has been involved, this love is still held out to us, encouraging us and
sustaining us for mission in God's world.

The end of this work does not mark the end of our conversations. It cannot
be finished because there is always more to be said about God and more
of God's love to be shared with other people. There are more questions
to be asked, more wondering and dreaming to be done. There are more
challenges waiting to undermine our simple assumptions and our
complacency. There is more work to be undertaken to see transformation
become a reality in the lives of the people around us. All of these things
inform our ministry as the whole people of God. Mission perspective and

mission focus help us make sense of trying to walk in God's way, not just because we are called to make a difference now, but because of the hope of heaven that is before us. It is not just our intellectual life, but our emotions and spirituality are invested as well: 'worshipping the Father and laughing with the Son and dancing in the Spirit'. For our desire to be a missionary people stems from gratitude, from thanksgiving for what God has done in Christ. If we can be grateful for all our theological education can give us, for study, fellowship and worship together, we can be responsive to the promptings of the Holy Spirit. Through Christ, we enter a missionary purpose that eternally comes to us, straight from the heart of God.

notes

Introduction

1. Quotations come from the report of the conference, *Making Christ Known: Mission in Ministerial Education and Training*, April 1994.
2. MTAG, *The Search for Faith and the Witness of the Church*, Church House Publishing, 1996.
3. Contact: Dr Anne Richards, Board of Mission, Church House, Great Smith Street, London, SW1P 3NZ or see www.ccom.org.uk

part 1 settings

chapter 1 the world we live in

1. We have had some discussion about how to refer to people outside Europe and North America. We are aware that the term 'non-western' is in use, but we hope to avoid this as it carries the implication that the West sets the norm. Consequently, we use 'world' Christianity and 'world' theology to include the life and insights of Christians beyond the western paradigm.
2. As suggested by Jo Moore, when special adviser to Stephen Byers, the former Transport Secretary.
3. Michael Moynagh, chapter 2: 'Hello, It-Must-Fit-Me World' in *Changing World, Changing Church*, Monarch/Administry, 2001.
4. Dr Peter May, a former member of the Board of Mission, cited the case of a patient who, having recovered from her symptoms, kept an appointment solely for the purpose of rebuking him for the length of his waiting list (personal communication).
5. So there is a proliferation of companies offering 'no win no fee' compensation for accidents.
6. All our stories are true illustrations from our own experience. Names have been changed in all instances.
7. So the Church of England has recently considered changing its regulations about where and how people can get married. See the report from the Aspects of Marriage Law Working Group, *Just Cause or Impediment*, General Synod paper 1436, Archbishops' Council, October 2001.
8. It is used by the European Value Systems Study Group in this way and so is used here. Note that Ivan Illich was writing about the notions of 'upper limits' in the 1970s.
9. Reported in the *Metro*, Wednesday 23 January 2002, p. 6.
10. So *Eternal Light, Music of Inner Peace*, by the Canonesses of the Holy Sepulchre, New Hall (Deutsche Grammophon, 2001) went to the top of the classical charts.
11. We have had some discussion of the right term to use here. Some writers use 'two-thirds world' or 'non-western world'. No phrase is perfectly accurate and we have opted for 'third' in inverted commas to indicate the provisionality of the description. We are aware that we cannot convey completely how those to whom we refer would describe themselves.
12. Professor Anthony Giddens, Reith Lectures 1999, no. 1, *Globalisation* – text downloaded from the Internet. See www.lse.ac.uk/Giddens/reith.htm.

13. *The Times*, 12 September 2001, pp. 1,2 and 4.
14. There are other interpretations of this parable, such as an argument from the lesser to the greater, as in the parable of the unjust judge. There are also different emphases in Matthew and Luke.
15. Finance companies often advertise suggesting that we should release our capital, or take out loans for gain 'now'. People may also donate money to charities that include a feel-good factor, children, animals, medical research. This means that *stewardship* becomes an important mission issue.
16. See Peter Selby, *Grace and Mortgage*, Darton, Longman & Todd, 1998.
17. Reprinted in the Board of Social Responsibility's *Crucible*, Spring 1999, p. 8.
18. See *Tertio Millennio Adveniente*, Catholic Truth Society, 1994.
19. Walter Brueggemann, *Theology of the Old Testament*, Fortress Press, 1997, p. 189.
20. See Michael Nazir-Ali, chapter 11: 'Jubilee: a theme for the Millennium' in *Citizens and Exiles*, SPCK, 1998, especially pp. 150–52.
21. Patrick Logan, *Biblical Reflections on the Political Economy of Jubilee*, Southwark Diocesan Board for Church in Society, 1997, p. 27.
22. See *Breaking New Ground: Church Planting in the Church of England*, General Synod report 1099, Church House Publishing, 1994, pp. 9–10.
23. Work by the Revd Dr Andrew Linzey, Professor of Theology and Animal Welfare in the University of Oxford, has particularly highlighted the importance of clarifying the Christian response to the place of animals within the creation and our responsibility towards and relationships with them.
24. Hans Küng, *Global Ethic for Global Politics and Economics*, SCM Press, 1997.
25. Robert Schreiter, *Reconciliation: Mission and Ministry in a Changing Social Context*, Orbis Books, 1992.
26. See the 'Powers' Trilogy: *Naming the Powers*, Fortress Press, 1994; *Unmasking the Powers*, Fortress Press, 1986; and especially part 2 of *Engaging the Powers*, Fortress Press, 1992.
27. We use this word following our discussion with Martin Palmer, who argued that people want something that is like, or of, Christ, but beyond our conventional christologies.
28. James Bennett interview with Tori Amos, *The Times* 'Metro' section, Saturday 11 April 1998, p. 8.
29. Centre for the Study of Human Relations, University of Nottingham, August 2000.
30. We ourselves have included contemplation of things as diverse as a piece of sculpture, Harry Potter novels and a Muppet video in our times of prayer and reflection.
31. For a report on the Millennium experience, see Stephen Lynas, *Challenging Time*, Churches Together in England/Church House Publishing, 2001.

chapter 2 the world as God sees it

1. John V. Taylor, *The Uncancelled Mandate, Four Bible Studies on Christian Mission for the Approaching Millennium*, Board of Mission Occasional paper no. 8, Church House Publishing, 1998, p. 19.
2. World Council of Churches document, 'Mission and evangelism in unity today', *International Review of Mission*, lxxxviii, Jan–Apr 1999, p. 111.
3. When it was first set up, the Church of England's Archbishops' Council notably had 'Ministry' in one unit and 'Mission' in a separate unit entitled 'Church and World'.
4. See *Building Missionary Congregations*, Church House Publishing, 1995.
5. See *The Gospel in a Pluralist Society*, SPCK, 1989.
6. Daniel W. Hardy, from his paper, discussed at MTAG, *The Orientation of STETS*, p. 3. His

thoughts on this matter are set out in full in *Finding the Church*, SCM Press, 2002.

7. See *Transforming Mission: Paradigm Shifts in Theology of Mission*, Orbis Books, 1991.

chapter 3 the 'marks' of mission

1. For example, the five marks of the Anglican Consultative Council (see below); the ten marks in MTAG's *The Measure of Mission*, Church House Publishing, 1987.
2. ACC 8, p. 101, *The Truth Shall Make You Free: Report of the 1988 Lambeth Conference*.
3. As argued by Robert Schreiter in *Reconciliation: Mission and Ministry in a Changing Social Context*, Orbis Books, 1992.
4. A Ridley Scott film, 2000.
5. Walter Wink recommends undertaking both kinds of analysis simultaneously. He suggests a kind of historical spirituality audit for determining the 'angel of a church', on the basis of which it is possible to make more informed and discerning judgements about what is appropriate mission in a given context. See his 'Powers' trilogy, especially *Unmasking the Powers*, pp. 69ff.
6. The necessity of building up the spirituality at the centre of a congregation is a central premise of Robert Warren's *Building Missionary Congregations*, Church House Publishing, 1995.

chapter 4 people in ministry and mission

1. He tells his story in *Faith in Life*, Churches Information for Mission, November 2001, p. 7.
2. 'Criteria for selection': excerpted from *The Report of a Working Party on Criteria for Selection for Ministry in the Church of England*, ABM Policy Paper no. 3B, October 1993, pp. 10, 12.

chapter 5 some stories

1. From 'Stories' sent in prior to the Lambeth Conference 1998, section 2.
2. So Mary speaks of her lifelong ministry in the church passing from doing a large number of things to a ministry of prayer, in *Faith in Life*, Churches Information for Mission, November 2001, p. 2.
3. For example, a Baptist minister opened his door to find a box on his doorstep. The box contained a sick dog. The accompanying note said: 'Please put my dog down and say a prayer'.
4. See, for example, Dong-Kun Kim, 'Korean Minjung Theology in history and mission' in *Studies in World Christianity*, vol. 2, part 2, 1996, p. 174.

chapter 6 styles of teaching and learning

1. For further examples, see the accounts of the importance of theological training given by individuals in Andrew Wingate, *Does Theological Education Make a Difference? Global Lessons in Mission and Ministry from India and Britain*, Risk series, World Council of Churches Publications, 1999.
2. We are grateful to Ian Stubbs for being part of our conversation on this subject and to Maxine Green for helping us understand the issues.
3. The philosopher and novelist Jostein Gaarder suggests that it is our job after death to tell God all we have seen and done. See *Through a Glass Darkly*, Orion, 1998, p. 153.
4. In the Roman Catholic Church, and in the Orthodox traditions, the Assumption provides a

picture of Mary, as the mother of Christ, bringing her life and experience back into God's presence. The crowning of the Virgin also provides an image of God's affirmation of that life and of Mary's part in nurturing and preparing Jesus for his ministry. Manifestly, the Ascension and the Assumption are not equivalent pictures, but these Christian traditions assert the meeting points between the Godhead and the human condition.

5. Or as Frank Kermode concludes: 'the world is our beloved codex. We may not see it, as Dante did, in perfect order, gathered by love into one volume; but we do, living as reading, like to think of it as a place where we can travel back and forth at will, divining congruences, conjunctions, opposites; extracting secrets from its secrecy, making understood relations, an approximate algebra. This is the way we satisfy ourselves with explanations of the unfollowable world – as if it were a structured narrative, of which more might always be said by trained readers of it, by insiders.' *The Genesis of Secrecy*, Harvard University Press, 1979, p. 145.

6. David Hay and Kate Hunt, *Understanding the Spirituality of People Who Don't Go to Church*, University of Nottingham, 2000.

7. David Hay and Rebecca Nye, *The Spirit of the Child*, HarperCollins (Fount), 1998, p. 109.

8. Janice Price, *Telling our Faith Story*, Church House Publishing, 1998.

9. This does not mean that we should dismiss the importance of learning effectively from people who know more than ourselves. Indeed, our own practice has been to invite experts in different fields to talk to us so that we can learn from their wisdom. The difference for us has existed in the capacity for dialogue and discussion and for our own reflection to help determine and evaluate and to own what we have learned. The learning experience is therefore much more than 'banking', for in the process as mission 'experts' we have learned a great deal about what we ourselves do not know.

10. See, for example, the discussion of how people are recognized and affirmed for a ministry of evangelism in *Good News People*, Church House Publishing, 1999.

11. P. Freire and A. Faundez, *Learning to Question: a Pedagogy of Liberation*, World Council of Churches Publications, 1989, p. 40.

12. Jenny Savage, Pastoral Placement Report to the Board of Mission, 1998.

13. The Revd Dr Peter K. Stevenson of Spurgeon's College, London (personal communication).

14. This quotation comes from the Anglican Diocese of Chelmsford's leaflet. The purpose of the groups is 'to grow a culture of care and support available to those in ministry accessible throughout the Diocese'. Further information from Dr Anne Richards.

15. Peter Price, *Telling it as it is: Interactive Learning for Churches Building Small Christian Communities*, New Way Publications, 1999, p. 17.

16. The opposition here between education for replication and for transference is not meant to imply that the theological education in the churches does not affect and transform individuals quite profoundly. It is rather attempting to point to what people have been enabled *to do* with what is undoubtedly a transforming experience.

17. The autobiography of Peter Owen Jones, written about his experiences at Ridley Hall, Cambridge, bears this out. See *Bed of Nails*, Lion Publishing, 1997.

18. Paulo Freire, *The Pedagogy of the Oppressed*, Penguin (new revised edition), 1993, p. 75.

19. For example, in 'Mission possible', Bishop Roger Sainsbury's attempts to become a truly missionary bishop, forming relationships for transformation of his diocesan area, are set out. See the paper by Steve Griffiths: 'Mission possible, reflections on the story of a Bishop's mission', November 2001. Permission to reproduce this and further details from RevSGriff@aol.com.

20. Steve Griffiths, 'Mission possible'.

21. See Robert Warren, *Building Missionary Congregations*, Church House Publishing, 1995, pp. 3–4.
22. As noted above, it is also a process question: how free are educators within the church to design their own programmes?

part 2 illuminations

chapter 8 mission and Church history

1. Francis Fukuyama, 'The end of history', *The National Interest*, no. 16, Summer 1989, pp. 3–18.
2. Simon Schama, *A History of Britain*, BBC Worldwide, 2000, pp. 16-17.
3. See Tom O'Loughlin, 'Theologians and their use of historical evidence: some common pitfalls', *The Month*, January 2001, pp. 30–35.
4. Our gratitude goes especially to the Revd Canon Vincent Strudwick and to Dr Brian Stanley for some lively debate and stimulating presentations.
5. Or 'wie es eigentlich gewesen', von Ranke, quoted in E. H. Carr, *What is History?*, Pelican, 1987, p. 8.
6. Murray G. Murphey, *Philosophical Foundations of Historical Knowledge*, State University of New York, 1994, p. 324.
7. See, for example, John Kent, *The Unacceptable Face: The Modern Church in the Eyes of the Historian*, SCM Press, 1987.
8. In cultures other than our own, with powerful oral traditions, the blending of human history, through stories of the ancestors, and faith in God, is often far more integrated.
9. See www.serve.com/thibodep/cr/jvanier.htm.
10. See *The German Ideology* by Karl Marx and Frederick Engels, International Publishing, 1971, reprinted 1993.
11. Elisabeth Schüssler Fiorenza, *Jesus: Miriam's Child, Sophia's Prophet: Critical Issues in Feminist Christology*, SCM Press, 1995, pp. 57–63.
12. So in chapter 5 of *The Search for Faith and the Witness of the Church* (Church House Publishing, 1996), we argued that we need to pay close attention to the history of ideas and in particular to those stories that are much less likely to get a hearing inside the Church.
13. Oliver Davies, *Celtic Christianity in Early Medieval Wales*, University of Wales Press, 1996, p. 1.
14. *Past Times* catalogue, Christmas 2001.
15. So the *Past Times* version of a 'Celtic Christmas' is 'a mystical midwinter celebration of fire and light', Christmas catalogue 2001, p. 6.
16. Lavinia Byrne (ed.), *The Hidden Journey: Missionary Heroines in Many Lands*, SPCK, 1993.
17. Andrew F. Walls, *The Missionary Movement in Christian History: Studies in the Transmission of the Faith*, Orbis Books/T & T Clark, 1996, p. 105.
18. Vincent Strudwick, 'The teaching of Church history with a missionary perspective in theological colleges', *Ambassador*, no. 18, Autumn 1999, pp. 4–8.
19. Brian Stanley, 'The history of mission in the theological curriculum', a paper presented at MTAG, 2 November 1999, p. 9.
20. Andrew Porter, 'Cultural Imperialism and the Protestant missionary enterprise 1780–1914', *Journal of Imperial and Commonwealth History*, 25/3, September 1997, pp. 367–91, quoted in Brian Stanley, 'The history of mission in the theological curriculum', 2 November 1999, p. 9.

21. Norman Davies, *The Isles*, Macmillan, 1999. See also *Europe, A History*, Oxford University Press, 1996, and Davies' assertion that 'History can be written at any magnification' (revised edition, 1997, p. 1).

22. See Schubert Ogden's 'Introduction' in Mary Potter Engel and Walter E. Wyman Jnr (eds), *Revisioning the Past*, Fortress Press, 1992, pp. 1–10, p. 6.

23. *Revisioning the Past*, 1992, p. 7.

24. *Revisioning the Past*, 1992, p. 5.

25. O'Loughlin is particularly talking about the Roman Catholic Church.

26. Tom O'Loughlin, 'Medieval Church history: beyond apologetics, after development: the awkward memories', *The Way*, no. 38, 1998 (pp. 65–76).

27. See above p. 27.

28. See Anne Hope and Sally Timmel, *Training for Transformation: A Handbook for Community Workers* (books 1–4, Mambo Press, Zimbabwe, 1984) for an education process that has applied Freire's 'problem-posing' rather than 'solving' methodology.

29. See John Hull's book of the same name, London, SCM Press, 1985.

chapter 9 mission and the Bible

1 the Hebrew Scriptures

1. Chaim Potok, *In the Beginning*, Penguin, 1976.

2. In this section on the Hebrew Scriptures, we have been particularly indebted to the Revd Dr Chris Wright, whose thematic approach we have most closely followed.

3. We have called this first part a study of the 'Hebrew Scriptures', rather than 'Old Testament', but this raises further questions. What might 'Hebrew Scriptures' mean to e.g. Arab Christians?

4. These questions parallel those in modern cosmology, where scientists are intrigued by the question 'Why does the universe go to the bother of existing?' and by versions of the so-called 'anthropic principle' which wonders if the way the universe is relates to our ability to observe it.

5. David Bosch, *Transforming Mission*, Orbis Books, 1991.

6. Walter Brueggemann, *The Prophetic Imagination*, Fortress Press, 1978, p. 97.

7. So Jesus refers to Jonah's final obedience to God and conversion of Nineveh as the only 'sign' to be given to a self-deceiving generation (Matthew 12.39; Luke 11.29).

8. Brian Keenan, *An Evil Cradling*, Vintage edition, 1993, p. 238.

9. See Walter Brueggemann, *Hopeful Imagination: Prophetic Voices in Exile*, Fortress Press, 1986, Part 1, pp. 9–47.

10. *Hopeful Imagination*, but also see Part 3.

11. Walter Brueggemann, *Biblical Perspectives on Evangelism: Living in a Three-storied Universe*, Abingdon Press, 1993, p. 15.

12. See Walter Brueggemann, *Theology of the Old Testament*, Fortress Press, 1997, chapter 10 'Ambiguity and the Character of Yahweh' pp. 359ff.

13. Norman Clayton, copyright © 1938, 1943 Wordspring, CopyCare. It is to be found in hymnbooks such as *Mission Praise*, Marshall Pickering, 1990.

14. Michael Nazir-Ali, *Mission and Dialogue: Proclaiming the Gospel Afresh in Every Age*, SPCK, 1995, p. 15.

15. See Raymond Fung, *The Isaiah Vision: Ecumenical Strategy for Congregational Evangelism*, Risk series, World Council of Churches Publications, 1992.

16. John V. Taylor, *The Uncancelled Mandate*, Church House Publishing, 1998, p. 21.

17. For example, see René Girard, *Things Hidden since the Foundation of the World*, Athlone Press, 1987.

18. See *Engaging the Powers*, chapter 7, and his critique of Girard, pp. 152ff.
19. This is the provocative description provided by Louis de Bernières in his introduction to the *Book of Job*, pocket canons, Canongate Books, 1998.

2 the New Testament

1. Alan Le Grys, *Preaching to the Nations: The Origins of Mission in the Early Church*, SPCK, 1998.
2. David Bosch, *Transforming Mission*, Orbis Books, 1991, pp. 15–16.
3. James Carleton Paget, 'Jewish proselytism at the time of Christian origins: chimera or reality?', *Journal for the Study of the New Testament* 62 (1996) pp. 65–103, p. 75.
4. We are indebted to the Revd John Proctor of Westminster College, Cambridge, for all his help to us at both these consultations.
5. Here we are following Richard Bauckham's ideas on *Mission as a Hermeneutic for Scriptural Interpretation*, using a paper synopsis from his Henry Martyn seminar, 1 November 1999.
6. Joan Bakewell writing in the *Guardian*, 30 April 2001, pp. 14–15.
7. N. T. Wright, *Christian Origins and the Question of God*, vol. 1, *The New Testament and the People of God*, SPCK, 1992; vol. 2, *Jesus and the Victory of God*, SPCK, 1996.
8. The section on N. T. Wright which follows is largely drawn from a paper given by John Proctor at a consultation set up by MTAG on Mission and the New Testament at Westminster College, Cambridge, in June 1999.
9. See, for example, Christopher Cocksworth, *Holy, Holy, Holy – Worshipping the Trinitarian God*, Darton, Longman & Todd, 1997.
10. *The New Testament and the People of God*, pp. 262–8, with references to numerous texts; *Jesus and the Victory of God*, pp. 308–10.
11. See, for example, works by Ann Morisey and Ken Leech, such as Ken Leech, *The Eye of the Storm: Spiritual Resources for the Pursuit of Justice*, Darton, Longman & Todd, 1999 (reprint).
12. And Chris Wright has pointed out to us that in Luke 24 Jesus gives his disciples a fundamental lesson in hermeneutic of the Hebrew Scriptures. His opening of the Scriptures, in all sections of the Hebrew canon, is both messianic and missiological.
13. See Robert Warren, *Building Missionary Congregations*, Church House Publishing, 1995, and *Being Human, Being Church*, Marshall Pickering, 1995.
14. We can argue that we see transmission of the 'suffering' idea to a theological exposition in the Pauline epistles and also in Hebrews, but here, the idea becomes something different and is annexed to eschatological expectations. Must we then use our hermeneutical key to determine how apostolic theology leads us to Jesus?
15. Richard Bauckham, *Mission as Hermeneutic for Scriptural Interpretation* lecture.
16. M. Goodman, *Mission and Conversion: Proselytizing in the Religious History of the Roman Empire*, Oxford University Press, 1994.
17. Carleton Paget comments on 'proselytism' as positing that other religions are unsatisfactory and thus starting dialogue in a negative light. On this reading proselytism is not possible where religions are tolerant of each other's presence. See p. 72.
18. *Jewish Proselytism* invites us to look again at the conversion to Judaism of Adiabene and his household in Josephus in respect of this, pp. 78,100.
19. Here again we can be helped by the theological reflection of cultures other than our own, reading back to us their hopes, expectations and fears when the Christian faith was shared among them. What did they expect to hear and to receive? See e.g. Teresa Okuré, *The Johannine approach to Mission: A Contextual Study of John 4.1-42*, Tübingen, Mohr, 1988.

chapter 10 mission and worship

1. J. G. Davies, *Worship and Mission*, SCM Press, 1967, pp. 12–13.
2. We are also grateful to the Liturgical Commission of the Church of England for the opportunity to discuss this material with them and for their helpful comments.
3. Daniel W. Hardy and David F. Ford, *Praising and Knowing God*, Westminster Press, 1985.
4. Additional Curates Society, *Good News*, Autumn/Winter edition 2001, p. 8.
5. St Augustine, *Confessions*, Book 1, 1.
6. For the Israelites, the cult was a liturgical extension of the historical ('saving') events of the Exodus and Sinai, just as for Christians it is a liturgical extension of the historical ('saving') events of the life of Jesus Christ. However, other religions surrounding the Israelites were founded upon mythic events.
7. See note 6.
8. See St Thomas Aquinas, *Summa Theologiae*, a Concise Translation, by Timothy McDermott (ed.), Methuen, 1989, pp. 131–9.
9. This is reflected in hymns such as George Herbert's 'Teach me, my God and King,' with the verse: 'A servant with this clause makes drudgerie divine ...'; in Charles Wesley's 'Forth in thy name, O Lord, I go, my daily labour to pursue' with the words: 'The task thy wisdom hath assigned, O let me cheerfully fulfil'; in John Keble's 'New every morning is the love' with the verse: 'The trivial round, the common task, will furnish all we need to ask.'
10. Dr Brian Castle remarked to MTAG that in his experience of residential theological colleges, the two most common causes of discontent are the chapel and the dining room. If there is contentment about worship and food, then other aspects of community life easily fall into place.
11. For a fuller development of this see Brian Castle, 'Mission: Curricular Issues', *Ministerial Formation*, January 1999.
12. For example, at a church with a mixed congregation in South London, the organist, who had a dislike of members he saw as 'catholic' stocked the choir with like-minded people and filled services with choruses and modern hymns. The justification for this was that it had attracted some new people to the church, but it also alienated the 'traditional' congregation who gradually defected to another church down the road, splitting the community.
13. See Anne Richards, on behalf of the MTAG, *The Toronto Experience: An Exploration of the Issues*, Board of Mission Occasional paper no. 7, Church House Publishing, 1997.
14. Norman J. Clayton, Norman Clayton Publishing Co/Word Music (UK)/CopyCare Ltd, 1971. *Mission Praise*, no. 374.
15. R. W. Dale, quoted by Horne, Silvester, 'Free Church history', p. 250, quoted in L. E. Elliott Binns, *Religion in the Victorian Era*, Lutterworth Press, 1946, p. 374.
16. David Bosch, *Transforming Mission*, Orbis Books, 1991.
17. 'Religious community' refers to communities of believers and not to specialist religious orders.
18. K. Kritzinger, 'Studying religious communities as agents of change', unpublished lecture, 8 June 1995.
19. For example, Deuteronomy 10.8; 24.17.
20. William Temple, *Christian Faith and Life*, SCM Press, p. 19.
21. *Common Worship: Services and Prayers for the Church of England*, CHP 2000, p. 182.
22. A. Yannoulatos in Ion Bria (ed.), 'Martyria-Mission: the witness of the Orthodox Churches today', World Council of Churches Publications, 1980 p. 67, quoted in Ion Bria, *The Liturgy After the Liturgy*, World Council of Churches Publications, 1996, p. 20.

23. Report from Section III of the World Council of Churches' 1980 conference on world mission and evangelism in Melbourne, para. 31 in *Your Kingdom Come: Mission Perspectives*, World Council of Churches Publications, p. 205, quoted in Brian Castle, 'Mission: Curricular Issues', *Ministerial Formation*, January 1999, p. 21.
24. M. Kinnamon (ed.), *Signs of the Spirit: Official Report of the WCC Seventh Assembly*, World Council of Churches Publications, 1991, p. 119, quoted ibid. p. 21.
25. See Note 8, p. 4.
26. Walter Wink, *Engaging the Powers*, Fortress Press, 1992, p. 299.
27. *Faith in Life*, the Church Life Profile found that 'traditional forms of worship' rated highly on a list of what people enjoyed about church. Unsurprisingly, this response came mainly from the older age groups (Churches Information for Mission, November 2001).
28. Don E. Saliers, *Worship Come to Its Senses*, Abingdon Press, 1996, p. 50.
29. So *Faith in Life* found personal devotion going on outside church but not at the same frequency as worship in church, pp. 15, 19.
30. See www.jesuit.ie/prayer/

chapter 11 mission and pastoral care

1. Stephen Pattison, *Pastoral Care and Liberation Theology*, SPCK (paperback edition), 1997, p. 67.
2. The rubrics referred to in the following section were written up in a paper entitled 'A brief review of the development of the relationship between Psychology, Pastoral Theology and Mission as viewed through the development of the Oxford Bachelor of Theology Rubric', by Revd Dr Brian Castle and presented to MTAG in 2000.
3. David Bosch, *Transforming Mission*, Orbis Books, 1991, p. 390.
4. David Hay and Kate Hunt, *Understanding the Spirituality of People who don't go to Church*, University of Nottingham, 2000, especially, p. 35.
5. Again, David Hay and Kate Hunt show that while there may be great bitterness towards the institution which is seen as controlling and judgemental, there might be great desire for and goodwill towards Christian faith. The missionary task in reaching out to such people requires sensitive and appropriate pastoral care, in order to make healing of the bitterness possible and to allow that residual goodwill to allow connection with the spiritual search. See especially their reflections on 'mission', op. cit., pp. 37–42.
6. John V. Taylor, *The Uncancelled Mandate*, Church House Publishing, 1998, p. 13.
7. David F. Ford, *The Shape of Living*, HarperCollins, 1997, pp. 103–4.
8. David Hay and Rebecca Nye, *The Spirit of the Child*, HarperCollins (Fount), 1998.
9. As James Joyce puts it, after a graphic description of a hell-fire and damnation sermon in *A Portrait of the Artist as a Young Man*, Triad/Panther edition, 1977, p. 115.
10. *The Uncancelled Mandate*, in the chapter on 'God's time'.

chapter 12 mission and doctrine

1. *Third Way*, December 1989/January 1990, vol. 12. no. 12, p. 44.
2. J. S. Mbiti, 'Theological Impotence and the Universality of the Church' in G. Anderson and T. Stransky (eds), *Mission Trends No. 3* (Paulist Press/Eerdmans, 1976), p. 17.
3. 'There is no indication in the advertising that theological reflection exists in other languages.'
4. David Ford, *Theology: A Very Short Introduction*, Oxford University Press, 1999, p. 31.
5. This deliberately echoes Anselm's definition of theology, *fides quaerens intellectum* (faith seeking understanding).

6. See Michael Nazir-Ali, *From Everywhere to Everywhere: A World View of Christian Mission*, Collins, 1991.

7. For further elaborations on this theme see Graham Kings, 'Evangelicals in search of Catholicity: theological reflections on Lausanne II', *Anvil*, vol. 7, no. 2, 1990, pp. 115–28, and 'The redress of mission' *Anvil*, vol. 16, no. 1, 1999, pp. 7–11.

8. This may be too comfortable a figure for some, since a great deal of creative mission and theological thinking is done amidst violence and poverty and oppression, but it has various profound biblical resonances.

9. *The Search for Faith and the Witness of the Church*, Church House Publishing, 1996, pp. 154–5. Readers interested in an overview of the development of Christian doctrine in relation to heretical thought will find this in Chapter 5 as we have not repeated the material here, but rather concentrated on mission in relation to contemporary thought.

10. Kwame Bediako, 'African theology' in David F. Ford, *The Modern Theologians* (Blackwells, 1989 and 1997) pp. 435–6. It is worth comparing the two editions. The newer edition is more global in scope: a chapter on theology of mission (by Lamin Sanneh) is included together with detailed chapters on Asian and Latin American theologies as well as Africa.

11. So John Pobee writes: 'this attempt to construct an African theology in the English language is the second best, even if it is convenient if it should secure as wide a circulation as possible.' *Toward an African Theology*, 1973, p. 23, quoted in Bediako, 'African theology' (n. 10), p. 436.

12. Hans Frei, *Types of Christian Theology*, edited by George Hunsinger and William C. Placher, Yale University Press, 1992, cited in Ford, *Modern Theologians*, p. 14 (see pp. 2–3 for a summary); and Ford, *Theology*, pp. 23-32. In *Modern Theologians*, Ford explains why, in that book, he numbers the types in reverse order.

13. See Ford, *Modern Theologians*, pp. 2–3, for further examples considered in that book.

14. For another typology, which focuses on contextual theologies and has fascinating missiological comments, see Stephen Bevans, *Models of Contextual Theology*, Orbis Books, 1992. In the updated edition Bevans includes a 'counter-cultural' model with John Milbank as an example.

15. Earlier Ford had commented that this type 'frequently displays ... the "superiority complex" of much modernity'. Ford, *Theology*, p. 24.

16. Ford, *Modern Theologians*, p. 3.

17. Raymond Panikkar, *The Unknown Christ of Hinduism*, Darton, Longman & Todd, 1964. His revised and enlarged edition, Raimundo Panikkar, *The Unknown Christ of Hinduism: Towards an Ecumenical Christophany*, Orbis Books, 1981, makes a considerable move into 'pluralist' mode.

18. Kwame Bediako, *Theology and Identity: the Impact of Culture upon Christian Thought in the Second Century and Modern Africa*, Regnum Press, 1992, and *African Christianity: the Renewal of a Non-Western Religion*, Edinburgh University Press, 1995. For a critique of Bediako see the review of *African Christianity* by John Parratt in *International Review of Mission*, lxxxiv, nos 332/333 (Jan/Apr 1995).

19. David Bosch, *Transforming Mission*, Orbis Books, 1991, pp. 492–6. For a critique and appreciation see Willem Saayman and Klippies Kritzinger (eds), *Mission in Bold Humility: David Bosch's Work Considered*, Orbis Books, 1996.

20. Warren was General Secretary of the Church Missionary Society from 1942–63 and Taylor succeeded him from 1963–74. See Graham Kings, 'Mission and the meeting of faiths: the theologies of Max Warren and John V. Taylor' in Kevin Ward and Brian Stanley (eds), *CMS and World Christianity, 1799–1999*, Curzon Press, 1999. See also David Wood, *Poet, Priest and Prophet: Bishop John V. Taylor*, CTBI, 2002.

21. David Tracy, *The Analogical Imagination: Christian Theology and the Culture of Pluralism*, SCM Press, 1981.
22. David F. Ford, *A Long Rumour of Wisdom: Redescribing Theology*, Cambridge University Press, 1992.
23. Kenneth Cragg, *Troubled By Truth: Life-Studies in Inter-Faith Concern*, The Pentland Press, 1992.
24. Vincent Donovan, *Christianity Rediscovered: An Epistle from the Maasai*, SCM Press, 1978 and 1982.
25. Ford, *Theology*, pp. 141–2, concerning Frances Young and David F. Ford, *Meaning and Truth in 2 Corinthians*, SPCK, 1988.
26. David F. Ford, *Self and Salvation*, Cambridge University Press, 1999.
27. Which is very different from 'self-worship' cf. the quip, 'He is a self-made man who worships his maker'.
28. It is interesting that Thérèse's writings and conversations included frequent specific mention of missionaries and missions. Her bad health prevented her from going to Hanoi to work, but she kept in constant prayer two key missionaries Maurice Bellière (Africa) and Adolphe Roulland (China). In 1927 both she and Francis Xavier were together affirmed as 'patrons of all missions'. See Mary Fröhlich, 'Mission patrons' in Karl Müller *et al.* (eds), *Dictionary of Mission: Theology, History, Perspectives* Orbis Books, 1997, pp. 311–14.
29. David Ford, *Self and Salvation*.
30. Paul Ricoeur, *Figuring the Sacred: Religion, Narrative and Imagination*, Fortress Press, 1995, pp. 116–17 in Ford, op. cit., p. 83.
31. T. S. Eliot, 'The Waste Land', lines 159–65, *Complete Poems and Plays of T. S. Eliot*, Faber, 1969, p. 73.
32. John V. Taylor, *The Primal Vision*, SCM Press, 1963, pp. 34–5.
33. Max Warren, *Theology of Attention*, Christian Literature Society and Indian SPCK, 1971, p. 6.
34. Bernard Lonergan, *Insight: A Study of Human Understanding*, Longman, Green, 1957; *Method in Theology*, Darton, Longman & Todd, 1972.
35. For an example, see Graham Kings, 'Facing Mount Kenya: the Bible and African traditional religion', *Anvil*, vol. 4, no. 2, 1987, pp. 127–43.
36. This is published as chapter 18 in Daniel W. Hardy, *God's Ways with the World: Thinking and Practising Christian Faith*, T & T Clark, 1996, pp. 311–27. See also chapter 29 for a profound sermon on mission and chapter 3, 'The Future of Theology in a Complex World' (which considers 'context' in particular). Hardy has been involved in centring the new theological curriculum on mission of the Southern theological training course – STETS – and from the autumn of 1999 is co-chairing a new series of seminars on Theology and Mission for the Currents in World Christianity project in Cambridge.
37. Theology 'wearing its heart on its sleeve'?
38. 'It seems ... that the SCG did not have a Christian audience in view but rather, through the teaching of Christian missionaries, an intellectual Arab audience.' Anton C. Pegis in the introduction to the *Summa Contra Gentiles*, Book 1, University of Notre Dame Press, 1975, p. 26.
39. See Winrich Loehr, 'Mission in the first millennium', *Mission Studies*, vol. xv 2/30, 1998, pp. 29–39.
40. J. S. Mbiti, 'Theological impotence ...', p. 17. In this regard, two important contextual theological networks are The Ecumenical Association of Third World Theologians (EATWOT) who publish a series through Orbis Books, Maryknoll, New York, and the International Fellowship of Evangelical Mission Theologians (INFEMIT) who publish a series through Regnum Press, Oxford.

part 3 heartenings

chapter 13 mission as prophecy

1. See S. Kim, doctoral thesis on *A study of debates on religious conversion in India 1947–1999 from the perspective of Christian mission*, University of Cambridge, 2001.
2. Bert Hoedemaker, 'Mission beyond modernity' in *Christian Mission in Western Society*, eds Simon Barrow and Graeme Smith, Churches Together in Britain and Ireland, 2001, pp. 230–31.
3. Domingo Llanque Chana, 'Ritual and the Christian life of Andean people', *Studies in World Christianity*, vol. 1, 1977, p. 64. The whole of this article is worthy of study in order to understand Domingo Llanque Chana's argument.
4. Andrew F. Walls, *The Missionary Movement in Christian History: Studies in the Transmission of Faith*, Orbis Books/T & T Clark, 1996, chapter 1.
5. Vincent J. Donovan, *Christianity Rediscovered: An Epistle from the Maasai*, SCM Press, 1978 and 1982, p. 31.
6. *Christianity Rediscovered: An Epistle from the Maasai,* SCM Press, 1978 and 1982, p. 16.
7. This is also a stated intention of, for example, Jerome Berryman's *Godly Play* programme, in which children are encouraged to dream about, look for and encounter God, aided but not blocked by adults.
8. We are indebted to Dr Brian Stanley for calling our attention to the work of Dr Porter and Jane Sansom, below.
9. Andrew Porter. '"Cultural imperialism" and Protestant missionary enterprise, 1780–1914', *Journal of Imperial and Commonwealth History*, 25/3, September 1997, pp. 367–91.
10. Jane Sansom, *Imperial Benevolence: Making British Authority in the Pacific Islands*, University of Hawaii Press, 1998.
11. Brian Stanley, *The History of Mission in the Theological Curriculum*, 2 November 1999.
12. Sophie Gilliatt-Ray, *The Theological Education of Anglican Clergy for Ministry in a Multi-faith Britain*, research project 1996–2001, University of Warwick.
13. Ann Davison, doctoral thesis on interfaith training in the Diocese of Chelmsford, St Mary's College, University of Surrey, 2000.
14. F. Knaggs, personal communication.
15. Janice Price, *Telling Our Faith Story*, Church House Publishing, 1998.
16. This is available as a resource (*Transparencies*) from autumn 2002.
17. The *Alpha* course is pioneered by Holy Trinity, Brompton and is a 13-week course exploring some of the basics of the Christian faith. *Emmaus: The Way of Faith* is a set of six resource books covering all aspects of the evangelistic process from initial contact through to growth as a Christian. Published by National Society/Church House Publishing, 1996.
18. Daniel W. Hardy, *Finding the Church*, SCM Press, 2002, p. 170.
19. See Michael J. Walsh, *Archbishop Oscar Romero: The Voice of the Voiceless*, Orbis Books, 1995, and http://rrnet.com/~sedagah/oarpry.htm

Conclusion

1. Marion Mort, 'Contributions from a consultant', *Making Christ Known: Mission and Evangelism in Ministerial Education and Training*, April 1994.

bibliography

works cited in the text

Bediako, Kwame, *African Christianity: The Renewal of a Non-Western Religion*, Edinburgh University Press, 1995.

Bediako, Kwame, *Theology and Identity: The Impact of Culture upon Christian Thought in the Second Century and Modern Africa*, Regnum Press, 1992.

Bevans, Stephen, *Models of Contextual Theology*, Orbis Books, 1992.

Elliott Binns, L. E., *Religion in the Victorian Era*, Lutterworth Press, 1946.

Bosch, David, *Transforming Mission*, Orbis Books, 1991.

Bria, Ion, *The Liturgy After the Liturgy*, World Council of Churches Publications, 1996.

Brueggemann, Walter, *Biblical Perspectives in Evangelism: Living in a Three-storied Universe*, Abingdon Press, 1993.

Brueggemann, Walter, *Hopeful Imagination: Prophetic Voices in Exile*, Fortress Press, 1986.

Brueggemann, Walter, *The Prophetic Imagination*, Fortress Press, 1978.

Brueggemann, Walter, *Theology of the Old Testament*, Fortress Press, 1997.

Byrne, Lavinia (ed.), *Hidden Journey: Missionary Heroines in Many Lands*, SPCK, 1993.

Carleton Paget, James, 'Jewish proselytism at the time of Christian origins: chimera or reality?', *Journal for the Study of the New Testament*, no. 62, 1996.

Carr, E. H., *What is History?* Pelican, 1987.

Chana, Domingo Llanque, 'Rituals and the Christian life of Andean people' in *Studies in World Christianity*, vol. 3, part 1, 1997.

Cocksworth, Christopher, *Holy, Holy, Holy: Worshipping the Trinitarian God*, Darton Longman & Todd, 1997.

Cragg, Kenneth, *Troubled By Truth: Life-Studies in Inter-Faith Concern*, The Pentland Press, 1992.

Davies, J. G., *Worship and Mission*, SCM Press, 1967.

Davies, Norman, *Europe: A History*, Oxford University Press, 1996 (revised edition, 1997).

Davies, Norman, *The Isles*, Macmillan, 1999.

Davies, Oliver, *Celtic Christianity in Early Medieval Wales*, University of Wales Press, 1996.

de Bernières, Louis, introduction to the *Book of Job*, Pocket Canons Series, Canongate Books, 1998.

Eliot, T. S., 'The Waste Land', in *Complete Poems and Plays of T. S. Eliot*, Faber, 1969.

Engel, Mary Potter, and Wyman, Walter E. Jnr (eds), *Revisioning the Past*, Fortress Press, 1992.

Fiorenza, Elisabeth Schüssler, *Jesus: Miriam's Child, Sophia's Prophet: Critical Issues in Feminist Christology*, SCM Press, 1995.

Ford, David F., *Self and Salvation: Being Transformed*, Cambridge University Press, 1999.

Ford, David F., *Theology: A Very Short Introduction*, Oxford University Press, 1999.

Ford, David F., *The Shape of Living*, HarperCollins, 1997.

Ford, David F., *A Long Rumour of Wisdom: Redescribing Theology*, Cambridge University Press, 1992.

Ford, David F., *The Modern Theologians*, Blackwells, 1989 and 1997.

Frei, Hans, *Types of Christian Theology*, Hunsinger, George, and Placher, William C. (eds), Yale University Press, 1992.

Freire, Paulo, *The Pedagogy of the Oppressed*, Penguin, 1993.

Freire, P., and Faundez, A., *Learning to Question: A Pedagogy of Liberation*, World Council of Churches Publications, 1989.

Fukuyama, Francis, 'The end of history', *The National Interest*, no. 16, Summer 1989.

Fung, Raymond, *The Isaiah Agenda: Ecumenical Strategy for Congregational Evangelism*, Risk series, World Council of Churches Publications, 1992.

Gaarder, Jostein, *Through a Glass Darkly*, Orion, 1998.

Girard, René, *Things Hidden since the Foundation of the World*, Athlone Press, London 1987.

Goodman, M., *Mission and Conversion: Proselytizing in the Religious History of the Roman Empire*, Oxford University Press, 1994.

Griffiths, Steve, 'Mission possible: reflections on the story of a bishop in mission', May 2001. Contact RevSGriff@aol.com.

Hardy, Daniel W., *Finding the Church*, SCM Press, 2002.

Hardy, Daniel W., *God's Ways with the World: Thinking and Practising Christian Faith*, T & T Clark, 1996.

Hardy, Daniel W., and Ford, David F., *Praising and Knowing God*, Westminster Press, 1985.

Hay, David, and Hunt, Kate, *Understanding the Spirituality of People Who Don't Go to Church*, University of Nottingham, 2000.

Hay, David, and Nye, Rebecca, *The Spirit of the Child*, HarperCollins (Fount), 1998.

Hoedemaker, Bert, 'Mission beyond modernity' in Barrow, Simon, and Smith, Graeme (eds), *Christian Mission in Western Society*, Churches Together in Britain and Ireland, 2001.

House of Bishops working party, *Good News People*, Church House Publishing, 1999.

Hull, John, *What Prevents Christian Adults From Learning*, SCM Press, 1985.

Joyce, James, *A Portrait of the Artist as a Young Man*, 1916, Triad/Panther edition, 1977.

Keenan, Brian, *An Evil Cradling*, Vintage edition, 1993.

Kent, John, *The Unacceptable Face: The Modern Church in the Eyes of the Historian*, SCM Press, 1987.

Kermode, Frank, *The Genesis of Secrecy*, Harvard University Press, 1979.

Kim, Dong-Kun, 'Korean Minjung theology in history and mission' in *Studies in World Christianity*, vol. 2, part 2, 1996.

Kings, Graham, *Christianity Connected: Hindus, Muslims and the World in the Letters of Max Warren and Roger Hooker*, Mission series 31, Zoetermeer, Boekencentrum, 2002.

Kings, Graham, 'Facing Mount Kenya: the Bible and African traditional religion', *Anvil*, vol. 4, no. 2, 1987.

Küng, Hans, *Global Ethic for Global Politics and Economics*, SCM Press, 1997.

Le Grys, Alan, *Preaching to the Nations: The Origins of Mission in the Early Church*, SPCK, 1998.

Leech, Ken, *The Eye of the Storm: Spiritual Resources for the Pursuit of Justice*, Darton Longman & Todd, 1999 (reprint).

Loehr, Winrich, 'Mission in the first millennium', *Mission Studies*, vol. 15 2/30, 1998.

Logan, Patrick, *Biblical Reflections on the Political Economy of Jubilee*, Southwark Diocesan Board for Church in Society, 1997.

Lonergan, Bernard, *Insight: A Study in Human Understanding*, Longmans, Green, 1957.

Lonergan, Bernard, *Method in Theology*, Darton, Longman & Todd, 1972.

Lynas, Stephen, *Challenging Time*, Churches Together in England/Church House Publishing, 2001.

Marx, Karl, and Engels, Frederick, *The German Ideology*, International Publishing, 1971, reprinted 1993.

Mort, Marion, 'Contributions from a consultant', *Making Christ Known: Mission and Evangelism in Ministerial Education and Training*, April 1994.

Moynagh, Michael, *Changing World, Changing Church*, Monarch/Administry, 2001.

MTAG, *The Search for Faith and the Witness of the Church*, Church House Publishing, 1996.

Müller, Karl (ed.), *Dictionary of Mission: Theology, History, Perspectives*, Orbis Books, 1997.

Murphey, Murray G., *Philosophical Foundations of Historical Knowledge*, State University of New York Press, 1994.

Nazir-Ali, Michael, *From Everywhere to Everywhere: A World View of Christian Mission*, Collins, 1991.

Nazir-Ali, Michael, 'Jubilee: a theme for the Millennium' in *Citizens and Exiles*, SPCK, 1998.

Nazir-Ali, Michael, *Mission and Dialogue: Proclaiming the Gospel Afresh in Every Age*, SPCK, 1995.

Newbigin, Lesslie, *The Gospel in a Pluralist Society*, SPCK, 1989.

Okuré, Teresa, *The Johannine Approach to Mission: A Contextual Study of John 4.1-42*, J. C. B. Mohr, 1988.

O'Loughlin, Tom, 'Medieval church history: Beyond apologetics, after development: the awkward memories', *The Way*, 38, 1998, pp. 65–76.

O'Loughlin, Tom, 'Theologian and their use of historical evidence: some common pitfalls', *The Month*, January 2001.

Owen Jones, Peter, *Bed of Nails*, Lion Publishing, 1997.

Panikkar, Raymond, *The Unknown Christ of Hinduism*, Darton, Longman & Todd, 1964.

Pattison, Stephen, *Pastoral Care and Liberation Theology*, SPCK (paperback edition), 1997.

Pegis, Anton C., Introduction to *Summa Contra Gentiles*, Book 1, University of Notre Dame Press, 1975.

Porter, Andrew, '"Cultural Imperialism" and the Protestant Missionary Enterprise 1780–1914', *Journal of Imperial and Commonwealth History*, 25/3, September 1997.

Potok, Chaim, *In the Beginning*, Penguin, 1976.

Price, Janice, *Telling Your Faith Story*, Church House Publishing, 1999.

Price, Peter, *Telling It as It Is: Interactive Learning for Churches Building Small Christian Communities*, New Way Publications, 1999.

Richards, Anne, *The Toronto Experience: An Exploration of the Issues*, Board of Mission Occasional paper no. 7, Church House Publishing, 1997.

Ricoeur, Paul, *Figuring the Sacred: Religion, Narrative and Imagination*, Fortress Press, 1995.

Saayman, Willem, and Kritzinger, Klippies (eds), *Mission in Bold Humility: David Bosch's Work Considered*, Orbis Books, 1996.

Saliers, Don E., *Worship Come to Its Senses*, Abingdon Press, 1996.

Sansom, Jane, *Imperial Benevolence: Making British Authority in the Pacific Islands*, University of Hawaii Press, 1998.

Schama, Simon, *A History of Britain*, BBC Worldwide, 2000.

Schreiter, Robert, *Reconciliation: Mission and Ministry in a Changing Social Context*, Orbis Books, 1992.

Selby, Peter, *Grace and Mortgage*, Darton, Longman & Todd, 1998.

Strudwick, Vincent, 'The teaching of Church history with a mission perspective in theological colleges', *Ambassador*, vol. 18, Autumn 1999.

Taylor, John V., *The Primal Vision*, SCM Press, 1963.

Taylor, John V., *The Uncancelled Mandate: Four Bible Studies on Christian Mission for the Approaching Millennium*, Board of Mission Occasional paper no. 8, Church House Publishing, 1998.

Temple, William, *Christian Faith and Life*, SCM Press, 1963.

Tertio Millennio Adveniente, Catholic Truth Society, 1994.

Tracy, David, *The Analogical Imagination: Christian Theology and the Culture of Pluralism*, SCM Press, 1981.

Walls, Andrew F., *The Missionary Movement in Christian History: Studies in the Transmission of Faith*, Orbis Books and T & T Clark, 1996.

Ward, Kevin, and Stanley, Brian (eds), *CMS and World Christianity, 1799–1999*, Curzon Press, 1999.

Warren, Max, *Theology of Attention*, Christian Literature Society and Indian SPCK, 1971.

Warren, Robert, *Being Human, Being Church*, Marshall Pickering, 1995.

Warren, Robert, *Building Missionary Congregations*, Church House Publishing, 1995.

Wingate, Andrew, *Does Theological Education Make a Difference?: Global Lessons in Mission and Ministry from India and Britain*, Risk series, World Council of Churches Publications, 1999.

Wink, Walter, *Powers Trilogy: Naming the Powers*, Fortress Press, 1994; *Unmasking the Powers*, Fortress Press, 1986 and *Engaging the Powers*, Fortress Press, 1992.

Wright, N. T., *Christian Origins and the Question of God*; vol. 1, *The New Testament and the People of God*, SPCK, 1992; vol. 2, *Jesus and the Victory of God*, SPCK, 1996.

some resources

suggested further reading

ACCM, *Education for the Church's Ministry* (ACCM paper 22), 1987.

Advisory Board of Ministry, *Servants and Shepherds* (Ministry paper 19), Church House Publishing, 1998.

Advisory Board of Ministry, *Shaping Ministry for a Missionary Church* (Ministry paper 18), Church House Publishing, 1998.

Arbuckle, Gerald A., *Grieving for Change*, Geoffrey Chapman, 1991.

Barrow, Simon, *Presence and Prophecy Study Guide* (for MTAG), Church House Publishing/CTBI, 2002.

Barrow, Simon (ed.), *Expanding Horizons: Learning To Be the Church in the World*, Church in Society Publications, 1995.

Bennett Moore, Zoe, 'Pastoral theology as hermeneutics', *British Journal of Theological Education*, 12/1, 2001, pp. 7–18.

Bosch, David, *Believing in the Future: Toward a Missiology of Western Culture*, Trinity Press International, 1995.

Bowen, Roger, *So I Send You: A Study Guide to Mission*, SPCK, 1996.

Brown, Callum G., *The Death of Christian Britain: Understanding Secularisation 1800–2000*, Routledge, 2001.

Brueggemann, Walter, *Hope for the World: Mission in a Global Context*, Westminster/John Knox Press, 2001.

Clark, David (ed.), *Changing World, Unchanging Church?* Mowbray, 1997.

Cracknell, K., and Lamb, C. (eds), *Theology on Full Alert*, British Council of Churches, 1986.

Davie, Grace, *Religion in Modern Europe: A Memory Mutates*, Oxford University Press, 2002.

Evans, Gillian, *The Reception of the Faith: Reinterpreting the Gospel for Today*, SPCK, 1997.

Fukuyama, Francis, *The Great Disruption: Human Nature and the Reconstitution of the Social Order*, Profile Books, 1999.

Greenwood, Robin, *Practising Community: The Task of the Local Church*, SPCK, 1996.

Hastings, Adrian, *A History of English Christianity 1920–1990*, SCM Press, 1991.

Hinton, Jeanne, *Changing Churches: Building Bridges in Local Mission*, Churches Together in Britain and Ireland, 2002.

Jenkins, Philip, *The Next Christendom*, Oxford University Press, 2002.

Kim, Kirsteen, 'Mission studies in Britain and Ireland: Introduction to a

World Wide Web', *British Journal of Theological Education*, 11/1, 2000, pp. 72–86.

Leech, Kenneth, *Soul Friend: Spirituality and Pastoral Care*, Darton, Longman & Todd, 1994.

Marriage, Alwyn, *The People of God: A Royal Priesthood*, Darton, Longmann & Todd, 1995.

Ministry Division, *Reader Ministry and Training 2000 and Beyond*, Church House Publishing, 2000.

Ministry Division, *Mission and Ministry: The Churches' Validation Framework for Theological Education*, Church House Publishing, 1999.

Mission Theological Advisory Group, *Transparencies*, Church House Publishing/CTBI, 2002.

Mission Theological Advisory Group, *Good News in Our Times: The Gospel and Contemporary Cultures*, Church House Publishing, 1991.

Moltmann, Jürgen, *God for a Secular Society: The Public Relevance of Theology*, SCM Press, 1999.

Montefiore, Hugh (ed.), *The Gospel and Contemporary Culture*, Mowbray, 1992.

Nazir-Ali, Michael, *Citizens and Exiles: Christian Faith in a Plural World*, United Church Press, 2000.

Nazir-Ali, Michael, *Shapes of the Church to Come*, Kingsway, 2001.

Newbigin, Lesslie, *Truth and Authority in Modernity*, Trinity Press International, 1996.

Nissen, Johannes, *New Testament and Mission: Historical and Hermeneutical Perspectives*, Peter Lang, 1999.

Okuré, Teresa (ed.), *To Cast Fire upon the Earth: Bible and Mission Collaborating in Today's Multicultural Global Context* (A project of BISAM – an interest group of IAMS), Cluster Publications, 2000.

Page, Ruth, *God With Us: Synergy in the Church*, SCM Press, 2000.

Sanneh, Lamin, *Religion and the Variety of Culture: A Study in Origin and Practice*, Trinity Press International, 1997.

Schreiter, Robert, *Mission in the Third Millennium*, Orbis Books, 2001.

Schreiter, Robert, *The New Catholicity: Theology between the Global and the Local*, Orbis Books, 1997.

Shorter, Aylward, *Evangelization and Culture*, Geoffrey Chapman, 1994.

Wessels, Antonie, *Secularized Europe: Who will Carry off its Soul?* World Council of Churches Publications, 1996.

Williams, Rowan, *Lost Icons: Reflections on Cultural Bereavement*, T & T Clark, 2000.

Wood, David, *Poet, Priest and Prophet: Bishop John V. Taylor*, CTBI, 2002.

Wright, Chris, 'The Old Testament and Christian mission', *Evangel* 14/2, 1996, pp. 37–43.

Wright, Chris, 'Christ and the mosaic of pluralisms', in Taylor, W. D. (ed.), *Global Missiology for the 21st Century: The Iguassu Dialogue*, Baker Academic, 2000, pp. 71–99.

Wright, Chris, *Knowing Jesus through the Old Testament*, Marshall Pickering IVP-USA, 1997.

Wright, Christopher J. H., *Deuteronomy*, New International Biblical Commentary, Hendrikson; Paternoster, 1997; Introduction, 'The missiological significance', pp. 8–17.

Yates, Timothy (ed.), *Mission: An Invitation to God's Future*, Cliff College Publishing, 2000.

Yates, Timothy, *Christian Mission in the Twentieth Century*, Cambridge University Press, 1994.

organizations

British and Irish Association for Mission Studies
Henry Martyn Centre
Westminster College
Cambridge CB3 0AA
www.martynmission.cam.ac.uk/BIAMS

Centre for Missiology and World Christianity
Graduate Institute for Theology and Religion
University of Birmingham
Elmfield House, Bristol Road
Selly Oak
Birmingham B29 6LQ
www.bham.ac.uk/theology/cwmc

Churches' Commission on Mission
Churches Together in Britain and Ireland
Inter-Church House
35–41 Lower Marsh
London SE1 7SA
www.ccom.org.uk

Currents in World Christianity Project
Westminster College
Cambridge CB3 0AA
www.divinty.cam.ac.uk/CARTS/cwc/default

Oxford Centre for Mission Studies
PO Box 70
Oxford OX2 6HB
www.ocms.ac.uk

Partnership for World Mission
Partnership House
157 Waterloo Road
London
SE1 8UU

Further information, resources, web sites and contact information can be obtained from:

Dr Anne Richards
Mission Theology Adviser
Church House, Great Smith Street
London SW1P 3NZ

index

related titles from the Mission Theological Advisory Group

Presence and Prophecy Study Guide

A heart for mission in theological education

This study guide aims to help a variety of groups, including local churches, tackle the issues raised in *Presence and Prophecy*. It sets out ways of engaging with the ideas in the book, linking the themes and joining in an important conversation about how the Churches in mission can make a difference in people's lives.

£3.95 0 7151 5549 0

Transparencies

Pictures of mission through prayer and reflection

What do Sister Wendy, the Muppets, Harry Potter and a sculpture of Jesus on the cross have in common? The answer is that they can all provide a focus for prayer and reflection on mission which in turn can be used to help us see more clearly how God is at work in and through our contemporary culture.

This imaginative collection of prayers and reflections, road tested by the ecumenical Mission Theological Advisory Group, is suitable for all kinds of prayer and study groups and can be adapted to a Lent or Advent course.

'Shows that prayer is the heart of our witness.'
David Atkinson, Bishop of Thetford

'Helps us to think afresh about God's mission.'
David Kerr, Belfast Central Mission, Northern Ireland

£6.95 0 7151 5550 4